WORLD OPINION AND THE EMERGING INTERNATIONAL ORDER

WORLD OPINION AND THE EMERGING INTERNATIONAL ORDER

Frank Louis Rusciano

With Roberta Fiske-Rusciano, Bosah Ebo,
Sigfredo A. Hernandez, and John Crothers Pollock

Praeger Series in Political Communication

Westport, Connecticut
London

Library of Congress Cataloging-in-Publication Data

Rusciano, Frank Louis, 1954–
    World opinion and the emerging international order / Frank Louis
    Rusciano ; with Roberta Fiske-Rusciano . . . [et al.]
        p.   cm.—(Praeger series in political communication, ISSN
    1062–5623)
    Includes bibliographical references and index.
    ISBN 0–275–95449–8 (alk. paper)
    1. Public opinion. 2. Group identity. 3. International
relations.   I. Fiske-Rusciano, Roberta. II. Title. III. Series.
HM261.R79   1998
303.3′8—DC21   97–50040

British Library Cataloguing in Publication Data is available.

Library of Congress Catalog Card Number: 97–50040
ISBN: 0–275–95449–8
ISSN: 1062–5623

First published in 1998

Praeger Publishers, 88 Post Road West, Westport, CT 06881
An imprint of Greenwood Publishing Group, Inc.

Printed in the United States of America

The paper used in this book complies with the
Permanent Paper Standard issued by the National
Information Standards Organization (Z39.48–1984).

10 9 8 7 6 5 4 3 2 1

Copyright Acknowledgments

The author and publisher gratefully acknowledge permission to use the following previously published material:

Portions of the Introduction were first published in Frank Louis Rusciano, Roberta Fiske-Rusciano, and Minmin Wang, "The Impact of 'World Opinion' on National Identity," *The Harvard International Journal of Press/Politics*, 2:3 (Summer 1997), pp. 71–92. © 1997 by the President and Fellows of Harvard College and the Massachusetts Institute of Technology.

Portions of Chapter 1 were first published in Roberta Fiske-Rusciano, "Towards a Notion of World Opinion," *International Journal of Public Opinion Research*, Vol. 2, No. 4 (1990), pp. 305–322.

Portions of Chapter 2 were first published in (1) Frank Louis Rusciano, "Media Perspectives on 'World Opinion' During the Kuwaiti Crisis," pp. 71–87 in *Media and the Persian Gulf War*, ed. Robert E. Denton, Jr. Copyright © Robert E. Denton, Jr. Praeger Publishers, an imprint of the Greenwood Publishing Group, Inc., Westport, CT, 1993. Reproduced with permission. (2) Frank Louis Rusciano, "Media Observations on World Opinion During the Kuwaiti Crisis: Political Communication and the Emerging International Order," *Southeastern Political Review*, Vol. 23, No. 3 (1996), pp. 505–530. (3) Frank Louis Rusciano and John Crothers Pollock, "Media Observations on World Opinion During the Recent Bosnian Crisis," Current World Leaders *International Issues*, Vol. 40, No. 2 (April 1997). Current World Leaders, 5385 Hollister Avenue #210, Santa Barbara, CA 93111–2305, USA, 805–683–4927 (phone), 805–683–4637 (fax), info@iasb.org (e-mail).

Portions of Chapter 6 were first published in Frank Louis Rusciano, "First and Third World Newspapers on World Opinion: Imagined Communities in Cold War and Post-Cold War Eras," *Political Communication* 14 (1997), pp. 171–190.

This book is dedicated to Francesco Fiske Rusciano,
who is already a citizen of the world.

Contents

Series Foreword

Those of us from the discipline of communication studies have long believed that communication is prior to all other fields of inquiry. In several other forums I have argued that the essence of politics is "talk" or human interaction.[1] Such interaction may be formal or informal, verbal or nonverbal, public or private, but it is always persuasive, forcing us consciously or subconsciously to interpret, to evaluate, and to act. Communication is the vehicle for human action.

From this perspective, it is not surprising that Aristotle recognized the natural kinship of politics and communication in his writings *Politics* and *Rhetoric*. In the former, he established that humans are "political beings [who] alone of the animals [are] furnished with the faculty of language."[2] In the latter, he began his systematic analysis of discourse by proclaiming that "rhetorical study, in its strict sense, is concerned with the modes of persuasion."[3] Thus, it was recognized over twenty-three hundred years ago that politics and communication go hand in hand because they are essential parts of human nature.

In 1981, Dan Nimmo and Keith Sanders proclaimed that political communication was an emerging field.[4] Although its origin, as noted, dates back centuries, a "self-consciously cross-disciplinary" focus began in the late 1950s. Thousands of books and articles later, colleges and universities offer a variety of graduate and undergraduate coursework in the area in such diverse departments as communication, mass communication, journalism, political science, and sociology.[5] In Nimmo and Sanders's early assessment, the "key areas of inquiry" included rhetorical analysis, propaganda analysis, attitude change studies, voting studies, government and the news media, functional and systems analyses, technological changes, media technologies, campaign techniques, and research techniques.[6] In a survey of the state of the field in 1983, the same authors and Lynda Kaid found additional, more specific areas of concerns such as the presidency, political polls, public opinion, debates, and advertising.[7] Since the first study, they have also noted a shift away from the rather strict behavioral approach.

A decade later, Dan Nimmo and David Swanson argued that "political communication has developed some identity as a more or less distinct domain of scholarly work."[8] The scope and concerns of the area have further expanded to include critical theories and cultural studies. Although there is no precise definition, method, or disciplinary home of the area of inquiry, its primary domain comprises the role, processes, and effects of communication within the context of politics broadly defined.

In 1985, the editors of *Political Communication Yearbook: 1984* noted that "more things are happening in the study, teaching, and practice of political communication than can be captured within the space limitations of the relatively few publications available."[9] In addition, they argued that the backgrounds of "those involved in the field [are] so varied and pluralist in outlook and approach, . . . it [is] a mistake to adhere slavishly to any set format in shaping the content."[10] More recently, Swanson and Nimmo have called for "ways of overcoming the unhappy consequences of fragmentation within a framework that respects, encourages, and benefits from diverse scholarly commitments, agendas, and approaches."[11]

In agreement with these assessments of the area and with gentle encouragement, in 1988 Praeger established the series entitled "Praeger Series in Political Communications." The series is open to all qualitative and quantitative methodologies as well as contemporary and historical studies. The key to characterizing the studies in the series is the focus on communication variables or activities within a political context or dimension. As of this writing, over seventy volumes have been published and numerous impressive works are forthcoming. Scholars from the disciplines of communication, history, journalism, political science, and sociology have participated in the series.

I am, without shame or modesty, a fan of the series. The joy of serving as its editor is in participating the dialogue of the field of political communication and in reading the contributors' work. I invite you to join me.

Robert E. Denton, Jr.

NOTES

1. See Robert E. Denton, Jr., *The Symbolic Dimensions of the American Presidency* (Prospect Heights, IL: Waveland Press, 1982); Robert E. Denton, Jr., and Gary Woodward, *Political Communication in America* (New York: Praeger, 1985; 2d ed., 1990); Robert E. Denton, Jr., and Dan Hahn, *Presidential Communication* (New York: Praeger, 1986); and Robert E. Denton, Jr., *The Primetime Presidency of Ronald Reagan* (New York: Praeger, 1988).

2. Aristotle, *The Politics of Aristotle*, trans. Ernest Barker (New York: Oxford University Press, 1970), p. 5.

3. Aristotle, *Rhetoric*, trans. Rhys Roberts (New York: The Modern Library, 1954), p. 22.

4. Dan Nimmo and Keith Sanders, "Introduction: The Emergence of Political Communication as a Field," in *Handbook of Political Communication*, eds. Dan Nimmo and Keith Sanders (Beverly Hills, CA: Sage, 1981), pp. 11-36.

5. Ibid., p. 15.

6. Ibid., pp. 17-27.

7. Keith Sanders, Lynda Kaid, and Dan Nimmo, eds. *Political Communication Yearbook: 1984* (Carbondale, IL: Southern Illinois University, 1985), pp. 283-308.

8. Dan Nimmo and David Swanson, "The Field of Political Communication: Beyond the Voter Persuasion Paradigm," in *New Directions in Political Communication*, eds. David Swanson and Dan Nimmo (Beverly Hills, CA: Sage, 1990), p. 8.

9. Sanders, Kaid, and Nimmo, *Political Communication Yearbook: 1984*, p. xiv.

10. Ibid.

11. Nimmo and Swanson, "The Field of Political Communication," p. 11.

Acknowledgments

This book grew out of a seminar I taught at the University of Mainz, during my tenure as an Alexander von Humboldt Fellow for the 1985-86 academic year. I have been privileged during the intervening decade or so to receive the support, advice, and contributions of a number of individuals on world opinion. The initial discussions began with my wife, Roberta Fiske-Rusciano, and resulted in the first chapter of this book. We were aided in the design of our questionnaire by Doris Kolesch and Anna and Bernd Niedermann, all students at Mainz in 1986. Robert Archibald and Kim Griffith also did extensive work on the content analyses for Chapter 2.

Professor Wolfgang Donsbach, presently of the University of Dresden, contributed helpful advice over the years, particularly on the first chapter, in his capacity as Managing Editor of the *International Journal of Public Opinion Research*.

Professor Robert Worcester of MORI in Britain provided useful commentary on the subject of world opinion and the global market, which I incorporated into Chapter 4. Professor Jennifer Hochschild of Princeton University provided an exhaustive review of Chapter 3, concerning the relationship between world opinion and the construction of national identity. I trust that I have done justice to these scholars' extensive efforts in the final product.

In the area of financial support, I am greatly indebted to Rider University, which provided me with a sabbatical and three summer fellowships to complete this book. I am similarly grateful to the Alexander von Humboldt Foundation which funded three research leaves in the German Federal Republic to allow me to pursue this research. My colleagues at the Institut für Demoskopie Allensbach in Germany also deserve special thanks. They always greeted my seemingly endless requests for data with patience and good humor, and they willingly lent advice or a sympathetic ear when I was attempting to work out theoretical or empirical problems in the research. Closer to home, the work done by Betty Vanheekhoven and Susan Petruzzi on the tedious tasks of correcting the edited manuscript were greatly appreciated.

A special note of thanks is in order to Professor Elisabeth Noelle-Neumann, who not only offered her support on the von Humboldt applications and opened the doors of the Institut to my investigations, but also provided lodging for my family and I when we visited Allensbach to pursue this topic. Her contribution can perhaps best be summarized by the simple advice she gave to me in 1991: "You must continue this work on world opinion." That declarative statement, and the underlying faith it reflects, helped sustain me through many of the frustrations in the research process. I truly believe there would have been no book without her support and advice.

Finally, I have had the privilege of writing this book with the most gifted of collaborators: Roberta Fiske-Rusciano of the Department of Anthropology at Rider University, Bosah Ebo of the Department of Communication at Rider University, Sigfredo Hernandez of the Department of Marketing at Rider University, and John Crothers Pollock of the Communications Studies Department at the College of New Jersey. If true collaboration is necessarily greater than the sum of its parts, it would be difficult to go wrong with as diversely talented a group as this. Also, I would like to thank some of my colleagues who are not represented in these pages, but whose comments and advice have sustained our efforts. Professors Minmin Wang and Jonathan Millen of the Department of Communication discussed our research and the issues in this book at seminars over the past three years. Similarly, Professor Jonathan Mendilow of the Department of Political Science maintained the valuable balance between harsh critic and friend, which one needs to produce their best work. If it takes a village to raise a child, it takes colleagues like Professors Ebo, Wang, Mendilow, Millen, and Fiske-Rusciano—all members of the Rider School of inquiry into global issues and social construction—to make a book.

Portions of the Introduction first appeared in *The Harvard International Journal of Press/Politics*. Portions of Chapter 1 first appeared in the *International Journal of Public Opinion Research*. Portions of Chapter 2 first appeared in *Media and the Persian Gulf War* (Robert E. Denton, Jr., ed.), the *Southeastern Political Review*, and Current World Leaders: *International Issues*. Portions of Chapter 6 first appeared in *Political Communication*.

Introduction

Frank Louis Rusciano

Our identities are formed primarily through encounters with "the Other." Our recorded history began when the single individual realized he belonged to a "we," and not just an "I," thereby endowing his actions with significance beyond his individual life span. Such a worldview contrasts sharply with that of the prehistoric man described by J.-J. Rousseau as a creature existing in isolation, recognizing neither the "we" in his fellows nor the value of his labors beyond the immediate moment. For man "without speech . . . without liaisons, with no need of his fellow men . . . perhaps never recognizing anyone individually" had "only those sentiments and intellect suited to that state" (Rousseau, 1964:137). His activities were his own only. Absent any social sense, there could be no passing of lessons or legacy between generations:

> If by chance he made a discovery, he was all the less able to communicate it because he did not even recognize his own children. Art died with the inventor . . . and every always starting from the same point . . . the species was already old, but man remained a child (137).

Rousseau acknowledged that man would never return to such a state of innocence; our worldview is irrevocably changed through our participation in history. But the changes in consciousness that accompany the origins of history point to a primary force in its development. Our historical consciousness demands that our identity and society take on a dialectical relationship from the beginning—otherwise, we would have no need to know our fellows or what came before as a means of knowing ourselves. Further, as the original "we" we have constructed is challenged by subsequent encounters with various "Others," our history as a people and our identities change in response. Such contacts add, color, or modify our sense of ourselves, and our history appears to conform to the Hegelian paradigm of thesis versus antithesis, resulting in a synthesis of worldviews (Hegel, 1954:28-29). The multiple identities in which we participate, often without thinking—as members of families, ethnic or religious groups, or nations—derive from our accumulation of historical contacts. As we extend these contacts to include new "Others," new historical epochs are potentially in the making.

Some encounters with "the Other" resonate so deeply within a people that the contacts in time acquire the power of myth. Even when the records of these contacts are faithful to historical events, their narratives often achieve the status of folklore, of parables describing adaptation, extinction, or stages of process in the ongoing lives of the people touched by them. Also, it is seldom that all parties involved in the encounter perceive it in the same way.

When Europeans first encountered the indigenous peoples of North America, for instance, the natives were hardly moved. Native Americans were accustomed to a plurality of tribes and a variety of languages, and simply regarded the newcomers as people of lighter skins, who needed to bathe more frequently. The Europeans, however, had left a continent which was much less diverse: "almost everyone spoke Indo-European related languages, and shared the same cosmological worldview" (Erdrich and Dorris, 1989:462). As a result, they searched desperately for a means to understand Native Americans, to fit them into the Adam and Eve schema, and to discover whether they had souls. Finally, after the subject had been debated in Spanish universities for 80 years, the Pope had to settle the question by decree—Indians indeed had souls. But by that time the encounter had "changed the European worldview" (462).

Other contacts were less benign. The Aztecs, who prior to their encounters with the Spanish existed virtually in isolation, perished in large part because they were ill-prepared to adapt their worldview to repel the hostile opposing force. The Aztec world was so circumscribed, and they knew so little of what existed beyond the boundaries of their empire, that the Spanish arrival "paralyzed" them, making resistance nearly impossible (Fuentes, 1989:507-508). Carlos Fuentes draws a moral from this tragedy:

> cultures that exist in isolation perish, and only cultures that communicate and give things to one another survive . . . Greeks communicated. They felt the presence of the Other . . . Having an identity means you accept the challenges and influences from everywhere. The great cultures of this world have been formed by this contagion of other cultures and not by their isolation (507-508).

But sometimes communication is difficult, particularly when the dominant group in a society resists contacts which threaten their identity. James Baldwin notes how the "interracial drama" that has been continually played out in the United States created a break with the European past more radical than the establishment of American democracy (Baldwin, 1986:87). For Baldwin, this drama has its roots in the American denial of the role of race—particularly the African race—in the creation of American identity. The Africans' loss of history due to slavery forced them to define themselves in terms of the terrible conditions of their lives in a new land. Hence, black history becomes key to understanding American history; the American identity is forged, in part, from the struggles of this people to create a new identity in the absence of their familiar surroundings, customs, and social networks. The denial of the black person's presence through slavery, forced segregation, second-class citizenship, and the silence of the history books has thereby prevented all Americans from knowing themselves.

The change in worldview has already occurred, but the dominant society still resists acknowledging it: "the interracial drama acted out on the American continent has not only created a new black man, it has created a new white man too . . . the world is white no longer, and will never be white again" (Baldwin, 1986:90). But the cost of this denial does not come cheap: "People who shut their eyes to reality simply invite their own destruction" (89). Still, the process of adaptation to the American racial encounter continues; nearly 50 years after Baldwin wrote these words, and four hundred years since Africans first arrived on the American continent, an American president has once again called for a dialogue on race.

In each case, encounters occurred and resulted in adaptation (Native Americans), extinction (Aztecs), or an ongoing process (American blacks). As different as they are, all three examples describe a contact with "the Other" which affects the worldview of at least one of the participants, marking a defining point in their history. These past encounters yield clues to our peculiar condition at the end of the twentieth century, for we now face contact with a global public, defined and bounded by the force of world opinion. What can we expect from this encounter? Looking backward, we may first unravel the dialectic between individuals and society that creates identities and prompts historical movement. In this Introduction I argue that opinion publics within the society affect identity in the same manner regardless of the size of the reference group. But contact with a global public has greater ramifications, for this group's overarching reach has the potential to transform our consciousness, our identities, and the very notions we have of history. These and other unique features of world opinion and the emerging global public will occupy us for the rest of the book.

THE CONSTRUCTION OF IDENTITY

Individual identity is constructed with an eye to the relevant reference groups in a person's life: "Identity is a phenomenon that emerges from a dialectic between the individual and the society" (Berger and Luckman, 1966:160). Reference groups change depending upon the relevant contacts in which one participates at any given time. Hence, individuals may be in contact with several reference groups providing separate messages about their identities. "People have levels of identity" so that a resident of Rome is at once "a Roman, an Italian, a Catholic, a European, a Westerner" (Huntington, 1993:24).

Public opinion is a phenomenon constructed, in a similar manner, with reference to specific groups, or "publics" (see Hennessey, 1985:9-10; Yeric and Todd, 1983:2-4; and Childs, 1965:12 as examples). A continuing controversy in public opinion research has been the exact nature of interactions between specific publics and the opinions expressed by their members. This discussion is directly relevant to the construction of identity on all levels—national, group, familial, and so on. If public opinion involves the communication of attitudes, norms, and beliefs among specific reference groups, it becomes the primary means by which identity is disseminated, shared, and reinforced within those groups.

Past researchers have tended to encounter a twofold problem in investigating these relationships: first, how does one describe the interaction between individual and group identity as a process?; and second, what is the primary group which generates an individual's identity by determining the process within which they will participate? This question is particularly relevant to discussions about encounters with "the Other" which transform identity, since the reference group in which a people decides to participate, and their interactions within that group, will determine the identity which emerges.

This introductory section responds to the two questions in the following manner. First, it argues that the process of public opinion which guides the construction of identity tends to be similar regardless of the reference group one considers; hence, encounters between groups that affect identity occur according to similar processes. Second, it argues, following John Zaller's thesis (1992), that since opinions need not be fixed, identity need not be fixed either. Instead, identity is "negotiated" when relevant reference groups clash in their interpretations. Further, this negotiation follows a pattern determined by the public opinion processes which structure the construction of identity on any given level. This insight will prove particularly important in the discussion of world opinion and the emerging global public. For the transformations in worldview and identity that we experience from contact with an international reference group follow the same patterns as previous contacts which occurred throughout history.

I describe this process of change in three steps. First, I discuss the controversies regarding the creation of group identity and its relationship to public opinion. Second, I propose a solution whereby issues of identity are negotiated, through communication processes that may be reflected in the media. Finally, I conclude by arguing that identity is at present being challenged on a global level, by the introduction of individuals to a global public defined by world opinion, the exploration of which will occupy the remainder of this book.

THE CONSTRUCTION OF IDENTITY AND PUBLIC OPINION:
THE CONTROVERSIES

Karl Deutsch argues that national identity is a form of social communication (Deutsch, 1966). One may expand this observation, since all forms of social identity—familial, national, ethnic, or global—are constructed as forms of social communication between the individual and a reference group. I define this communication process as part of the general process of public opinion. Elisabeth Noelle-Neumann describes public opinion as those opinions which an individual can or must display in public in order to avoid social isolation (Noelle-Neumann, 1992). Although certain critics take issue with this definition, it is generally accepted that any process of public opinion involves interactions between the individual and a group:

> The social psychologist interested in public opinion seeks fundamentally to explain how "opinion" is modified by the fact that it is "public"—to explain, in other words, the various ways in which ideas and opinions are shaped and altered through interaction among people and the social groups they constitute (Price and Oshagan, 1995:178).

The authors also note that writers who defined this tradition such as William James (1890), J.M. Baldwin (1893), and George Mead (1934) assumed that a person's very identity is a product of social interactions such as those described above.

Mapping the interaction between the individual and the relevant "public" on any level, then, is key to understanding how identities are formed. At all levels, "macrolevel information exchange [occurs] within 'interpretive communities,'" which in turn exercise the control of public opinion and culture that plays a role in . . . hegemonic models" such as those defining national or group identity (Beniger and Gusek, 1995:235).

Noelle-Neumann argues, in her "spiral of silence" theory, that these interactions are governed by three specific tendencies in societies: (1) individuals become aware that opinion is strengthening or weakening on a particular issue, often guided in part by messages from the media; (2) individuals react to these changes with more confident speech in support of the emerging position, or silence in opposition to it; and (3) individuals fear isolation, which causes them to heed the emerging opinion in the society (Noelle-Neumann, 1992; Price and Oshagan, 1995:203). If, however, "public" is defined as exposure to the opinions of others, how can one be sure that the society, and not some other group (ethnic, religious, familial, etc.) is the relevant one affecting and defining the individual's opinion? This question is particularly relevant to questions of identity, which has currency within and between all levels of groups. How does one define the group that has primary influence upon identity?

IDENTITY AS A CONSTRUCT WITHIN OPINION PROCESSES

The question raised concerns identity on all levels, from familial to ethnic to national and beyond. Individuals interact with a plurality of groups that may affect their opinions and identities:

> We can conceptualize interpersonal relations as constituting smaller opinion publics that may work in concert with or against the larger, systemic debate over policy issues. In such a confluence of *potential* normative forces, only certain ones become operative over the course of an individual's social interaction concerning a given issue. An important empirical issue to be sorted out is the determination of which particular norms become salient for various people (Price and Oshagan, 1995:205).

Researchers have identified various "smaller opinion publics" which affect an individual's attitudes on specific issues. These reference groups include communities (Canache, 1995), ideological groups (see Taylor, 1982 and others on "pluralistic ignorance"), and the small experimental groups used by Solomon Asch (1952) and referenced by Noelle-Neumann. The opinion processes, including the fear of isolation and the tendency of individuals to heed the opinions of others, must operate even as the reference groups change, as must competing descriptions of group effects upon individual opinions. Hence, a common criticism of theories of public opinion like the spiral of silence, or other models of social interaction between an individual and a "public," is that none prove that a given society is the relevant public to which the individual is responsive. Individuals come in contact with multiple reference groups; it seems arbitrary to argue that one specific group or another is solely responsible for affecting a person's opinion or identity.

The model necessarily becomes more complicated when an individual comes into contact with two or more levels of reference groups at one and the same time. For instance, ethnic identity is not formed solely with reference to one group in a given nation; the national society, and indeed the world at large, may have an image of the ethnic group which affects the way in which its members view themselves. As such, ethnicity may have relevance on several levels. Opinions about an individual's ethnic background, those signals which supposedly indicate whether a person should express or silence their identity in "public," may be complementary or conflictual on these different levels.

Consider again, for example, Samuel Huntington's resident of Rome, who is Roman, Italian, Catholic, European, and Westerner at the same time. It seems naive to assume that reference groups based around city, ethnicity, religion, continent, and region of the world would not give conflictual messages with regard to identity. How then is the individual to manage these varying signals? One model could argue that identity is formed as an n-dimensional space, in which each dimension (d^1, d^2, d^3, . . . d^n) represents the influence of a different reference group upon a person's opinions and identity. The different levels of "public," then, are represented as vectors in this space, and a person's opinion or identity is the sum total of the direction and force of each of these vectors.

I perceive three problems with this model. First, it seems overly complex as a thought process, and there is little evidence to suggest that individuals constantly operate on so many different levels. Second, the combination of identities would be so unique to each individual that any attempt at collective identity would be virtually impossible. Third, the model assumes that identity is settled, or fixed, as a sum of all forces at any given time. In fact, it is unlikely that all levels of reference groups, or "publics," are active at any one time for an individual.

Models that attempt to trace opinions or identities back to specific reference groups imply that these phenomena are fixed. I would suggest as an alternative that norms or identities that emerge from the public opinion process vary with the time and context which define their influence. This approach follows Zaller's thesis that individuals do not have fixed opinions; instead, they carry within them varying "considerations" about an issue which reflect the social circumstances in which they find themselves at the time. As Zaller notes: "Response variation is rooted in an important substantive phenomenon, namely the common existence of ambivalence in people's reactions to issues" (Zaller, 1992:75). This "ambivalence" is affected by reference groups and the "priming effects of media" (78). I add that these factors interact in a manner one may measure in the potential conflict between different levels of "publics" which may define a person's identity.

The notion of "ambivalence" suggests this interpretation etymologically: "ambi" refers to "both," while "valence" refers to the "capacity of an entity to unite or interact" with another. Ambivalence in attitudinal structures implies a suspension between potentially conflictual forces (such as reference groups, which may be mediated by media), all of which have the capacity to attract and influence the individual's attitudes.

Instead of conceptualizing reference groups as valence forces in space, it is more useful to model them as "layers" of identity which may or may not be activated at a given time in an individual's life. These layers may be organized in terms of ever-increasing levels of breadth, so long as this organization is not assumed to reflect the importance of these groups for an individual's identity. To return to the example given above, the individual who is at once Roman, Italian, Catholic, European, and Westerner has layers of reference groups defined by city, nationality, religion, continent, and region of the world.

I would emphasize that it is possible all of these reference groups, and the potential identities for individuals they represent, will not conflict at any given time. Indeed, following Zaller's thesis, only one or a few may be relevant as "considerations" in the formation of opinions or identity, depending upon the context. Moreover, the list of reference groups is far from inclusive; there are several others (familial, organizational, etc.) that could be included here. Nor does the breadth of a group indicate its probable influence on an individual's identity. Depending upon the circumstances, groups of greater breadth, such as one's country, might be more important to an individual's sense of self than groups of lesser breadth, such as one's state. Conversely, one's state may be more important to one's identity than one's nation. Robert E. Lee, for example, decided to join the Confederate cause during the Civil War when his home state of Virginia seceded from the Union. Lee, who had been offered command of the Union forces before his decision, considered his state a more important reference group in his decision than the nation (Wills, 1979:440-442).

Regardless of the relevance of particular groups at any given time to an individual's identity, however, the addition of a new reference group carries with it the potential for affecting a person's sense of self. New groups portend new encounters with "the Other." In this book, I will explore the possible ramifications of the addition of a new reference group—*a global public*—to the lexicon of human experience. Because of the potential scope and reach of this public, its potential effects range from changes in individual identity to adjustments in the behavior of nations. All of these changes are prompted by a process of attitudinal and identity formation—*a world opinion*—that defines the international public.

ORGANIZATION OF THE BOOK

World opinion defines the boundaries of an international public; it creates global markets and global identities; it affects the behavior of nations. I approach such a broad concept by beginning the first chapter with a few basic questions: What are the fundamental components of world opinion? What allows for its influence over human activity? Some preliminary answers emerge from a content analysis of common usages of the term or its equivalent, in stories and editorials in the *International Herald Tribune* and the *Frankfurter Allgemeine Zeitung*. This study derives six primary components of world opinion: a moral component, a pragmatic component, the threat of international isolation, and references to the power of world opinion, a nation's image, and the world considered as a unit. The power of world opinion derives primarily from the moral component, which allows the world community to threaten errant nations with international isolation. From these findings comes a preliminary definition of the concept: *"world opinion" refers to the moral judgments of observers that actors must heed in the international arena, or risk isolation as a nation.*

The second chapter describes how this notion of world opinion changes our perceptions of the manner in which relations between nations are to be organized. What emerges is a new "international order," which resembles neither the Cold War's ideological conflict between East and West, nor the Utopian promise of a "New World Order" heralded by the Bush administration in the wake of the Persian Gulf War. Rather, the new configuration is properly conceived as a social construct, a "system of intelligibility" for "separation of the world into different kinds of space" (Shapiro, 1989:13). It is based upon a competition among various interpretations of "world opinion," advanced by nations with different perspectives on an issue.

I trace this competition by focusing upon two crises that prompted an international response, the Persian Gulf War and the Bosnian conflict. By using content analyses of major first and third world newspapers and United Nations documentary records, I trace the apparent emergence of international consensus on these issues. The evolution of consensus, and international cooperation, may be traced in the intersection of references to world opinion in various media outlets and international forums. Indeed, because each nation reflects its own dominant and regime interests in the way they construct world opinion, the potential for international collective action appears to depend upon the convergence, in date and content, of the different perspectives on world opinion into a working consensus. Absent such a convergence, the chances for an international response to crises become slim.

Is it reasonable, however, to describe the integrative function of world opinion in a new international "order" when the rise of nationalism threatens the peace in the post-Cold War era? Nationalism relies upon a sharp (and often violent) differentiation between peoples and nations, giving lie to notions that an "international community" exists across countries' borders. The third chapter addresses this issue by exploring the roots of the recent rise of nationalism, and linking it to the concept of a nation's "reputation" and "status" in world opinion. It begins by noting that the collapse of Marxist interpretations not only portended the demise of a system; it also signalled the end of a model of historical development. Prior to the collapse of communism, Eastern bloc nations which lagged behind according to capitalist measures of development such as Gross National Product could claim to be more developed historically, in terms of progress within the inevitable trends of history. This claim not only made scarcity more endurable within these systems, it also served as a source of status or pride for their citizens. With the collapse of the Marxist model, however, these citizens suffered status dislocations, as they fell subject to a model of development which ranked their nation lower than the position to which they were accustomed. Their national identity thus became less of a source of pride, and many of these citizens sought alternative means such as nationalism to regain their lost pride.

This chain of events must be understood in terms of world opinion, for two reasons. First, one basis for citizens' pride in this model is their country's international status or reputation; nations derive their standing from the manner in which they are viewed in world opinion. Second, because international status is so critical to the pride served by national identity, this identity can no longer be created in isolation within a nation's borders. Rather, national identity becomes a negotiated construct between a nation's *Selbstbild* (or self-image, the image citizens have of their country) and its *Fremdbild* (or international image, the reputation of their nation in world opinion). Crises of status anxiety from the collapse of the Eastern bloc can therefore be traced through the effects of world opinion on the construction of national identity. This chapter analyzes Germany after reunification as a case study of the construction of national identity in the midst of such crises.

Many analysts have argued that the rise of a global market, which would bind nations' economies into mutually profitable exchanges, will forge ties that render destructive forms of nationalism obsolete. The fourth chapter takes issue with these benign views, noting that global consumer tastes are merely one form of world opinion, and the global market just one part of the emerging global public. International consumer tastes have the same structure as world opinion. The fear of social isolation is a motivating force for the global consumer as well as the member of the global public. Finally, the global market is a subsystem within an emerging "international community" of individuals with similar tastes, attitudes, and opinions. Any analysis of the integrating effects of the global market must therefore be placed within the larger context of world opinion.

We use the growth of the global market as a means of discovering an "attentive public" for world opinion in the fifth chapter, by focusing upon information as a commodity within the global public. We assume that individuals who seek out information or discussion about world opinion define a potential market for media that disseminate material on the subject. These consumers, in turn, might define an attentive public, described as those persons who actively seek information about international public opinion.

Our media market approach begins with a comparative analysis of four newspapers, from which we construct a Cumulative Index of World Opinion, which measures the depth of coverage of world opinion as a concept in each of the papers. We then correlate the readership characteristics for each paper with the depth of coverage provided, assuming that readers who are most interested in world opinion will gravitate toward the newspapers that provide the most comprehensive analysis. We isolate three demographic characteristics of these readers in this section of the analysis.

In the next section, we test whether these individuals do indeed form a potential "attentive public" of like-minded individuals which crosses national borders. To this end, we construct five scales dealing with attitudes toward economic inequality from the 1992 International Social Survey. We discover that individuals who share the described demographic characteristics are more alike in their opinions on these issues than individuals who do not. We conclude by describing a possible model for the dissemination of world opinion, using this attentive group as a link between elites and the mass of citizens.

In the final chapter, I tackle the implications of all of these findings for the emergence of an "imagined international community," to paraphrase Benedict Anderson (Anderson, 1992). I discover that nations tend to construct world opinion according to their nations' dominant interests, as Edward Herman and Noam Chomsky argue, by comparing first world and third world newspapers (Herman and Chomsky, 1988). However, I also discover an "imagined community" of nations which exists alongside of national interests in the discourse on world opinion, by comparing Cold War and post-Cold War newspapers. These findings raise fundamental questions about the whole concept of world opinion: Can it be said to exist if its interpretations vary with time and historical era? What are we to make of the emergence of an imagined international community alongside the nation-states that hold sway over individuals' loyalties?

These questions are addressed in the Conclusion, where I revisit some of the themes regarding history and identity that begin this book. Because the construction of world opinion is mutable, the definition of "the Other," as well as the boundaries of the international community and the nations isolated from it, shift with the events and issues being considered. Hence, the status of individuals versus "the Other" is always in a potential state of flux. The spread of values internationally through world opinion heralds neither the end of man's search for identity, nor the "end of history," despite the claims of certain authors (see Fukuyama, 1996). Instead, it heralds the end of an idea of history as evolutionary, and replaces it with a series of encounters defined by constantly shifting definitions of "the Other." The challenge for the nation-state in the emerging international order is to remain a relevant entity in the midst of changes wrought to identity and human history in the new era. I discuss the role world opinion might play in the new politics that may result in the concluding pages of this book.

1

Toward a Notion of "World Opinion"

Frank Louis Rusciano
and Roberta Fiske-Rusciano

The phrase "world opinion" enjoyed widespread use before it had been adequately defined. Despite common reference by social scientists, journalists, and world leaders, it eludes consistent or systematic definition. While it draws its inspiration from the term "public opinion," it is not quite clear which public is referenced in the world context, and whether there are any attitudes or preferences that may be attributed to this public. Hence, certain critics charge that "world opinion" is merely a metaphor carelessly constructed from public opinion, and falsely extended to a "world public" or "world community" that does not exist.

One speaks easily of public opinion in the United States, France, or West Germany, for example, attributing to each nation's citizens distinct cultures and values.[1] This assumed existence of national public opinion would appear to preclude the existence of a public for world opinion. If public opinion draws its meaning from specific state boundaries, world opinion, by definition, may not. Hamid Mowlana, for instance, argues:

> As the complexities of the modern world grew, it became fashionable in the literature to apply a variety of terms to the *world stage* as a whole, with phrases such as "international community" and "international system." It is, however, doubtful whether the aggregation of states alone possess the *common values and assumptions*, which are by definition the essential conditions of community, and whether or not the working of a world society is in some way analogous to a mechanical system. The result has been to emphasize the tangible, the formal, and the measurable (Mowlana, 1986:176; emphases added).

Nevertheless, he seems to acknowledge the existence of a "world stage as a whole" upon which citizens and leaders of nations act. And it is from this notion of an open arena for international action, observation, and judgment that a different notion of "world opinion" emerges. This meaning moves from the notion of "public" as a defined group, toward a notion of "public" as a state of relations between nations or citizens.[2]

Noelle-Neumann introduces an alternative notion of "public" in her definition of public opinion: a feeling of exposure to the observation and judgments of others (Noelle-Neumann, 1992:61-62). This provides a key for discussing "world opinion." The existence of a "world stage" implies an arena in which citizens or leaders of nations act openly, exposed to the judgments of other nations and leaders. Furthermore, just as Noelle-Neumann's analysis includes the sanction of the "threat of isolation" for those who violate the dictates of public opinion, so too does world opinion include a threat of isolation for those who run afoul of it. The critical aspect of "social control," central to Noelle-Neumann's study of this notion of "public," also often appears connected with the public in world opinion. However, it is important to note that world opinion need not preclude the existence of "publics" defined by individual nations, any more than public opinion precludes the existence of publics within individual nations. Rather, the judgments of specific nations (the "audience" for the "world stage") are directed toward the actions, statements, and beliefs of others appearing in this arena. World opinion refers to another realm of activity linked, to be sure, with any "publics" defined by national boundaries or shared cultures.

This approach raises a myriad of questions: Who serves as the "audience" for actions on the "world stage"? How are actions or statements attributed to nations or leaders as "actors"? Who renders judgment on these actions? Upon what moral basis are these judgments rendered? But before one may begin to address these questions, or even speculate further on the actual existence of world opinion, one must know more about the nature of the term as it is commonly used in discourse.

This chapter derives initial hypotheses concerning the common usage of "world opinion" by studying its appearance in the stories and editorials of two quality newspapers—the *International Herald Tribune* (United States) and the *Frankfurter Allgemeine Zeitung* (German Federal Republic)—for the months of February, March, and April 1986. A content analysis of all pieces referencing world opinion during this period found that the concept was commonly used in both newspapers. It was referenced 103 times in the *International Herald Tribune* and 67 times in the *Frankfurter Allgemeine Zeitung*. The primary source of these references (73% in the *IHT* and 66.1% in the *FAZ*) were the newspapers' own reporters; other sources included wire services such as API, UPI, Reuters, and AFP (9% in the *IHT* and 13.2% in the *FAZ*), and guest writers, notably editorial and syndicated columnists (18% in the *IHT* and 20.3% in the *FAZ*). These data indicate no significant difference in the sources for references between the two newspapers; the eta value for the relationship equaled only .047.

This finding does not "prove" the existence of world opinion. Rather, it allows the researcher to search out clues to the manner in which the American and West German newspapers used the term. The study of such clues is a first step toward deriving hypotheses about the meaning of "world opinion," enabling the study of its existence and nature. The derivation of these hypotheses follows in five steps. First, the study's methodology and limits are described, to circumscribe the extent to which the results may be generalized. Second, the perceived agenda for world opinion is discussed in terms of subjects referenced, appearances in one or both newspapers, and the dates on which stories appeared. Third, the possible influence of world opinion is studied, with emphasis upon its relationship to the moral and pragmatic components of actors' behaviors. Fourth, the notion of "isolation" as a punishment in world opinion is analyzed with reference to its relationship to the other components. The chapter concludes with a preliminary organization of these themes into a theory of the process of world opinion. This process is then compared with the public opinion process within nations. Suggestions for further testing of the hypotheses are advanced, along with some reflections on the possible stakes involved in understanding the concept of world opinion.

THE SAMPLE AND THE STUDY DESIGN

This project's purposes guided four decisions in the research design. First, only those articles that referenced world opinion in some form were included in the study. Hence, comparisons of subjects that prompted citation with those that did not, and comparisons of the times when specific issues prompted citation and when they did not, were excluded.[3] Second, the choice of newspapers represented a compromise between cross-national analysis and comparability of media. The newspapers are from different nations: the *International Herald Tribune* is American (although it is published and distributed primarily in Western Europe) and the *Frankfurter Allgemeine Zeitung* is West German. The two papers do have several similarities. Both are quality newspapers covering national, international, and financial events, and both are published from Western, advanced industrial societies with common interests and international commitments. We desired a cross-national sample for an initial study, but also wished to control other factors of comparability as much as possible. The addition of further variables for comparison (e.g., studying third world newspapers or Western tabloids) was left for a later analysis.

Third, any study performed in a given period is limited by the state of world affairs during that time. In these terms, the period running from February through April of 1986 was a busy time. Major events included reevaluation of U.S. policy toward South Africa and that nation's declaration of a news blackout, Mikhail Gorbachev's consolidation of power in the Soviet Union and his activist world leadership, a peak in terrorist activities, revolts against leadership in the Philippines and Haiti, and the Kurt Waldheim election in Austria. The number of references to world opinion (103 in the *IHT* and 67 in the *FAZ*) might not be typical of a quieter time in world affairs. This condition should be viewed as an opportunity rather than a problem. Exploratory research is best performed on the richest lode of information possible. The hypotheses derived may then be tested during quiet and active periods in world affairs.

Fourth, references to "world opinion" included both implicit and explicit citations. Explicit citations reference the phrase or its equivalent directly. Examples include "world opinion," "world public opinion," "international opinion," and "international public opinion" in English, and *Weltmeinung* and *Weltöffentlichkeit* in German. Such citations constitute 17.4% of the references in both papers. More common (82.6% of references) were implicit citations, which did not use synonyms for world opinion, but included attitudes, opinions, or reactions attributed to the world or all nations together. Such citations include "world support," "international outrage," "international scorn," *Welt Besturtzung* (international consternation), *Internationale Verurteilung* (international judgment), and *Ansehen im Ausland* (appearance in foreign nations). The following quotations illustrate examples of these constructions:

> In Costa Rica and Honduras, rebel-related border incidents have caused concern that the guerillas are exacting a high cost in *international prestige* and domestic security (*IHT*, 3/3/86).

> The television images that dominated the nightly news last summer and helped crystallize Western anger against South Africa have all but disappeared, replaced by something less frequent and less powerful. . . .
> The result has not reduced the level of violence in South Africa—and January had two of the highest death tolls in 18 months of unrest—but it has helped give South Africa something of a respite from the intense *world attention and opprobrium* it incurred last year, and officials seem very satisfied as a result (*IHT*, 3/4/86).

> Before announcing the proposal, Mr. Gorbachev accused the United States of aggression against Libya and said its actions were a "*challenge to the world public*" (*IHT*, 3/27/86).

Implicit citations also were often dynamic constructions, as if "the world" were expressing an opinion or judgment: "turning its attention," "observing," or "expecting." The following quotations illustrate examples of these constructions:

> Quadaffi *remains isolated.* . . . But even if Quadaffi possesses complete power in Libya, *he must continue to live with the rest of the world. That has become more difficult for him* (*FAZ*, 4/18/86).

> *The entire world was able to observe* . . . as Benigno Aquino was being shot. . . . For the Aquino murder and the election fraud Marcos paid a high price, *isolation at home and abroad* (*FAZ*, 2/19/86).

The public hearing has given the Afghans the feeling that *the outside world has not completely forgotten them* (*FAZ*, 3/24/86).

While the attribution of an attitude or opinion to any "public" or group remains a debatable proposition (see Mackie, 1967, quoted in Hardin, 1982:1), such references to the world properly belong in a study of world opinion.

THE AGENDA FOR WORLD OPINION

An apparent agenda for world opinion emerged during this time, centered around six issues, representing 64.1% of the references in the American paper and 68.7% of the references in the West German paper. These issues were: (1) nations' reevaluations of their policies toward Apartheid in South Africa; (2) talks on nuclear arms between the superpowers, prompted in part by Gorbachev's consolidation of power; (3) an American review of their policies toward Central America, especially Nicaragua; (4) the presidential election in the Philippines, in which Ferdinand Marcos was replaced by Corazon Aquino; (5) the clashes between the United States and Libya, which culminated in the U.S. bombing of Tripoli; and (6) the revelations about Kurt Waldheim's past as he approached election to the Austrian presidency.

These topics, which were driven by particular events during the period studied, dominated two-thirds of the world opinion references. Figure 1.1 shows that the allocation of total references to each of the six topics was also remarkably similar. The average difference in percentage of references between the two newspapers[4] was only 4.6%; the chi-square value for the table equaled .135, indicating no discernible relationship between the percentage of references on each topic and the paper in which they appeared. The largest gap in total references occurs concerning the Waldheim affair, which occupied 10.4% of the *FAZ*'s references to 1.4% of the *IHT*'s references. An obvious explanation for this difference is that the West German press was more sensitive to the issue than the American press and, hence, was more likely to emphasize it earlier (the story was beginning to break as the period under study ended). Such sensitivity to particular issues should be regarded as a factor in the nation's possible awareness of world opinion. However, the overall finding stresses *continuity* and *similarity* in total citations and emphasis regarding the six issues.

This continuity extended to the dates upon which the citations to world opinion appeared in several cases. The percentage of total references on each issue was calculated for the two newspapers for two-week periods between February and April 1986.[5] Table 1.1 shows the chi-square values and their significance levels for the relationship between newspaper and the dates at which references appeared for each issue. In no cases do the measures indicate that the newspapers had significantly different patterns, for these references appeared in each issue. All significance levels are well above the .05 value necessary to denote a significant difference between the two papers' patterns of reporting

Figure 1.1. Percentage of Total References on Major Issues, by Newspaper

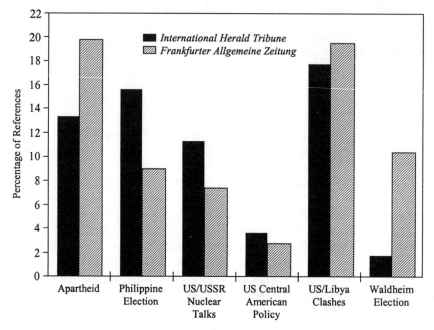

Table 1.1. Relationship Between Newspaper and Date of References to World Opinion, by Issue

Issue	Chi-square value	Significance	(n)
Apartheid in South Africa	6.100	.296	(27)
Marcos and the Philippines	2.670	.445	(22)
US/USSR Nuclear Talks	5.920	.205	(17)
US Central American Policy	.833	.659	(5)
US Clash with Libya	.454	.797	(30)
Waldheim Election in Austria	3.210	.200	(9)

references. The data indicate a marked similarity for the timing of agenda items between the two newspapers.

A plausible reason for the two newspapers' similar emphasis might have lain in common wire service sources. However, only 1 reference out of the 107 represented by these topics derived from the same wire service. The primary sources for citations (79.4% for the *IHT* and 65.9% for the *FAZ*) on these issues were the papers' own reporters.

Of the remaining citations, three other subjects were referenced in both newspapers: the Iran-Iraq war (1% of references in the *IHT*, 1.5% in the *FAZ*), the changes in the Politburo leadership and the possible effects on world affairs (1% of references in the *IHT*, 3% in the *FAZ*), and the Swiss referendum rejecting membership in the United Nations (1.9% of references in the *IHT*, 3.5% in the *FAZ*). All other references are cited in only one of the newspapers, and are scattered among a variety of topics.

The citations are notable because few issues receive more than one citation, and only three subjects (human rights in the USSR in the *IHT*, and the Olaf Palme assassination and the conference of neutral nations in the *FAZ*) represented barely more than 4% of the total references from each paper. Dissimilarities in emphases between the papers tend to occur among issues receiving the fewest references.

Our preliminary hypothesis therefore stresses the similarity in the choice of critical issues in world opinion, the emphasis laid on these issues, and the timing of the citations. When an issue was event-driven, dealing with a specific policy or action that demanded almost immediate response, the pattern of citations tended to be most similar. When an issue was developing, or as a nation was considering the ramifications and reactions to an ongoing situation, the citations tended to appear first in the newspaper whose nation was more directly involved. Beyond these considerations, there appeared to be general agreement on the content of world opinion between the two newspapers.

THE MORAL AND PRAGMATIC COMPONENTS
OF WORLD OPINION

The notion of "world opinion" implies evaluation of issues or events. We classified these judgments in two ways: moral and pragmatic. Moral evaluations were based upon *values* which relevant nations were supposed to share, where issues are discussed in terms of right or wrong patterns of behavior. Some articles made specific references to morality; one stated that sanctions against South Africa were useful as "moral gestures of foreign policy." Other articles referenced morality indirectly; one quoted the criticism that "the developed world has lost its sense of the sacred." Pragmatic evaluations were based upon *interests* which relevant nations were supposed to share, where issues were discussed in terms of practical costs or benefits. Some articles referenced shared interests directly; one stated that "the Soviets do deserve credit for rational calculation of important international interests." Other articles referred indirectly to positive benefits all nations would receive by heeding world opinion, as when one writer advocated "the international cooperation upon which market stability will rely." The moral component was cited with comparable frequency in the two newspapers, included in 69.1% of references in the *IHT* and 76.8% of references in the *FAZ* (eta = .083). References to the pragmatic component were less common, but also similar in frequency in the two newspapers, included in 45% of references in the *IHT* and 40.7% of references in the *FAZ* (eta = .046).

In 36.4% of the cases, world opinion had both moral and pragmatic components; behavior defined as moral was also in a nation's best interests. In 35.1% of cases, the moral component was mentioned alone; the pragmatic component was mentioned alone in only 5.3% of cases. In one-quarter of the cases, neither component was mentioned. The results imply the central importance of the moral component for world opinion. The moral component was referenced in 71.5% of cases; the pragmatic component in just 41.7% of cases. Furthermore, the moral component was nearly seven times more likely to be referenced alone than the pragmatic component (by a margin of 35.1% to 5.3%, respectively). These patterns did not vary by newspaper. As Table 1.2 indicates, the pattern of references to the two components was virtually the same between the two newspapers.

This finding raises important issues in cross-national analyses; discussing shared values is more difficult and problematic than discussing shared interests among nations. The consideration of cross-national—and hence, cross-cultural—moral references forces us to confront two seemingly contradictory principles. Moral principles are commonly considered to be contextually defined and culturally specific within nations. Behavior sanctioned in one culture is often forbidden in other cultures. On the other hand, a moral component of world opinion implies the existence of value judgments which cross national borders

Table 1.2. Relationship Between Newspaper and Date of References to Moral and Pragmatic Components of World Opinion

	IHT Percent	*FAZ* Percent
Moral and Pragmatic	38.5 (37)	32.7 (18)
Moral Alone	30.2 (29)	43.6 (24)
Pragmatic Alone	6.3 (6)	3.6 (2)
Neither Mentioned	25.0 (24)	20.0 (11)

Chi-square = 2.949, significance = .399

and cultures. The conflict is not new, and has figured prominently in nineteenth- and twentieth-century debates over nationalism. Charles Maier, for instance, notes that before German reunification under Otto von Bismarck, the "historical community was divided over whether or not the existence of a unified nation required renouncing ethical commitments to the international community" (Maier, 1989:4). The creation or existence of a "national character" has often precluded discussion of values common to separate nations.

But even if "national character" (like "public opinion" within nations) implies a general ethical consensus in a country, nations still embrace a wide variety of cultural and ethical perspectives. Diversity does not prevent research- ers from identifying value judgments or other general traits that bind individuals or societies into a "national character" or a "public" (Maier, 1989:150-151). Likewise, the diversity of national cultures does not preclude the existence of shared values to bind nations into a "world opinion." The level of analysis is shifted, but the justification for shared values amid diverse ethical systems is similar.

THE POWER OF WORLD OPINION

Our analysis indicated that the moral component of world opinion partially explained its influence over international affairs. Indeed, morality was central to discussions of the influence of world opinion. For this analysis, the "power of world opinion" was indicated by use of a synonym for "power," such as "force" or "influence"; examples include when Mrs. Winnie Mandela argued that the South African government would have to release Nelson Mandela to "relieve international *pressure*." This power was also defined in terms of specific effects that world opinion was assumed to have; examples include Arafat's statement that "terrorism outside Israel had become counterproductive— had turned opinion against the Palestinians."

The matrix in Table 1.3 shows the relationship between this power and the moral component of world opinion. References to moral judgments were signifi- cantly correlated with references to the power of world opinion ($r = .2531$, sig- nificance $= .001$). Moral references also correlated significantly with references to the threat of isolation directed against international actors or nations ($r = .1234$, significance $= .064$), and references to a nation's international image ($r = .1923$, significance $= .009$). The moral component occupies a central posi- tion among these three factors; while there was a slight correlation between references to the power of world opinion and a nation's image ($r = .1164$, sig- nificance $= .065$), neither factor correlated with references to the threat of isolation ($r = .0366$ for the power of world opinion, and $r = -.0053$ for the nation's image). Furthermore, the relationship between the power of world opin- ion and the nation's image became insignificant with a control for references to the moral component of world opinion; the product moment value fell from .1164 to .0714 after the moral component was introduced.

Table 1.3. Relationships Between Different Components of World Opinion

	Pragmatic Component	Power of World Opinion	Nation's Image	Threat of Isolation
Moral Component	.2958 (.000)	.2531 (.001)	.1923 (.009)	.1234 (.064)
Pragmatic Component		.1715 (.016)	.1224 (.064)	.0299 (.356)
Power of World Opinion			.1164 (.065)	.0366 (.318)
Nation's Image				.0053 (.472)

Correlation coefficients (Pearson) and level of significance

Table 1.4. Relationship Between Different Components and the Moral and Pragmatic Components of World Opinion

	Zero-order Values	Control for Moral Component
Pragmatic Component with:		
Power	.1715 (.016)	.1416 (.0694)
Image	.1224 (.064)	.0694 (.198)
Isolation	.0299 (.356)	.0072 (.465)
	Zero-order Values	Control for Moral Component
Moral Component with:		
Power	.2351 (.001)	.2151 (.004)
Image	.1923 (.009)	.1646 (.022)
Isolation	.1238 (.064)	.1204 (.071)

References to the pragmatic component of world opinion are also significantly related to the power of world opinion (r = .1715, significance = .016) and the nation's image (r = .1224, significance = .064), but not to the threat of isolation (r = .0299). However, the first two correlations are misleading; they arise due to the common occurrence, and intercorrelation, between the moral and pragmatic components in many of the references. Table 1.4 illustrates this finding. Here, references to the power of world opinion, a nation's image, and the threat of isolation are correlated with the pragmatic component with a control for the moral component, and with the moral component with a control for the pragmatic component. When one controls for the presence of the moral component, the relationship between the other factors and the pragmatic component becomes insignificant. However, when one controls for the presence of the pragmatic component, the relationship between the three factors and the moral component is hardly reduced. The central importance of the moral component is reconfirmed—any relationship between the pragmatic component and the other factors occurs because of its shared presence with the moral component.

As a preliminary hypothesis, we assume world opinion derives power from its capacity to affect a nation's image, or threaten a nation with isolation, due to the moral judgments it renders on acceptable forms of behavior. Defining the exact principles for these moral judgments is beyond the limits of a preliminary study. But the hypotheses regarding the moral power of world opinion are underscored by a closer examination of the threatened punishment of isolation.

ISOLATION AND WORLD OPINION

In one article in the *International Herald Tribune*, a reporter noted how a "fear of isolation" from the rest of the world often prompted a reluctant South African government to allow normally censored messages to enter the nation through the international television and radio media. Isolation proved to be a critical concept in our analysis of world opinion, appearing in 29.5% of the citations and giving rise to three questions: (1) What does "isolation" mean for world opinion? (2) When is it likely to occur? and (3) Why would nations or leaders fear it?

Isolation was more likely to be referenced in the *FAZ* (34.8% of citations) than in the *IHT* (25.9% of citations), but the citations were strikingly similar regarding the sources of citations and the issues referenced. The primary source of references to isolation (75% in the *IHT* and 66.7% in the *FAZ*) were the newspapers' own reporters; other sources included wire services (12% in the *IHT* and 14.3% in the *FAZ*), and guest editorial and syndicated columnists (12% of references in the *IHT* and 19% in the *FAZ*). As the data indicate, there were no significant differences in the sources for references between the two newspapers.

Of the references to isolation, 77.1% cited topics that appeared in both newspapers. Only 10.4% and 12.5% of the references cited topics that appeared solely in the *IHT* and the *FAZ*, respectively. The six major issues referenced above also tended to receive similar emphases regarding references to isolation. Figure 1.2 shows the percentage of total references to isolation on these issues for the two newspapers. As the lines indicate, the distribution of references is strikingly similar between the two papers, indicating some degree of consensus about subjects likely to prompt a threat of isolation.

Like "world opinion," "isolation" was cited in explicit (39.6%) as well as implicit terms (60.4%). Explicit citations reference the word or its equivalent directly: "isolation in an increasingly integrated world," "diplomatically isolated," "political isolation," "isolation in foreign nations." Implicit references referred to gestures or phrases describing a nation separated from, or avoided by, other nations in the world. Examples include "America may make itself the bogeyman," "this process makes it difficult to look at [Israel] just like any other nation in the world," and "flouting the norms of international conduct has made him the target of widespread . . . scorn."

Isolation was discovered to have two related meanings here. First, it reflected the disruption of *tangible* relationships of trade, diplomacy, and business. These included the denial of landing rights or recognition of leadership, the closing of embassies and recall of ambassadors, and the boycotting of a nation's goods. But isolation also had a more *general* meaning—the message that a nation's citizens were unwelcome in foreign countries, or that their leaders were snubbed by other leaders in the world. The isolated nation or individual feels as a pariah to other nations. One article noted how Marcos faced "increasing diplomatic isolation" after his fraudulent presidential election, and how Yasir Arafat appeared "more isolated than ever" in his role as Palestine Liberation Organization chief. This sensibility may manifest itself when a nation's reputation causes citizens to feel ashamed of their national identity (for example, see Noelle-Neumann and Koecher, 1989).

Isolation was also perceived as an interaction between a nation's government and citizens, and the other nations in the world. In 27% of the cases where isolation was mentioned, other nations were described as a *unit*. "World community," "world public," or "civilized nations" are examples of these references. Indeed, world opinion was commonly attributed to an "international order," however loosely defined. The world was also referenced as a unit through its reactions to an event or action: "the world observes," "the whole world waits," "the world holds its breath." Finally, Mowlana's concept of a "world stage" also appears in a variety of forms: nations operate on an "international stage," in an "international theater," or in a "world theater" (Mowlana, 1986:176). All these concepts define the isolated nation's estrangement from a common sensibility other nations apparently share.

The primary source for references to the world as a unit (75.7% in the *IHT* and 65.5% in the *FAZ*) were the newspapers' own reporters; other sources included wire services (10.8% in the *IHT* and 13.7% in the *FAZ*), and guest editorials and syndicated columnists (13.5% in the *IHT* and 20.7% in the *FAZ*). As the data indicate, there were no significant differences in the sources for references between the two newspapers.

Figure 1.2. Percentage of Total References to Isolation on Each Issue

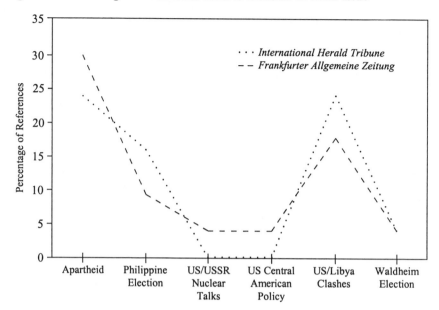

Isolation was characterized as a key to the *power* of world opinion in 30% of the cases, carrying its message to leaders and citizens. The punishment was cited in 31.8% of cases where leaders were aware of world opinion, and 20% of cases where citizens were aware of world opinion; it was cited in none of the cases where neither were aware of world opinion.[6] A nation's *image*, referenced in 28.4% of cases where isolation was cited, was presented at risk when a nation was faced with isolation.

Isolation appears as a key element in the world opinion process, as it appears in the two newspapers. A nation's actions on the "world stage" earn it an international reputation. If a nation's image is tarnished, the nation risks being threatened with isolation. According to the data, the likelihood of this threat increased according to certain criteria. Isolation was more likely to be referenced in cases when a moral issue was at stake than when it was not, by a margin of 28.2% to 16.3%, respectively (r = .124, significance = .064). Isolation was also more likely to be referenced when a nation's moral and pragmatic interests regarding world opinion conflicted, by a margin of 66.7% to 23.2%, respectively (r = .304, significance = .013).[7] Finally, isolation was more likely to be referenced when world opinion conflicted with a nation's public opinion, by a margin of 40% to 15.4%, respectively (r = .278, significance = .031).[8]

These findings are hardly surprising. Countries would be expected to conform to world opinion when it served their national interests. The threat of isolation is required to encourage conformity only when world opinion conflicts with national interests, or internal opinion. As noted above, there are instances where world opinion carries with it a pragmatic component that appeals to the *shared* interests of all nations involved. But this is not the case when isolation is threatened. Here, nations do not share common interests, and the country in question has national interests that conflict with world opinion. The threat of isolation is invoked when an appeal on pragmatic grounds alone will not work; the threat is necessary to attempt to alter the nation's equation of their interests. In this case, a nation's options include tempering the single-minded pursuit of their interests, or ignoring world opinion and risking disruption of economic, political, and diplomatic ties to other nations. China's brutal suppression of the prodemocracy movement in Tiananmen Square, and the country's resulting condemnation and isolation by other nations, is a stark example of the latter strategy. According to some analysts, world reaction to this event influenced the Soviet Union's decision to follow a cautious approach to prodemocracy movements in the Eastern bloc nations.[9] Such events suggest that the process of world opinion described in the two newspapers provides ample justification for nations to fear isolation.

CONCLUSION

This analysis began with a reflection on the notion "public" in "public opinion" as a guide to analyzing a similar notion for "world opinion." Further examination of Noelle-Neumann's use of the notion public in public opinion provides a heuristic device for organizing our hypotheses about world opinion. Noelle-Neumann describes three steps in the public opinion process: (1) the capacity for individuals to sense when an opinion strengthens or weakens in a society; (2) their reactions to this sense, leading them toward more confident speech or silencing; and (3) the common fear of isolation, which prompts individuals to be mindful of their opinions of others (Noelle-Neumann, 1984:62). Her definition of public opinion follows from these steps: "public opinion" consists of attitudes or behavior that an individual can or must express publicly in order to avoid social isolation (63). Our analysis of world opinion generated complementary hypotheses regarding the agenda for world opinion in the two newspapers, and the role of isolation in the process. The two newspapers reflected a general consensus regarding:

1. the *major issues* which formed the content for world opinion;

2. the *relative emphasis* on these issues during the three-month time period; and

3. the *dates* when event-driven issues were suitable topics for discussion in world opinion.

Regarding the role of isolation, the two newspapers agreed that

4. when a nation's interests, actions, statements, or public opinion conflict with the moral imperatives of world opinion, the nation may be threatened with isolation by other nations. Consequently, actors may consider tempering their pursuit of goals which could earn them international condemnation.

Both newspapers shared a sense of when issues were waxing or waning as suitable topics for world opinion. Both papers also shared a sense of which issues were likely to prompt isolation, and the risks of ignoring this threat. A preliminary definition of world opinion following from these findings would therefore be: *World opinion refers to the moral judgments of observers which actors must heed in the international arena, or risk isolation as a nation.*

In an increasingly integrated world, a nation's actions, statements, and image are subject to closer scrutiny than in previous times. Such scrutiny invites, or demands, reactions to issues that had previously seemed to be matters of concern just within nations.[10] Consider this argument regarding the Waldheim election in Austria:

> In the wake of the election, *the world cannot remain silent.* It must severely condemn some Austrians' deliberate exploitation of the Waldheim affair, during the election, to prompt anti-Jewish sentiments (*IHT*, June 11, 1986; emphases added).

If world opinion demands certain statements or reactions, it demands reconsiderations of the boundaries and significance of national behavior. What was once only a matter of parochial or national concern (like an election) becomes a "public" matter on the "world stage." Such reflections lend a new perspective to such high-sounding phrases as the "global village." The notion of "village" implies an openness to opinion which invites the scrutiny and judgment of one's neighbors. The notion of a "global village" may similarly expose a nation's citizens and leaders to the judgments of others and, hence, to the vagaries of world opinion in demanding and disturbing ways.

NOTES

1. Indeed, even a publication like *World Opinion Quarterly*, whose title suggests a discussion of "world opinion," is concerned with describing opinion distributions on comparable questions in various different nations.

2. In order to understand this transition, one must briefly reexamine accepted notions of "public opinion." Defining a "public" for public opinion as a national society bounded by specific borders is itself a questionable assumption. Many social scientists have abandoned this notion, instead describing "publics" defined by shared characteristics such as race, ethnic background, and social class within a nation's specified borders (see Hennessey, 1985:9-10; Yeric and Todd, 1983:2-4; and Childs, 1965:12 as examples). This, however, raises a number of other definitional problems regarding the boundaries of groups to be described as publics, and the proportion of persons who must ascribe to an attitude before this description is legitimate (see Rusciano, 1989:2-4).

3. However, an initial study aimed at deriving hypotheses about world opinion must concentrate on the term's *presence*; analyses of the term's *absence* are best left for a future testing of these hypotheses.

4. This measure was derived by averaging the difference in the percentage of total references between the two newspapers on each topic.

5. The last time period is slightly longer, including four days left in the month for the period under study.

6. Although it must be noted that where the issues of leaders' awareness ($N = 87$) or citizens' awareness ($N = 27$) was discussed, there were only two cases in each instance where leaders or citizens were not aware of world opinion.

7. Isolation was not more likely to be referenced when a pragmatic issue was at stake than when it was not.

8. The correlations refer to data for both newspapers combined; however, none of the correlations were significantly reduced with a control for the newspaper.

9. In fact, one analyst makes this point in analyzing Gorbachev's motives in an article for the *Washington Post Weekly Edition* (January 8, 1990:9).

10. World opinion may have critical effects within nations as well. Because identity is an interactive process on the individual and collective levels, national image is a key element in national identity. Our sense of identity reflects how we see ourselves and how others perceive us (see Gilligan, 1982:159). As such, a nation's reputation beyond its borders can affect its citizens' perceptions of the values and culture that characterize their country. World opinion thereby might explain why citizens of nations with tarnished international reputations can be reluctant to display a sense of national pride (see Noelle-Neumann and Koecher, 1987).

2

World Opinion During Times of Crisis

*Frank Louis Rusciano
and John Crothers Pollock*

Following the momentous events of 1989-1991, the international media (e.g., Unger, 1991; Ullman, 1991) were quick to declare the existence of a "post-Cold War order." However, doubts about the existence of such an order have arisen since the heady days following the fall of the Berlin Wall. Events in Bosnia and many of the former Eastern bloc nations have prompted the observation that the Cold War's legacy is a "new world disorder" in the absence of accustomed conflicts defined by superpower competition (Hinckley, 1991).

The problem here is one of definition. The end of the Cold War did disrupt a "world order" by breaking alliances that had previously defined international relations. But a "world order" is also a social construction—a "system of intelligibility" for the "separation of the world into kinds of space" (Shapiro, 1989:13). The Cold War order, considered in these terms, was a clash of liberal versus Communist ideologies. There are indications that a new paradigm is emerging in the post-Cold War era.

Descriptions of this emerging system, while less than explicit, tend to include two primary features. First, they assume a *consensus*, real or perceived, exists regarding acceptable behavior in international affairs. Second, they assume leaders may invoke the sanction of *international isolation*, in various ways, to punish nations that violate this consensus. Both features relate directly to the concept of "world opinion." Consensus implies that nations generally share opinions about proper behavior in the international sphere, while the threat of isolation implies that these nations are willing to act upon this consensus to punish errant countries or leaders.

The "post-Cold War order" grows out of a competition between different constructions of world opinion regarding acceptable international behavior. However, as noted in the previous chapter, some analysts have claimed that "world opinion" is entirely an individual construct, serving the values of those who

invoke it (see Bogart, 1966; and Morgenthau, 1962).[1] As such, it cannot serve
as the basis for a "system of intelligibility" or collective action in global affairs.
The concept moves from individual to social construction when it is communicated to others: "once we attempt to articulate what there is [in the 'world out
there'] we enter the world of discourse. At that moment the process of construction begins" (Gergen, 1992:171).

This chapter studies different sources of discourse regarding world opinion
during the Kuwaiti crisis preceding the Persian Gulf War and the Bosnian crisis
during 1995. The sources on the Gulf War include media observations from different areas of the world and documents regarding United Nations' discussions
about international collective action to address the crisis. The analysis of the
Bosnian crisis depends solely on media observations.

We advance three conclusions regarding the emerging international
"order." First, this "order" grows out of a consensus among various nations on
how world opinion is constructed on specific issues. Second, it is less fixed than
the Cold War competition between superpowers. It occurs as a process of opinion formation, rather than as a conflict between defined ideologies or interests.
Finally, the process is reflected when the timing and content of different forms
of public discourse on world opinion converge. The discourse is made public
through national and international media outlets and global forums like the
United Nations. As such, various forms of political communication facilitate,
reflect, and define the growth of the emerging "order" at any given time. These
processes are evident in both "successful" and problematic cases of international
cooperation.

THE STUDY DESIGN AND QUESTIONS FOR RESEARCH
ON THE KUWAITI CRISIS

The first analysis has two purposes. First, it studies the common usage of
the concept of "world opinion" in *The New York Times* (*NYT*, representing a
major Western nation's newspaper) and the *Times of India* (*TOI*, representing
a third world nation's newspaper). The notion of "representation" must be
understood here. The two dailies were selected as examples of quality newspapers in their respective venues. Both are independent of ties to foreign media
outlets; the *Times of India* was originally a British publication during the colon-
ial era, but it became a purely Indian enterprise after the nation gained independence in 1947. However, it is not assumed that *The New York Times* or the
Times of India express the perspectives of the United States or India, or of the
first or third world, respectively, regarding world opinion. Rather, it is assumed
that the manner in which each newspaper socially constructs the concept of
world opinion is affected by their nation and region of origin. A newspaper's
national origin may explain, but not determine, its perspective on world opinion.

Comparative content analyses of world opinion are necessary because
Herman and Chomsky argue that newspapers in particular nations (notably the

United States) tend to "manufacture consent" by "filtering" news according to the perspectives of the government and dominant private interests. Factors contributing to this filtering include concentrated ownership of mass media, media dependence on advertising revenues, media reliance on government and corporate sources for information, criticisms of objectivity as a means of disciplining the media, and anti-communism as an accepted ideology (Herman and Chomsky, 1988:2). The last factor has declined in importance in the post-Cold War era, but the other factors might have retained or increased their influence in recent years. A comparative analysis can reduce the influence of these factors by introducing information from another nation's newspapers.

Consider Herman and Chomsky's argument that news coverage of a Soviet pilot's downing of a Korean jetliner in 1983 deliberately emphasized the American government's interpretation of "world opinion." *The New York Times* reported on August 31, 1984, that U.S. officials "assert that *worldwide criticism* of the Soviet handling of the crisis has strengthened the United States in its relations with Moscow" (Herman and Chomsky, 1988:32; emphases added). It is unclear whether all or even most foreign newspapers echoed this interpretation of world opinion. It is reasonable to assume that the *Times* primarily echoed the American government's perspective on world opinion. A comparative analysis of different nations' newspapers should clarify whether, and how, media observations on world opinion are bound by national interests.

It is also possible that the national factors described by Herman and Chomsky, if accurate, affect the Indian newspaper. Furthermore, American news "filters" might have the capacity to affect the news media of other nations, given the influence of the United States in international media systems. However, the analysis indicates that the two newspapers approached the subject of world opinion on the crisis in a different manner. Indirect effects of American influence on foreign governments' interpretations of world opinion will be discussed in this chapter's conclusion.

This project performs a content analysis on all stories and editorials referencing world opinion during the prewar Kuwaiti crisis, from August 1, 1990, through January 16, 1991. During this period, the American daily referenced the concept 67 times and the Indian daily, 65 times. Explicit citations included such usages as "world opinion," "international opinion," or "world public opinion." Implicit citations, which comprise more than 93% of both newspapers' references, attribute attitudes, preferences, opinions, or reactions to the world or to all nations considered together. Two examples follow.

There probably would have been little world reaction had it not been for the oil and wealth at stake (Lewis, 1990:A27).

Bowing to international . . . pressure and condemnation and the threat of punitive economic sanctions, Iraq today started withdrawing its troops from Kuwait, three days after it invaded the country (*TOI*, 1990a:1).

Implicit references also included active constructions, as if "the world" were stating an opinion, or passing judgment on an action or event: "condemning," "applauding," or "expecting" some phenomenon. Two examples follow.

All nations have reason to be outraged by a violation of frontiers tantamount to armed robbery. . . . The only rational response is to isolate Iraq and compel its unconditional pullout (*NYT*, 1990:E18).

What these various pressures add up to is a refusal by the international community . . . to endorse the fait accompli that Iraq presented it with by forcibly taking over Kuwait (*TOI*, 1990b:10).

These and similar citations form the basis for the first part of the comparative analysis of the two newspapers' references to world opinion. This section of the study concentrates on four major subjects: (1) the timing of references to world opinion on the crisis in the two newspapers; (2) the relative emphasis both newspapers place on the moral component of world opinion (which stresses values shared by nations) and the pragmatic component of world opinion (which stresses interests shared by nations); (3) the two newspapers' evaluations of world reactions to the crisis; and (4) the manner in which both papers describe the timing and extent of Iraq's isolation from the world community.

R.L. Doty notes that if "the same kinds of subjects, objects, and relations are found to exist in different texts, this is indicative of a particular logic at work . . . if differences are constructed according to the same logic in a variety of texts, we can reasonably suggest there is a dominant discourse" (Doty, 1993: 308). Analysis of the two newspapers reveals a somewhat different "logic" in each regarding world opinion. The similarities and differences in the "dominant discourse" on the subject between the two newspapers reflect the relative positions of the United States and India in the international community.

The second part of the analysis studies the construction of world opinion as it emerges out of a different set of discursive practices. This section analyzes discussions in the United Nations regarding punitive sanctions against Iraq during the period under study. The timing of references to sanctions converges with the timing of references to world opinion on the subject in *The New York Times* and the *Times of India* eight weeks into the crisis. This finding is discussed in terms of the relationship between media perspectives on world opinion and international collective action, and the meaning of competition between different discursive constructions of world opinion.

Exploring the Agenda and Timing of References to World Opinion

For the period studied, the Kuwaiti crisis dominated the agenda for world opinion in both newspapers; all of *The New York Times'* references and 45 (or 69.2%) of the *Times of India*'s references dealt with the crisis. Despite the dominant position accorded this topic in both papers, the Indian daily clearly

Figure 2.1. Percentage of Total References to the Kuaiti Crisis, by Date (N = 112)

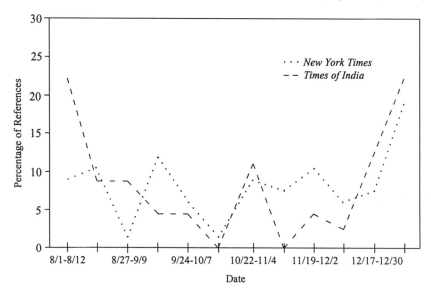

perceived a more diverse agenda for world opinion.[2] Topics not referenced in *The New York Times*, but found in the *Times of India*, include the Pakistanis' development of atomic weapons and Israel's treatment of the Palestinians on the West Bank. This pattern of general similarity with specific, and important, variance also applies to the date of references to world opinion on the Iraqi invasion.

Figure 2.1 shows the distribution of citations on the crisis for both newspapers, by date, divided into two-week periods.[3] As the graph indicates, there is little correspondence between the dates of reference in the first eight weeks; however, the correspondence increases dramatically in the next 16 weeks. The Cramer's V values verify these observations, indicating a significant difference in the first period, and no significant difference in the second period.[4]

The similarity after the first eight weeks does not stem from similar wire service sources for stories and editorials, since the two papers shared sources in only 9% of cases in the early and later periods. Other significant differences in the two newspapers' perspectives on world opinion indicate reasons for the convergence of references. First, the two newspapers displayed significant differences in their measures of world opinion. The *Times of India* cited leaders' reactions as a primary source for world opinion in 64.4% of cases; *The New York Times* mentioned leaders' reactions as a source in only 12% of cases. In most cases (58.2%) the American daily cited no measure for world opinion; the Indian daily cited no measure in few cases (9%).

This significant difference[5] applies for citations before and after the first eight weeks of the crisis. But the signals given by world leaders shifted dramatically between these two periods, altering the perception of world opinion in the Indian newspaper. In the first eight weeks of the crisis, the Indian newspaper was more likely than the American newspaper to feature the Iraqi perspective on the invasion in its descriptions of world opinion. While the *Times of India*'s stories and editorials condemned the Iraqis' actions as morally wrong, the Indian daily cited Iraqi public opinion in 50% of the references in the first eight weeks. By contrast, the American daily cited Iraqi public opinion in only 4.5% of these cases. Not surprisingly, Iraqi public opinion in the Indian paper disagreed with other interpretations of world opinion in nine out of ten cases.

After the first eight weeks of the crisis, though, references to Iraqi opinion in the *Times of India* (4% of citations) actually drop to a lower level than references in *The New York Times* (8.9% of citations). Other evidence suggests that the disparity between the two newspapers' interpretations of world opinion was greater in the first eight weeks of the crisis than afterward. At the beginning of the crisis, the *Times of India* ascribed "indirect motivations" to the United States, accusing its leaders of "trying to turn the whole world against Iraq" and "trying to humiliate and overthrow Mr. [Saddam] Hussein because he is an uppity insubordinate Arab" (Jansen, 1990:1). The newspaper also predicted that the U.S. troop presence in Saudi Arabia might dissipate "Arab and world hostility" by making Hussein an "underdog and a hero," despite his initial isolation (*TOI*, 1990b:10).

One may explain early differences in the timing and tone of references to the Kuwaiti crisis by comparing the relative positions of India and the United States in the world, and to the continuing development of an international consensus during this period. *The New York Times* repeatedly indicated that world opinion favored the American demonization of Hussein on the invasion, with little specific reference to other nations' reactions. The *Times of India* reflected and cited a greater variety of sources, including other world leaders and Iraqi public opinion, in its construction of world opinion. After the first eight weeks, an international consensus appears to emerge.

Several factors no doubt contributed to this change. First, Hussein's appearance with two British children on August 23, intended to illustrate the supposedly humane treatment of Westerners barred from leaving Iraq, probably affected this shift. The image of the frightened children served to project a cruel and vivid picture to the international media.

Second, Soviet support of American actions against Iraq, granted when George Bush and Mikhail Gorbachev met in Helsinki on September 9, also underscored the unity of world leaders against the invasion of Kuwait. The agreement of the two former antagonists signaled that the Cold War divisions on such crises were past; the support also had special significance in India, which traditionally enjoyed a friendly relationship with the Soviet Union.

Third, the United Nations Security Council passed nine resolutions during the first eight weeks of the crisis, condemning the invasion and defining Iraq's economic and diplomatic isolation. Furthermore, the United States was clearly attempting to assume the role of world opinion leader from the beginning of the crisis. Polls taken in several European nations in August 1990 indicate the American strategy was successful. Majorities in Britain, France, and Germany felt it was appropriate for the United States to "take the lead in responding to the Iraqi invasion" (Hinckley, 1991:Table 5).[6] Similarly, support in August 1990 for the U.S.-sponsored sanctions against Iraq was strong in Britain, France, Germany, and Italy (Table 6).[7]

Opinions in the international media reflected a similar consensus regarding actions against Iraq. Support was high in newspapers in Western Europe, Latin America, and the Soviet Union; while some Asian and African newspapers questioned American motives in the Gulf, they still strongly condemned Iraqi aggression (USIA, 1990). As the *Times of India* monitored other nations' leaders as one indicator of world opinion, it received a clear message of support against Iraq and for economic sanctions. The convergence of references to world opinion on the crisis reflects this emerging consensus. The consensus had different ramifications for the United States and India, though, given their different positions and interests during the crisis. These differences are reflected in the manner in which the two papers described the moral and pragmatic components of world opinion, and the threat of isolation, in their stories and editorials.

The Moral and Pragmatic Components of World Opinion During the Kuwaiti Crisis

The search for a dominant discourse regarding world opinion must necessarily focus beyond its agenda to the concept's component parts. Our initial analysis focused on two critical elements: the moral and pragmatic components of world opinion. The two newspapers balanced the moral and pragmatic components of world opinion in a way that corresponds to the patterns of general convergence and specific variance described above. *The New York Times* and the *Times of India* projected similar perspectives on the moral component of world opinion during the crisis, condemning the Iraqi invasion as ethically wrong. Even when the Indian newspaper qualified this condemnation by citing such actions as Kuwait's refusal to adhere to limits on oil production set by the Organization of Petroleum Exporting Countries, it still described the invasion as an affront to all nations' moral sensibilities. As such, the moral component is ubiquitous in references to world opinion on the crisis in both papers, appearing in 95.5% of stories in *The New York Times* and in 93.2% of stories in the *Times of India*. These citations were equally likely to occur before and after the first eight weeks of the crisis in both newspapers. As noted in the previous chapter, references to the moral component tend to correspond with references to the power of world opinion to compel nations to accept its judgments.

The pragmatic component, though highly correlated with references to the moral component, is less important in developing an international consensus. World opinion is primarily about moral suasion. This insight is relevant to the present discussion, since the two newspapers reflected much less agreement on the pragmatic issues in world opinion regarding the invasion of Kuwait. The American newspaper repeatedly claimed that action against Hussein served the interests of all nations; the Indian newspaper remained more ambivalent regarding the interests of its nation and other third world nations. An editorial in the *Times of India* makes clear the conflict between the moral and pragmatic components of world opinion for India and other third world countries:

> India fully endorses the U.N. Security Council's resolutions calling upon Iraq to vacate its occupation of Kuwait. . . . *India has refrained from any criticism, even indirectly, of the very large forces deployed against Iraq around its borders . . . it recognizes that each state has an inherent right of self-defense and to take measures it considers necessary towards this end.* . . . India is urging Iraq, a friend of long standing, to pull back its troops to clear the way for the redress of its grievances against Kuwait. . . . *If Iraq refuses to accept the peaceful alternative, the onus will be on it for the consequences that may follow will be disastrous not only for Iraq but for countries like India (TOI,* 1991a:12; emphases added).

The editorial clearly states the conundrum in the Indian newspaper's perspective on world opinion. On the one side, it defends the moral right of a nation to self-defense. On the other side, it acknowledges that the application of the principle in this case would violate the interests of India and "countries like it" (i.e., other third world nations). The implied solution is clear: the newspaper "refrains from any criticism," falls silent, and does not protest that its interests do not coincide with other nations regarding war, in deference to the power of the moral principle.

References to world opinion in the two newspapers indicate that once an international consensus developed, the moral component tended to silence discussion of the pragmatic component of world opinion in the *Times of India* relative to *The New York Times*. Overall, *The New York Times* referenced the moral and pragmatic components with equal frequency, in about 91% of cases; the *Times of India* referenced the pragmatic component in 61.4% of cases and the moral component in 93.2% of cases.[8]

Even more important, though, was the timing of these differences. In the first eight weeks of the crisis, both newspapers expressed their perspectives on the pragmatic component of world opinion with equal frequency; references appeared in 72.7% of cases in *The New York Times* and in 60% of cases in the *Times of India.*[9] Beyond the first eight weeks, though, references to the pragmatic component in the American newspaper increased to all cases, while references in the Indian daily stayed constant at about 62.5% of cases.[10] Hence, as the American newspaper defined and discussed the pragmatic component of world opinion more aggressively on the crisis, the Indian newspaper responded with a relative silencing of its perspective on the supposed "common interests" shared by all nations. Why did references to the moral component apparently supercede references to the pragmatic component in the Indian newspaper, but not in the American newspaper? One answer lies in the power of world opinion to enforce its moral imperatives through the threat of international isolation.

The Threat of Isolation and the Kuwaiti Crisis

As noted in Chapter 1, "isolation" in world opinion refers to implicit or explicit moves by nations to distance themselves from those who violate the dictates of world opinion. *The New York Times* referenced Iraq's isolation after the invasion in 79.1% of articles, while the *Times of India* referenced it in 72% of its articles. Isolation was referenced in explicit and implicit terms. Explicit references (34.7% of citations) used the word or some equivalent: "Mr. Saddam Hussein is almost completely isolated," "Hussein . . . struggles to break his international isolation," and "there will be no separate . . . paths for isolated nationalistic efforts" are examples of such usage. Implicit references (65.3% of citations) conveyed a sense that the leader or country is separated from, or shunned by, other nations. References to "embargoes" and "boycotts" of Iraqi goods after the UN resolutions barred trade with Baghdad are examples of such usage. Another example is this statement of the expected results of the Bush-Gorbachev summit in Helsinki, described in *The New York Times* of September 11, 1990:

> Conveying to Saddam Hussein the message that Moscow was standing with Washington and the rest of the world was meaningful in itself, of course; the chances of persuading him to pull out of Kuwait depend to a considerable degree on penetrating the Iraqi dictator's tough psychological carapace and *making him feel increasingly shunned, cornered, and friendless* (Apple, 1990:1; emphases added).

Isolation has two meanings in the above examples. It may involve the breaking of tangible relationships of commerce, diplomacy, or business. Other countries may close embassies, recall diplomatic personnel, or bar trade with the isolated nation. But isolation may also convey the vague, general sense that a country's citizens and leaders are pariahs to other nations, unwelcome as visitors or unrecognized as legitimate heads of state. *The New York Times'* quotation illustrates this latter notion—the feeling of being "shunned" and "friendless" in the world, without reference to any specific or tangible actions other nations may take against the target of isolation. References to isolation followed the same pattern by date in the two newspapers as references to world opinion on the crisis. These references were significantly different by date between the two

Figure 2.2. Percentage of Total References to Isolation on the Kuaiti Crisis, by Date (N = 72)

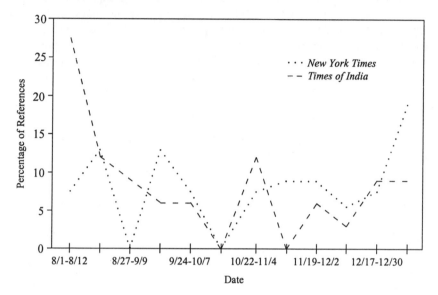

dailies before, but not after, the first eight weeks of the crisis.[11] These results are illustrated graphically in Figure 2.2.

References to isolation and references to world opinion follow a similar pattern; directing the threat of isolation toward a nation requires a clear international consensus. Indeed, the newspapers were often quite specific about the entity from which Iraq was isolated. Hussein's actions put him outside of the "international community," the "community of nations," and the "world community" in various articles and editorials. The recurrent pattern of early variance and later convergence reveals differences and similarities in the dominant discourses on world opinion in the two newspapers.

Once an international consensus appeared to form on the crisis, and moral considerations superceded pragmatic considerations in the *Times of India*, the timing of references to the issue and the threat of isolation converge between the Indian and American newspapers. But this convergence alone is insufficient evidence of a "new system of intelligibility" for the post-Cold War era. A new order implies more than just consensus and international isolation in descriptions of world opinion. It also implies that these forces have some power or influence over nations' actions. As such, there must be evidence of a link between international consensus and collective action. This chapter pursues this link by studying discourse within the United Nations regarding international reactions to the Iraqi invasion.

An Institutional Connection? Media Perspectives on World Opinion and United Nations Activity

Different means exist for the construction of world opinion. To this point, the analysis has defined characteristics of "dominant discourses" on the subject as reflected in two newspapers. But the concept may also grow out of practices of discourse which are not so self-consciously applied to the subject. The interaction of several nations' perspectives, if given an arena for expression, may also construct boundaries and a definition for world opinion on a given topic, making the concept a "reality." As Doty notes:

> Policy makers also function within a discursive space that imposes meaning on the world and thus creates reality (Shapiro, 1989:100, 116). . . . "foreign policy makers" need not be limited to prominent decision makers, but could also include rather anonymous members of the various bureaucracies who write the numerous memorandums, intelligence reports, and research papers that circulate within policy circles. The discourse(s) instantiated in these various documents produce meanings and in doing so actively construct "reality" upon which foreign policy is based (Doty, 1993:303).

On a theoretical level, though, one may argue that the discourse that occurs within institutions is different from the discourse which occurs in other venues, notably the news media. Institutional discussions, even within bodies like the United Nations, which does not enjoy the legitimacy and influence of national legislative bodies, are likely to be action oriented. Discourse on Iraqi sanctions within the UN certainly followed this pattern, including discussions of their legitimacy as well as proposals of how sanctions might be implemented and maintained. The discussion of linkages between media observations of world opinion and UN discourse, then, must assume a possible relationship between world opinion (however inadequately reflected) and international collective action to punish Iraq, respectively.

Establishing connections between constituent opinion and institutional responses has always been a difficult task for political scientists. This task is even harder in the present case, where media provides, at best, a reflection of world opinion. To establish a possible connection between opinion and response, this section borrows from other analysts' approaches to the problem. These approaches include testing the changes in direction of policy in institutional bodies in response to opinion (Page and Shapiro, 1983) or the correspondence between citizens' and elites' perceptions of the public agenda (Verba and Nie, 1972).

It is hypothesized that media observations on world opinion may reflect the priority of the Kuwaiti crisis at a given time, which in turn may relate to the priority of sanctions against Iraq on the UN agenda. The volume of media references to world opinion on the Kuwaiti crisis is one indicator of the subject's priority over time. The priority rises and falls across the various two-week periods graphically represented in Figures 2.1 and 2.2. If discussions within the

United Nations follow a similar pattern, it would suggest a link between the media-perceived agenda for world opinion and the UN institutional agenda. This connection could have various interpretations; it could indicate pressure placed upon the institution by world opinion or simply a convergence of discourse on world opinion from varying sources. In either case, the comparative timing of media observations and UN discussions can provide valuable insights for defining the role of political communication in the post-Cold War era.

This project studies UN documents regarding Iraqi sanctions to analyze construction of a "discursive space" for world opinion within that forum. These documents include letters from various nations to the UN secretary general and the Security Council, minutes of General Assembly and Security Council meetings, and press releases from the international body.[12] It seeks to link the timing of an apparent consensus about the agenda for world opinion (as reflected in the two newspapers) with the enforcement of consensus by international isolation (as reflected by UN documents). It asks whether the construction of an agenda for world opinion parallels the construction of an agenda regarding the means to implement it. This question is especially appropriate here. The embargo against Iraq confounded the generally accepted logic regarding international sanctions. It is usually assumed that such actions will fall victim to a version of the logic of collective action, as one or more countries "defect" from the boycott, and try to seize the isolated nation's markets for themselves.

The involvement of a critical resource like oil should further assure this failure (see, for example, Barry and Hardin, 1982; Schelling, 1958; Jervis, 1970; and Snidal, 1985 for various discussions of the collective action problem). The sanctions against Iraq violated these assumptions. Despite Iraq's control of about 20% of the world's known oil reserves after the invasion, the embargo against their goods was deemed 100% effective, costing that nation 48% in lost trade. As such, the boycott was approximately two to three times more effective than the most successful past actions of this sort.[13]

The emerging consensus regarding world opinion and isolation, reflected in *The New York Times* and the *Times of India*, parallels this success. For this analysis, all UN documents dealing with international sanctions against Iraq were analyzed for the dates between August 2, 1990, and December 31, 1990.[14] The documents were coded by date of arrival, and these dates were compared to the dates of references to world opinion and the isolation of Iraq in the two newspapers. The results of these comparisons are presented graphically in Figures 2.3 through 2.6.

A familiar pattern emerges from these results. The volume of UN documents on Iraqi sanctions does not follow the timing of references to world opinion or isolation in either newspaper in the first eight weeks of the crisis. However, the volume of documents converges with this timing in both newspapers after the first eight weeks.[15] This relationship does not occur because the newspapers were taking their cues on world opinion from the United Nations; the volume of UN documents does not correlate with the timing of

Figure 2.3. Percentage of References to World Opinion in the *New York Times* and UN Documents on Iraqi Sanctions, by Date (N = 409)

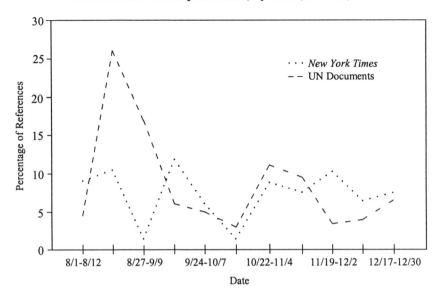

Figure 2.4. Percentage of References to World Opinion in the *Times of India* and UN Documents on Iraqi Sanctions, by Date (N = 390)

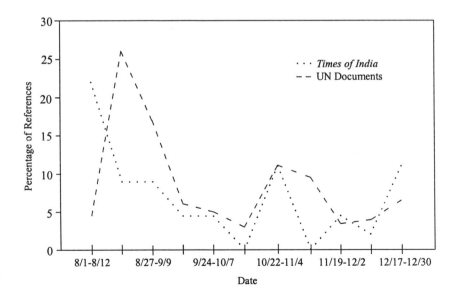

**Figure 2.5. Percentage of References to Isolation in the *New York Times* and
UN Documents on Iraqi Sanctions, by Date (N = 398)**

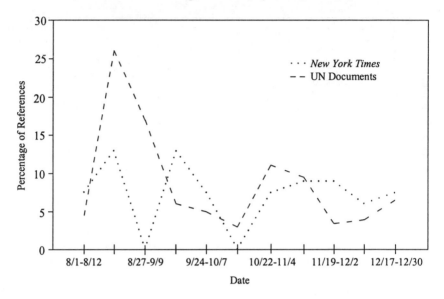

**Figure 2.6. Percentage of References to Isolation in the *Times of India* and
UN Documents on Iraqi Sanctions, by Date (N = 385)**

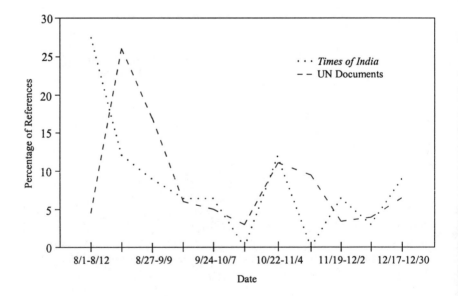

either newspapers' references until the two newspapers' references converge. Two possible explanations account for these results; both suggest significant implications for the role of political communication in the post-Cold War order.

First, the international media may provide a means by which world opinion is disseminated, and the threat of isolation expressed toward errant nations. The media therefore defines, or creates, a "public," considered as individuals or nations open to the threat of isolation. By this explanation, when media sources from different nations in the West or the third world construct the form and content of world opinion differently, this public is fragmented and ineffective in collective action. When a consensus forms within this "world public," countries within the United Nations respond with similar activity, following the pressures applied through the media over time.

A second explanation considers the volume of UN documents, and the references to world opinion and isolation in the two newspapers, as separate measures of discourse on world opinion. Each outlet would collect information about world opinion from somewhat different sources. When these sources converge, a consensus in international opinion has probably developed, and the chances for international collective action are enhanced. Here, all various forms of discourse on relevant subjects become potential inputs into the formation of a post-Cold War order. The question remaining is whether the combination of various constructions provides sufficient evidence and detail for describing a "system of intelligibility" for understanding conflicts in the present era. Before rendering judgment on this issue, we turn to the thornier example of the Bosnian crisis, and the challenges it presents to notions of a "system of intelligibility" in the post-Cold War era.

MEDIA OBSERVATIONS ON WORLD OPINION DURING THE RECENT BOSNIAN CRISIS

The Persian Gulf War represented a halcyon period for those who dreamed of a "new world order"; these dreams were soon dashed on a rock called Bosnia. The conflicts in the former Yugoslavia seemed well suited for international intervention. The events had been prompted by the demise of the Soviet Union, which removed a threat that theretofore had held together a fragile coalition of nationalist factions within Yugoslavia. The war also offended the world's moral sensibilities; its stories of "ethnic cleansing" conjured up memories of the Nazi exterminations during the Second World War. Finally, it seemed as though all nations had a historical imperative to make peace in this region; it was less than a century ago that the First World War had started due to violent actions in the Balkans.

Despite these conditions, the response of the international community to the Bosnian crisis was agonizingly slow and inadequate. The United Nations sent peacekeeping forces that were incapable of keeping peace, and set up an arms embargo that had little effect on the warring factions' abilities to cause each other harm. Finally, the major powers, including the United States and Germany, contributed little more than rhetoric condemning the violence. It appeared as though the Persian Gulf War had been an aberration, and that the post-Cold War condition was a "new world disorder" marred by unpredictable and brutal conflicts instead of superpower competition (Hinckley, 1991). The Bosnian conflict begged the question of whether a "post-Cold War order" based around world opinion could realistically be said to exist.

Upon initial observation, the prospects look bleak. The international community waited years to respond to conditions in the former Yugoslavian republic. We argue one reason is found by considering the twin features of world consensus and international isolation as preconditions for such a response. Put another way, prior to the bombing of the marketplace in Sarajevo, world opinion had not crystallized sufficiently to warrant a response, despite the horrible circumstances of the war. We explore this thesis by studying the usage of the concept of world opinion in two quality newspaper from two key players in the Bosnian crisis, players without whom an international response would have been impossible: the United States and Germany.

The Study Design and Questions for Research on the Bosnian Crisis

The following analysis studies all references to world opinion on the Bosnian crisis, from April 28, 1995, to November 28, 1995, in *The New York Times* (*NYT*) and the *Frankfurter Allgemeine Zeitung* (*FAZ*). The dates for the analysis were chosen with reference to the shelling of the marketplace in Sarajevo on August 28, 1995; the references are studied from 16 weeks before the shelling to 14 weeks after the shelling, through the signing of the Dayton peace accords. During this period, 98 references to world opinion on Bosnia appeared in the two newspapers: 35 references in *The New York Times* and 63 references in the *Frankfurter Allgemeine Zeitung*.

This portion of the analysis followed the same methodology and assumptions applied to the Kuwaiti crisis. As before, we assume newspapers in particular countries (especially the United States) tend to "manufacture consent" by "filtering" the news according to the perspectives of the government and prominent private interests (Herman and Chomsky, 1988:2). Further, these effects extend even to the discussion of world opinion, upon which nations are expected to agree. Newspapers can be expected to offer national perspectives on world opinion. Two hypotheses follow: one may partially explain a newspaper's usage of world opinion with reference to its nation's interests; and, when two or more newspapers converge in their perspectives on world opinion, an international consensus—and the potential for collective action—may become more likely. Absent any such convergence, world opinion will likely remain fragmented into the different nations' perspectives, making international collective responses unlikely.

Profiling the Usage of World Opinion in the Two Newspapers

The most immediate observation regarding coverage of world opinion on the Bosnian crisis is that the German newspaper contained more references to the subject than the American newspaper. One explanation of this finding could be that the German newspaper simply tends to reference world opinion more often than the American newspaper; however, the previous chapter suggests there are no general patterns in the number of times newspapers from Germany and America reference world opinion. A more plausible explanation is that the Bosnian crisis had more salience as an issue in world opinion in Germany, since the war was occurring so close to its borders, and historically Germany had been deeply involved in this region. It is therefore not surprising that the Bosnian crisis would be the subject of more references to world opinion in the German newspaper.

The greater salience of the issue for the German newspaper is underscored by a unique relationship that exists between the dates upon which the stories and editorials reference world opinion on Bosnia in the *NYT* and the *FAZ*. Figure 2.7 shows the percentage of references to world opinion in both newspapers, divided into two-week periods, for the period studied. The obvious mode for both newspapers' references occurs in the seventh week, which covers the dates of July 21, 1995, through August 3, 1995. Otherwise, references to Bosnia appear to occur earlier in the German newspaper than in the American newspaper. This relationship is statistically significant ($r = .248$, $p = .014$), indicating that references tend to occur earlier in this time period in the *FAZ*.

An even more unusual relationship underlies this finding. In Figure 2.8, the percentage of references for each two-week period in the *FAZ* is graphed against the percentage of references for the *next* two-week period in the *NYT*. Hence, the percentage of American references is compared with the percentage of German references from the previous two-week period. The resulting chart shows an amazingly similar pattern to the references, as if the *NYT* were "following the lead" of the *FAZ* in the timing of references by a lag of approximately two weeks. This finding is verified by the measures of association; the significant relationship between the newspaper and the date of reference disappears for the time-lagged data in the second chart ($r = .127$; $p = .213$). These results suggest that even while the issue was of greater salience to the German newspaper, both newspapers appeared to be reacting to the same stimuli and events, although the reaction time seems a bit slower for the American newspaper.

Yet another finding qualifies this tendency. When one divides the period under study into three discrete time segments, as shown in Figure 2.7, the results reveal a more complex relationship between dates of reference and newspapers. For the first period, from April 28, 1995, through July 6, 1995, the described pattern is confirmed; references to world opinion on the crisis occur significantly earlier in the German newspaper than in the American newspaper

**Figure 2.7. Percentage of References to World Opinion on Bosnia,
by Two-Week Periods and Newspaper**

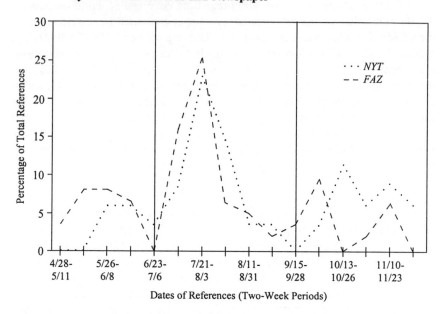

**Figure 2.8. Percentage of References to World Opinion on Bosnia,
by Lagged Two-Week Periods and Newspaper**

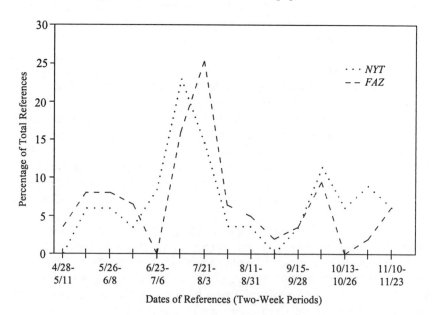

(r = .453; significance = .039; N=21). Similarly, for the third period, from September 15, 1995, through December 7, 1995, the pattern is also confirmed; references in the German newspaper again occur significantly earlier than in the American newspaper (r = .380; significance = .061; N = 25).

This pattern is disrupted during the crucial period of response by the North Atlantic Treaty Organization (NATO) between July 7, 1995, and September 14, 1995. Even though more than twice as many references (N = 52) occur in this period in the two newspapers when compared with the other two periods, the differences between the dates of reference are *not* significant (r = .140; significance = .321). This finding is confirmed by a visual examination of Figure 2.7, which indicates that for this period, the two newspapers' references to world opinion appear to follow the same pattern by date.

This convergence provides a potentially important insight into the creation of world consensus on an issue like Bosnia, at least as that process is reflected in the two newspapers. When the German newspaper led the American newspaper in the timing of references, little action occurred. When the timing of references converged in the two newspapers, the NATO forces took action and the Dayton peace process was initiated.

This finding regarding the timing of references provides only part of the comparative analysis of world opinion in the two newspapers. It is also notable that the generally greater salience of the issue in the German daily did not translate into a clearer judgment on world opinion than that of the American newspaper; indeed, the opposite appears true. In the *NYT*, 94.3% of the references to world opinion on the crisis occurred in news stories; by contrast, in the *FAZ*, only 49.2% of the references occurred in news stories, while just over 50% occurred in editorials, a significant difference (r = .454; p = .000). This difference suggests that while the German newspaper reflected a greater salience regarding the issue than the American newspaper, the *FAZ* also reflected a greater ambivalence about the content of world opinion, making it a subject more suitable for editorial discussion than reporting.

This finding is underscored by analyses of the content of world opinion. The *FAZ* rendered a judgment on the direction of world opinion—positive or negative—about the subject in 64.3% of cases; all other references were neutral on the direction. By contrast, the *NYT* rendered a judgment on the direction of world opinion in almost all the cases, a significant difference (r = .379; p = .000). The Bosnian issue was not only the subject of greater discussion regarding world opinion in the German newspaper; it was also the subject of greater indecision regarding the judgment of world opinion on the issue. To explore this relationship further, it is necessary to disaggregate the concept of world opinion into its component parts, and compare their usage in the two newspapers.

Comparative Analyses of the Components of World Opinion During the Bosnian Crisis

This ambivalence about world opinion in the *FAZ* carries over into discussions of its component parts. As above, we rely upon the components of world opinion described in Chapter 1: the moral component, the pragmatic component, and references to the power of world opinion, the threat of isolation, the nation's image, and the world as a unit. The two newspapers often differ on their use of these components in their descriptions of world opinion.

There are no significant differences in the percentage of references in either newspaper for five of the components of world opinion; both newspapers were equally likely to include the moral component, the pragmatic component, the threat of isolation, the world as a unit, and the nation's image in their references to world opinion on Bosnia. The American newspaper was more likely, however, to reference the power of world opinion than the German newspaper, by a margin of 25.7% to 9.5%, respectively ($r = .215$; $p = 033$). Similarly, the American daily was more likely to describe citizens' and leaders' reactions to world opinion than the German daily ($r = .277$; $p = .005$).

These findings are not surprising, given the previous results. It is difficult to speculate on citizens' or leaders' reactions to world opinion when the content and direction of opinion are unclear. Under these circumstances, it is also reasonable to assume that observers would perceive the power of world opinion as more diffuse, and less likely to influence citizens' or leaders' actions, since there is no consensus on which way individuals should be pressured to respond.

Another indication of the relative ambivalence in the German newspaper regards the threat of isolation. Isolation may have two meanings here. It can refer to specific actions, such as boycotts, embargoes, or the denial of diplomatic recognition to a regime. It can also refer to a vague, general sense that a country's leaders and citizens are considered as pariahs to the rest of the world.

This distinction is particularly important in the case of Bosnia. The international community imposed two "layers" of isolation upon Bosnia, each having different meanings within world opinion. First, the United Nations imposed specific sanctions, including an arms embargo, against all the warring factions in the former Yugoslavia. All the specific references to isolation refer to this embargo. However, the arms embargo came to symbolize the noninvolvement of foreign nations in the Bosnian crisis, for it gave an implicit advantage to the well-armed factions in the country. Second, in contrast to the Kuwaiti crisis, where isolation implied the engagement of the world community, isolation here implies the community's retreat from action or responsibility. The German newspaper was far more likely to reference this form of isolation than the American newspaper, by a margin of 62.5% to 21.4%, respectively ($r = .411$; $p = .058$). Even though an examination of references shows that both the German and American newspapers viewed "isolation" in this context as equivalent to the arms embargo, the German newspaper was more explicit in this regard. Isolation in this context translated into a nonjudgment regarding the actions of any of the warring factions—a position that became more controversial when the policies of "ethnic cleansing" were being pursued by the Bosnian Serbs.

Finally, there are indications of a change in the German position later in the period under study. The *Frankfurter Allgemeine Zeitung* became significantly more likely to reference the pragmatic component of world opinion and the power of world opinion the later the date of the article ($r = .310$ and $p = .017$, and $r = .228$ and $p = .073$, respectively). These results suggest that the *FAZ* was moving toward a more defined notion of world opinion on Bosnia in the latter part of this period. Further, this change is consistent with the findings regarding the timing of references to world opinion. It is in a later period that the references converge between the American and German newspapers. This convergence appears matched by a lessening of the *FAZ*'s ambivalence regarding the international interests at stake and the capability of world opinion to influence events. These results, the NATO response, and the start of the Dayton process all seem to indicate an emerging consensus in world opinion, at least as that concept is described in the two newspapers. The *FAZ*'s change is not surprising, given the worldwide outrage over the shelling of the Sarajevo marketplace, and the need for German approval of NATO bombing raids in response and German support for the Dayton peace accords.

National Perspectives on World Opinion I:
Disaggregating the Concept for the American Newspaper

The preceding analysis begs the question of why the German newspaper was more reluctant than its American counterpart to pass judgment on world opinion regarding Bosnia. One possible explanation lies in the relative positions of the United States and Germany in the world community. Further, these positions are revealed when one examines the manner in which the two newspapers combine the various components in their construction of world opinion. This study used a factor analysis to analyze these relationships.

For references in *The New York Times*, three significant factors emerged from the rotated analysis, as shown in Table 2.1:

- The first, which we shall designate the *Consensus Factor*, combines the moral component, the pragmatic component, and the power of world opinion, all with positive factor loadings. This factor describes the combined consensus on values and interests in the world that gives world opinion its power to influence events.

- The second, which we designate the *Intervention Factor*, combines the world as a unit with a positive loading, and isolation with a negative loading. Since isolation, in this case, refers primarily to the arms embargo, the factor describes a conflict between isolating the entire nation by means of a value-neutral arms embargo, and a unified world response that would further involve the international community in the crisis.

Table 2.1. Factor Analyses of Components of World Opinion

New York Times		*Frankfurter Allgemeine Zeitung*	
Factor 1: Consensus Factor		Factor 1: Nonintervention Factor	
Moral component	.52123	Pragmatic component	.61647
Pragmatic component	.88650	World as a unit	.76211
Power of world opinion	.79173	Nation's image	-.67342
Factor 2: Intervention Factor		Factor 2: Ambivalence Factor	
World as a unit	.82679	Moral component	-.79571
Isolation	-.78818	Isolation	.69460
Factor 3: Image Factor		Factor 3: Power Factor	
Nation's image	.94758	Power of world opinion	.74061

- The third, designated the *Image Factor*, contains only references to the nation's image; here, this factor refers to the U.S. image as a world leader, and the responsibility it must undertake in order to mobilize world opinion in response to the crisis.

Taken together, the three factors indicate that the American newspaper recognized the power of world opinion in its emerging consensus about Bosnia, the need for specific intervention to stop the carnage, and the role of the United States as world leader to rally an international response in world opinion. Several examples from news stories in *The New York Times* illustrate the particular position in which the United States found itself at various times in the crisis:

What does it say about America . . . that we are willing to go along with immoral and insane policies because the rest of the international community is doing so? (Whitney, 1995:A8).

Some [American] soldiers who took part in the exercise seemed enthusiastic about the prospect of deployment in Bosnia. . . . "This is a chance to do something positive, something humanitarian," Lieutenant Love said. "The people down there have been suffering, and if we can show them that we care about them, that the world cares about them, that may do some good" (Kinzer, 1995:A8).

Radovan Karadzic, leader of the Bosnian Serbs, said: "The whole world is celebrating peace, but we don't have peace. America has brokered this cease-fire, and it is obliged to stop the Muslims" (Hedges, 1995:A4).

After nearly four years of 250,000 people killed, two million refugees, atrocities that have appalled people all over the world, the people of Bosnia finally have a chance to turn from the horror of war to the promise of peace. . . .

All the parties have asked for a strong international force to supervise the separation of forces and to give them confidence that each side will live up to their agreements. Only NATO can do that job and the United States, as NATO's leader, must play an essential role in the mission. . . . We are at a decisive moment. The parties have chosen peace. America must choose peace as well (*NYT*, 1995:A11).

These quotations all illustrate the elements of the factors discussed. The Consensus Factor is reflected in the moral outrage over the atrocities in the Balkans, and the response of the international community, reflecting the power of a unified world opinion. The Intervention Factor is illustrated by the acknowledged failure of the arms embargo (in the first quotation), and the realization that a "strong international force" would be needed to keep the warring parties apart. Finally, the nation's image is present in the clear position of the United States as leader of world opinion; the necessity for the "United States to choose peace" to support the Dayton accords, and the acknowledged position of America as the leader of NATO, underscore this role.

The three factors are thus suitable for a nation that is viewed, both abroad and within, as the leader in world opinion. This position, of course, begs the question of why American intervention in the conflict took so long. The response is that world opinion exists alongside a nation's public opinion on particular issues, and while world opinion from the American perspective may have been urging intervention, the American public was reluctant to go along.[16] In this way, the convergence of timing in references to world opinion, and the increased clarity of the issues involved, may have reflected a growing international consensus that moved the United States into a leadership position. If so, the timing also reveals how briefly this "window of opportunity" was open. The convergence between newspaper references to the crisis lasts only a little over two months. If this convergence does indeed reflect some degree of consensus, that consensus lasted for a preciously short time.

This conclusion is particularly important given the U.S. position in the crisis. Nations tend to balance their own interests against the demands of world opinion. In this case, the American people viewed military intervention in Bosnia with skepticism. Therefore, any action by the US required the balancing of American public opinion with world opinion—a weighing of what is demanded of a nation externally against what the nation's citizens will accept. Had world opinion been less concentrated or consensual in the critical middle period under study, it might have been insufficient to compel a reaction by American leaders over the objections of a reluctant public.

National Perspectives on World Opinion II:
Disaggregating the Concept for the German Newspaper

Whereas *The New York Times* emphasized the role of the United States as a leader in world opinion, the *Frankfurter Allgemeine Zeitung* emphasized a more ambivalent role for Germany. At first, one might expect that Germany, as an emerging power in Europe after unification and as the linchpin of NATO, would take a strong stand to lead world opinion in the crisis. However, such an interpretation ignores the wariness with which Germans approach armed intervention in other nations, particularly after their country had just been reunified. Historically, of course, German armed intervention has been linked with aggression by the international community; given this reputation, it is not surprising that Germans were reluctant to lead an intervention in the crisis. It is also not surprising that while the German newspaper was concerned with world opinion on Bosnia earlier than the American newspaper, its judgments about world opinion were more ambivalent.

These considerations are reflected in three factor analyses of the construction of world opinion in the *FAZ*, as shown in Table 2.1:

- The first, which we designate as the *Nonintervention Factor*, combines the pragmatic component of world opinion and the world as a unit with positive loadings, and the nation's image with a negative loading. This factor indicates a nation whose image runs counter to intervention, even when the world community is united and appalled by the carnage and when the interests of all nations are recognized. Indeed, this factor seems to imply that Germany has a stake in the outcome along with all other nations, but mention of its image is a counterbalance to any considerations of intervention.

- The second, which we designate as the *Ambivalence Factor*, combines the notion of isolation with a positive factor loading, with the moral component with a negative factor loading. It is important to recall that "isolation" in the case of Bosnia dealt primarily with the arms embargo, which did not single out any particular side for moral condemnation. This particular factor indicates that when the moral issues in world opinion were being discussed in the German newspaper, they were incompatible with the position taken on the arms embargo. Since the embargo was the official German position, however, this factor reflects the ambivalence in stories regarding world opinion on Bosnia. At once, it was recognized that an international value consensus was emerging, while the official policy recognized no superior moral position on the conflict.

- The third, which we designate the *Power Factor*, includes the power of world opinion, with a positive loading. This factor indicates that the German newspaper realized that pressure was building for world opinion to influence events, even while the ambivalent position of Germany, given its international image, prevented its leaders from leading world opinion.

This ambivalence is reflected in several quotations from the *Frankfurter Allgemeine Zeitung* on this subject:

There is no international majority for a peacekeeping mission (Rueb, 1995a:6).

The Limits of Isolation: All the world had reached a turning point [on Bosnia] . . . all the world waits for a new mandate for the United Nations

troops, waits for the United Nations General Secretary of the Security
Council to state a new mandate for the troops (Rueb, 1995b:2).

Despite the energetic attempts . . . by NATO and the European Union to get
back the initiative [in Bosnia] . . . the world will not interpret [their efforts]
in this way (*FAZ*, 1995:14).

In each of these quotations, it is recognized that some action must be taken
(hence, the power component of world opinion). Yet, at the same time, the leadership of world opinion is left to other sources: the United Nations Security
Council, NATO and the European Union, or the "international majority." Also,
there is doubt concerning the reaction of these various entities, all of which
represent some portion of world opinion, regarding the appropriate action. The
sense conveyed is of all actors waiting for the others to react. Given Germany's
position in the world, and its historical and international reputation, this
interpretation of world opinion is not surprising.

CONCLUSION: DISCOURSE ANALYSES AND
THE DEFINITION OF THE POST-COLD WAR ORDER

Studying different forms of discourse on world opinion is one means of
approaching the definition of a post-Cold War order. The different forms illustrate the ambiguous position of nations in the new order. Consider the position
of India during the Kuwaiti crisis. As

bipolarity has ceased to be an organizing factor of the international political
structure . . . [this] causes problems for all countries, and not the least for
India, which is now faced with a variation of the challenge that confronted
it at independence: how to relate to a single dominant global power while at
the same time maintaining its own freedom of action and promoting a global
role for itself (Thornton, 1992:1067).

India can no longer claim status as a nonaligned nation, since nonalignment has
little meaning in the absence of superpower competition.

These circumstances also affect the United States, albeit in different ways.
For if the world has ceased to be bipolar, it is also not completely unipolar,
despite American military dominance. In political and economic terms, dominance is much more ambiguous. But many analysts still assume that the lack of
a Soviet presence means the United States will dominate the discourse and definition of any emerging order. This view argues that world opinion is just a
synonym for the interests of America and other major nations. The "post-Cold
war order" would therefore appear much like the old order to third world
nations. The major nations would simply retain, under a different name, hegemony over the interpretation of events. This perspective is reflected in a quotation
from an Indian peace activist in the *Times of India*:

We will be representing those *silent countries* whose economy will be most affected by the war. If there is a war, the poor countries of Asia and Africa will suffer the most. . . . However, surprisingly, these nations have no say in the Gulf controversy (*TOI*, 1991b:12; emphasis added).

American officials implied a somewhat similar perspective on their power to affect world opinion after the Gulf War:

Secretary of State James Baker III argued before Congress [that] "We remain the *one nation that has the necessary political, military, and economic instruments at our disposal to catalyze a successful response by the international community.*" Bush was to repeat the same theme in the State of the Union message: "Among the nations of the world *only the United States of America has had the moral standing* and the means to back it up [in the Gulf crisis]" (Cooper et al., 1991:391; emphases added).

These statements assume American hegemony over world opinion and the silencing of third world perspectives. If only the United States has the "necessary instruments" to "catalyze" an international response because of the nation's "moral standing," other countries without similar resources cannot influence the moral component which underlies the power of world opinion. Certainly, there is extensive evidence that the United States, as represented by the Bush administration, attempted to "manufacture" an international consensus regarding sanctions against Kuwait. As Bosah Ebo notes:

The Bush administration acquired support . . . by forgiving $8 billion in Egyptian debts to the United States. The well-documented Syrian history of terrorism was de-emphasized by the administration to gain Syrian support. The Soviet crackdown in the Baltic regions was virtually ignored in order to sustain Soviet support. . . . China was granted a high level diplomatic contact by the Bush administration (the United States had maintained only low level diplomatic contact with China after the Tiananmen Square massacre) to gain Chinese support (Ebo, 1992:5).

These actions might suggest that even though the United States did not have the power to compel other nations to follow their lead in the Gulf, America's unique position of power allowed them to "buy, bargain, or bribe" their way toward support. But if national considerations such as these stand alongside the moral force of world opinion as a means of generating consensus, can one study the consensus-building in isolation from other factors?

Further, can one speculate about the extent of American hegemony over world opinion just in terms of the dynamics of discourse from various sources on the issue? In response, Cooper et al. distinguish between "dominance" or "compliance induction [by] force, coercion, or manipulation," from "leadership" which compels the potential leader "to consult, to explain, to persuade . . . to cajole" (Cooper et al., 1991:396-398). Certainly, the analysis would not be complete without some mention of the Bush administration's efforts to build consensus. Yet, to interpret as hegemony the ability to "buy, bargain, or bribe" one's way to consensus is to define the term virtually out of existence. The need for such lobbying implies that other nations have bargaining power in return; this need also implies a shift in power relations from the Cold War era, when hegemony was described in terms of spheres of superpower influence. Put another way, there is a qualitative difference between *controlling* discourse on an issue, and *directing* discourse through various forms of persuasion. The former suggests *hegemony*; the latter suggests *opinion leadership*. The evidence from this study supports the latter interpretation.

The comparative content analyses of references to world opinion during the recent Bosnian crisis support this conclusion. Nearly all the differences in the usage of the concept of world opinion in *The New York Times* and the *Frankfurter Allgemeine Zeitung* may be explained with reference to the positions of the United States and Germany, respectively, regarding leadership in world opinion on the Bosnian crisis. These differences provide a plausible explanation for an apparent contradiction. The German newspaper observed the salience of given issues on Bosnia for world opinion approximately two weeks before the American newspaper; yet it was generally unable (or unwilling) to render as clear a judgment about world reaction to these events. The German desire to avoid a leadership position in international opinion reflects their close watch on events and their inability to judge them decisively.

This implies our second hypothesis: when newspaper coverage in different media converge in some manner, an international consensus may be forming regarding world opinion. When the German newspaper led the American newspaper in the timing of references to world opinion on Bosnia, there was little direct reaction by the world community, and by NATO, to the Bosnian crisis. Once these references converged in timing, as they did in the second period in Figure 2.7, action was taken to intervene in the conflict.

What is suggested here is a conflict between the perceived roles of nations in the international community, and their proximity to the crisis. The German newspaper appeared quicker to reference the implications of the crisis for world opinion, while reflecting the nation's reluctance to lead international opinion or action. The American newspaper, by contrast, reflected the perception that the United States needed to lead international opinion or action on the crisis, while remaining about two weeks behind the German newspaper in referencing the implications of world opinion. In the former case, the *FAZ* depicts a nation of origin with the *proximity* but not the international *position* (i.e., legitimacy) to act in world opinion; in the latter case, the *NYT* reflects a nation of origin with the *position* but not the *proximity* to act in world opinion. The results suggest that the United States was able to act only when its position and its proximity relative to the crisis intersected.

Analyzing the post-Cold War "order," as one means of "separating the world into different kinds of space," is not meaningful using only the perspective on world opinion offered by *The New York Times*, the *Frankfurter Allgemeine Zeitung*, or the *Times of India*. Actions and discussions in the United Nations during the first crisis did not follow the timing of the references to world opinion or isolation in either newspaper until both newspapers' perspectives converged. The American efforts may have affected this convergence, but the American newspaper's perspective alone did not correlate with the timing of discussions of Iraqi sanctions in the international body during the first eight weeks of the crisis. It is inarguable that certain nations may have more influence over world opinion in particular cases than others; but influence is not equivalent to control, just as leadership is not equivalent to dominance.

Regarding the Bosnian case, even though the various media reflected their national interests in their interpretations of world opinion, the earlier failures of the international community to respond suggested that *world opinion had not yet crystallized sufficiently on the issue to make a reaction possible*. When a German newspaper can remain ambivalent on world opinion on this issue, which affects its nation so closely, it also indicates a great potential for external discord among other nations regarding the issue. This internal and external discord must be resolved (or at least negotiated) before a consensus about the role and timing of international action can be reached in world opinion. The analysis suggests that such a consensus did emerge for a brief period, at least insofar as perceptions of the two nations' leaders and citizens on world opinion are reflected in the two newspapers analyzed.

Messages carried by the international media appear to influence the formation of world opinion during the post-Cold War era. However, a caveat is in order. The threat of isolation, or the application of that threat in tangible actions, will not necessarily alter a nation's or leader's behavior. This threat alone did not remove Hussein from Kuwait, or end the fighting in the Balkans. In other cases, the threat might not even be sufficient to compel nations to honor sanctions or support actions against an isolated country. Instead, media perspectives on international public opinion may have become an additional factor in a nation's calculation of the costs and benefits of international collective action.[17]

The findings suggest that the major change from the Cold War to the post-Cold War order may be the definition of a "new arena of discourse," in which world opinion remains open to different constructions from several corners. Of course, there is a distinction between constructing a "world order" and proving its existence, even as a heuristic model. If this were not so, a plurality of constructions of world opinion could not exist. Yet the evidence from the Persian Gulf War and the Bosnian case suggests that when various constructions overlap in a significant manner, a genuine "order" is created, albeit even for the brief period of convergence.

The very existence of competing constructions of world opinion on issues like Kuwait or Bosnia implies that all nations—major or minor—may need to construct world opinion from a perspective beyond their own ideological frameworks. Support for a given interpretation cannot be assumed, as when the world was split into well-defined alliances. Competition among varying versions of world opinion thus replaces competition between superpower ideologies. The situation is now more fluid, with a greater potential for influence by nations that might previously have been defined only in terms of their place in the superpowers' ideologies. Third world nations now have both a greater potential for self-definition and a greater risk of being ignored. However, the evidence suggests that the perspectives of other countries like India are important, even to a superpower like the United States. Otherwise, American officials would not court their opinions so assiduously.

The Bosnian case carries another lesson: the challenge for nations with the proximity and position to lead world opinion in a given crisis will be to forge a consistent global consensus regarding appropriate action by the international community. On Bosnia, a consistent consensus has, as yet, proved elusive. It appears that the international media can play a critical role in reflecting (and perhaps facilitating) the process of consensus building at times. Similarly, world opinion may facilitate collective efforts, as when it spurred actors to an international coalition against Iraq. But it may also disrupt integration, as when it encourages an international status competition that prompts the destructive expressions of nationalism discussed in the next chapter. The stability of the new "order" on any given issue will thus rest generally upon the creative capabilities of the international community, and specifically upon the abilities of the primary actors in any given case.

NOTES

1. Davison (1973:871) defends the concept by conceptualizing it in broader terms. More recently, Hill (1996) has given a serious critique of the concept's importance.

2. The difference between the two newspapers was statistically significant regarding the agenda for world opinion; the Cramer's V was .429 with a significance level of .012.

3. The last two-week period includes three extra days added in from the remainder of the six-month period under study. The two-week division for studying references proved to be useful in the previous chapter, and is used generally throughout the text.

4. The Cramer's V for the first 8 weeks was .412 with a significance level of .067. The Cramer's V for the next 16 weeks was .356 with a significance level of .427. While the value for the first 8 weeks fits the acceptable range for assuming a relationship (the symmetric lambda for this relationship was .196, verifying this conclusion), the value for the next 16 weeks clearly suggests no relationship (the symmetric lambda for this relationship was .000, verifying this conclusion).

5. The symmetric lambda value for the relationship is .36.

6. The percentages of respondents who felt "strongly" or "somewhat" that American leadership was appropriate were 58% in Britain, 52% in France, and 64% in Germany. Italy, by contrast, reflected more ambivalence on the issue, giving 40% support to American leadership on the crisis.

7. The percentages of respondents approving the economic embargo "strongly" or "somewhat" against Iraq were 83% in Britain, 79% in France, 79% in Germany, and 61% in Italy.

8. This difference between the two newspapers is significant; the product moment correlation r = .358 for the relationship, with a significance level of .000.

9. This difference is statistically insignificant; the product moment correlation r = .135, with an unacceptable significance level of .357.

10. This difference is statistically significant; the product moment correlation r = .530 with a significance level of .000.

11. The Cramer's V for the first 8 weeks was .487 with a significance level of .036, indicating a significant difference between the two newspapers. The Cramer's V for the next 16 weeks was .330, a significance level of .546, indicating no significant difference between the two newspapers.

12. There were 370 documents studied for the period between August 1, 1990, and December 31, 1990. Of these, 81.4% were letters from different nations to the secretary and the Security Council, 14.3% were published minutes of the General Assembly, 2.7% were press releases from the Security Council, and 1.6% were general statements by the General Assembly.

13. See Hufbauer and Elliot (1991:A17).

14. The last two-week period of newspaper studies was eliminated from the analysis of UN documents because it was during this period that the issue of sanctions became moot, with the UN decision to use force to remove Iraq from Kuwait, and the U.S. decision to support the UN resolution by going to war.

15. The Cramer's Vs for these periods confirm these results. For the first 8 weeks, the Cramer's V comparing references to world opinion with the date of UN documents equals .327 with a significance level of .000 for *The New York Times*; comparable values for the *Times of India* were .377 with a significance level of .000. Both results indicate significant differences between the date of document arrivals and references to world opinion. After the first 8 weeks, though, the values for *The New York Times* equal .199 with a significance level of .272; comparable values for the *Times of India* equal .219 with a significance level of .218. Both results indicate no significant difference between the date of document arrivals and references to world opinion in the second period.

References to isolation follow a similar pattern. For the first 8 weeks, the Cramer's V comparing references to isolation with the date of UN documents equals .303 with a significance level of .000 for *The New York Times*; comparable values for the *Times of India* equal .365 with a significance level of .000. Both results indicate significant differences between the date of document arrivals and references to isolation. After the first 8 weeks, though, the values for *The New York Times* equal .192 with a significance level of .345; values for the *Times of India* equal .187 with a significance level of .432. Both results indicate no significant difference between the date of document arrivals and references to isolation in the second period.

16. This reluctance still existed even after the Dayton accords had halted the fighting in Bosnia; in December 1995, 57% of Americans did not back President Clinton's plan to send troops to the region (see Sneider, 1995).

17. See a similar argument regarding public opinion and collective action within a given society in Rusciano (1989:80-140).

3

National Consciousness, International Image, and the Construction of Identity

Frank Louis Rusciano and Bosah Ebo

In a conference on Europe in the new world order held at Georgetown University, the noted political theorist Shlomo Avinieri observed how "the institutions we have had until now, and which will have great difficulties adapting to the new situation, were based on the concept that the West had to be defended, and if possible, things should be . . . rolled back . . . in the East" (Avinieri, 1991:25). The same critique applies generally to political analysis in the post-Cold War era. Until the collapse of the Soviet Union and the Eastern bloc, political theorists were often preoccupied with studies of the operations and shortcomings of liberalism or Marxism as defining principles for states. However, the end of the Cold War has prompted, among other things, a resurgence of nationalism and a scramble to redefine national borders that most observers had considered settled. To date, resurgent nationalism has been viewed as a latent syndrome previously suppressed by centralized control from the Soviet government, only to be unleashed once the center collapsed.

This chapter argues that this explanation is incomplete in three ways. First, it assumes the resurgence of nationalism can be understood in the same terms as earlier nationalistic movements, and that centralized control represented only an "interruption" in history regarding such movements. Second, it overestimates the ability of centralized authorities to control nationalistic movements, while ignoring the extent to which Soviet authorities (among others) used nationalism as a means of advancing their own ends (see Greenfeld, 1985). Finally, it ignores the general role national identity plays in the definition and maintenance of nations, and the reasons why this role has become important in the wake of the Soviet collapse.

This chapter attempts to present a two-part approach to these deficiencies. First, it studies the special circumstances for reconstructing national identity in the post-Cold War era. Second, it studies how identity (and social reality in general) is constructed regarding national entities, and how this construction is carried out in unique forms in the mass media within the post-Cold War context. We address the issue of the reemergence of nationalism in the new world order by studying the construction of national identity as political communication, involving a social/psychological process and an ongoing process of international negotiation.

What follows is divided into six sections. The first section describes the processes that led to the need for a reassertion of national identity and new means to define it. The second section describes how the national consciousness and international image of a nation become the primary factors in the negotiation of a nation's identity in world forums. The third, fourth, and fifth sections present an extended case study of the construction of national identity in Germany after reunification and the anti-immigrant violence which followed it. The final section discusses the relationship between the macro-level political communication involved in the negotiation of national identity and the micro-level psychic and material needs of citizens that are served by this negotiation.

DEFINING THE POST-COLD WAR CONTEXT

The post-Cold War context can perhaps be best understood by noting that prior to the economic and ideological collapse of the Soviet Union, analysts tended to divide the world into three parts: first world nations (the major industrial powers), second world nations (the Communist nations such as the Soviet Union, the Warsaw Pact countries, and China),[1] and third world nations (the less developed nations of Latin America, Africa, the Middle East, and Asia). In liberal economic theory, the stages of development are traditionally divided into preindustrial, industrial, and postindustrial levels, characterized by such factors as the main occupation of a majority of the workforce and the economic and natural resources available to the nation (Best et al., 1986). However, the typology of nations and the typology of levels of development do not correspond directly: first world nations may be industrial or postindustrial, second world nations may be industrial or preindustrial, and third world nations tend to be preindustrial. As such, the second world overlapped the first and third worlds in this hierarchy of economic development. The reasons for this overlap concern other ideological distinctions that formerly separated first and second world nations, and which thereby provided alternative definitions of "national development" and "national identity."

Much of liberal theory rests upon the notion that economic activity, and the related measures of growth and development, are objective standards, outside the realm of politics. Marxist theory, particularly as it was applied in this context by the former Eastern bloc, includes economic activity, and all related measures, within the context of political definition (see Talmon, 1960:1-2). This conflict delineates the previous ideological division of nations into first, second, and third world countries.

For first world nations, development was defined, and nations ranked, according to material satisfaction, measured in such terms as the per capita Gross National Product and the subsequent division of wealth in the society (Rostow, 1971).[2] For second world nations, material satisfaction was a political construct in the Marxist framework, relating to goals or desires deemed appropriate by centralized authorities; as such, "development" followed a different standard, as nations were ranked according to their progress toward the ultimate end of historical or material development—that is, the Communist society. Third world nations occupied different positions, depending upon which standard for development one used.[3] According to liberal theory, third world nations occupied the lowest position in the developmental hierarchy. However, third world nations were also potential battlefields upon which the clash of worldviews was pursued. Here, the West advanced the purely economic notion of development, wooing these nations with the promise of greater material wealth, a higher standard of living, and their attendant political liberties. The East pursued what J.L. Talmon describes as a "Messianistic" interpretation of development, wooing these nations with the status of being more advanced historically, if they embraced Communism, than the Western nations.[4]

The clash of these two visions included national identity, because, as Yael Tamir notes, "aspiring to national self-determination is . . . bound up with the desire to see communal space not only as an arena for cooperation for the purpose of securing one's interests, but as a place for expressing one's identity" (Tamir, 1991:587). National self-determination, or the claiming of a common culture leading to national identity, presents citizens with considerations of economic viability (how does citizenship serve my material interests?) and personal identity (what status do I derive from being a member of this nation?). The collapse of the second world portended the rise of nationalism because it removed a fundamental path by which nations could define their status in the world and defend their standing in a hierarchy of economic, social, and political development.

This work argues that the status deficiency that results from the loss of a nation's favored position in one hierarchy promotes a need among citizens to search for alternative means of delineating their country's status. This need tends to be more subconscious than articulated. Still, the ideological collapse, which accompanied the end of the Soviet Union's centralized control over the second world, is arguably of equal, or greater, importance than its power collapse. The power collapse provided the opportunity for the emergence of nationalism in its present form, but the ideological collapse provided its impetus.

According to Liah Greenfeld, "*National identity is, fundamentally, a matter of dignity. It gives people reasons to be proud*" (Greenfeld, 1992:487). As such, it provides a means of avoiding the condition of *ressentiment*, which

> refers to a psychological state resulting from suppressed feelings of envy and hatred . . . and the impossibility of satisfying those feelings. . . . [T]he structural basis of envy itself . . . is the fundamental comparability between

the subject and the object of envy, and the belief on the part of the subject in the fundamental equality between them. . . . [However] the actual inequality . . . rules out practical achievement of the theoretically existing equality. The presence of these conditions renders a situation *ressentiment*-prone irrespective of the temperaments and the psychological makeup of the individuals who compose the relevant population. The effect produced by *ressentiment* is similar to "anomie" (Greenfeld, 1985:15-16).

The collapse of the second world, and the resulting loss of one path to national identity and status, left both an assumption of equality and an actual inequality. In contrast to the Cold War era, in which the Western and Eastern blocs often did not recognize (or respect) as legitimate various governments allied with the opposite side, regimes in the post-Cold War order were generally to enjoy what O. Obasanjo (1991:94) refers to as "respect for the sovereignty of nations."

Yet the classification of nations into preindustrial, industrial, and postindustrial confers upon countries unequal standing in the world, which gives rise to the invidious comparisons Greenfeld describes. First, there are clear inequalities in resources and standards of living, exacerbated by "individual and collective expectations rising rapidly, especially as the world's rich want more of everything and the poor desire what the rich already have" (Brzezinski, 1993:24). Second, there are the related inequalities in the "social value" of national identity derived by nations according to their position in the developmental hierarchy. The "social value" of national identity lies in its ability to accord pride to its citizens, to confer upon them a sense of dignity and collective mission. However, within any hierarchy, only those occupying the top positions may derive status, and hence pride, from their station. By this international standard, the status of the most developed nations is defined, in part, by the fact that only a few countries may occupy the highest ranking at any given time. Fred Hirsch refers to this problem in societies as "social crowding," since the top positions would lose their social value as bases for national pride if all or most nations were able to achieve these positions (Hirsch, 1976).

Citizens of less privileged nations may thus suffer from a "national status deficiency" as the alternatives to liberal theory, which offered these countries a vision and a sense of collective mission and pride, have collapsed. Indeed, latent nationalist feelings probably hastened this collapse as the alternative model lost credibility. But this syndrome need not be confined only to the less developed nations; any nation that undergoes a status dislocation due to changes in the post-Cold War era is susceptible to the same psychological reactions from its citizens. Robert Reich describes how such dislocations may arise from comparisons between nations even in the midst of absolute gains in material well being:

Sociologists have long noted the phenomenon of relative deprivation, whereby people evaluate their well-being in light of others' wealth. The average citizen of Great Britain is better off than twenty years ago, but feels poorer now that the average Italian has pulled ahead. When I ask my students whether they would prefer living in a world in which every American is 25 percent wealthier than now and every Japanese was much wealthier than the average American, or one in which Americans were only 10 percent wealthier but still ahead of the average Japanese, a larger number of people usually vote for the second option. Thus, people may be willing to forego absolute gains to prevent their perceived rivals from enjoying even greater gains (Reich, 1991).

This chapter argues that a major problem in the restructuring of national identity in the post-Cold War era involves the struggle for citizens of a given country to define their status in the community of nations within the developmental hierarchy as it now exists.

THE SOCIAL CONSTRUCTION OF IDENTITY: FROM PROPAGANDA WAR TO NEGOTIATED CONSTRUCT

Since the end of the Cold War, the elements that go into the structuring of national identity have become bases for conflict. As *ressentiment* rises among nations, the tangible and intangible aspects of their national identity become issues in the struggle for status. The tangible aspects include the exact borders of the nation, its economic condition, and the peoples over which it has legitimate authority. The intangible aspects include a shared historical memory, a common cultural heritage, and a common ethnicity. But all of these factors are social constructions (Mazrui, 1986:23-28).[5] This chapter derives the elements involved in the generation of national identity and analyzes the manner in which these elements have emerged in the presence of a post-Cold War configuration.

In order to perform such a derivation, one must first examine the sources of "nationhood" as they have previously existed. Gyorgy Csepeli notes that

groups identifying themselves and others in terms of a national category are the products of a relatively recent historical development. The word "nation" is definitely not new but its uses as a category for self-identification for a particular assembly of people was unknown before the French revolution of 1789. . . . In this period the modern values of liberty, property, equality and the establishment of institutions aimed to realize these values (such as parliamentary democracy, the market and class society) invalidated previous categories of self-identification as successful means of social legitimation (Csepeli, 1994:326).

As such, "national identity as a modern means of self-identification can be analyzed as a set of affective and cognitive components" (327). Also, changes in the institutions created to realize certain values—such as the transition to a market economy and its attendant values from a socialist economy—should be expected to affect the nature of national identity and, in turn, the psychological state associated with it.

But there is more to identity than the citizens' cognitions; for the social construction of identity to take place, the "national dreams and dangerous myths" (Pross, 1993:342) which make up national identity must be communicated to others. The individual cognitive "map" of identity therefore moves to national identity when it is shared and ultimately accepted or rejected by others within and beyond the national society; the social construction of the concept depends upon discourse between those who wish to create an identity and those who must acknowledge the identity for it to have legitimacy (Gergen, 1992:171). The construction of national identity thereby involves the interaction between individual psychology and political discourse. As Eric Waddel notes,

> group identity does not exist in isolation, but rather is based on the notion of culture difference, and hence, organized around boundaries and interactions across boundaries. . . . In such a dialectical context, group identity is both self-ascribed (by those within the group) and ascribed by those beyond the boundary (the other group).
> The degree of concordance between ascription and self-ascription and, indeed, the very recognition of one or the other group depends upon the relations of power existing between the two (Waddell, 1990:61).

When the primary conflict over national identity involved the competition between two notions of development, political communication served mainly as a venue for the propaganda battle between East and West. A variety of (often anomalous) structures resulted as the two sides created borders for nations which served this conflict. Entities which shared ethnic and historical identities, such as Germany and Korea, were divided; others which shared few discernible characteristics, such as the Soviet Union, Czechoslovakia, Yugoslavia, and many nations in Africa and the Middle East, were combined or created.

In the post-Cold War era, the elements that go into the structuring of national identity have changed as the propaganda battle has receded. This change requires that we reconsider the processes by which identity in general, and national identity in particular, are constructed.

Like individual identity, national identity is defined "in the context of a relationship" (Gilligan, 1992:160). Identity consists of the notion one has of oneself, and the recognition of that notion by others. Similarly, national identity arises from a negotiation between the idea citizens have of their nation (their self-image or *Selbstbild*), and their nation's image among citizens and leaders of other nations (their international reputation or *Fremdbild*).

If national identity is to provide a sense of dignity for individual citizens, if it is to have some "social value" to those who claim it, it must command the respect of others. This respect must necessarily arise out of a process by which citizens' perceptions of their country are reconciled with other nations' images of it. Hence, national identity grows out of an interactive process, a negotiation

Figure 3.1. The Construction of National Identity

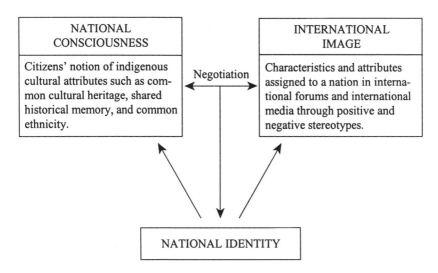

between national consciousness and international image that is conducted in world forums such as the United Nations and global media outlets. This process is illustrated in Figure 3.1.

National identity clearly serves the material and psychic needs of the citizens or leaders associated with it. But what defines a nation's international image and, hence, its status? In individual societies, public opinion and reputation define the status of particular objects and the individuals associated with them (Rusciano, 1989:79-110). In the global community, world opinion and the international reputation of a nation define the basis for this status and the citizens and leaders associated with it.

World opinion no longer conforms to the structures set by the ideological conflict in the Cold War; a nation does not automatically command status with a significant portion of the world merely by declaring itself Communist or democratic. Instead, world opinion has become a more free-floating phenomenon, whose meaning for each nation must be negotiated.

The major variable in a nation's success in asserting its own vision of its national identity is its ability to convince other nations, particularly the major powers, that this vision does not conflict with the norms or interests of the international community. "International image" is therefore primarily determined by the moral and pragmatic components of world opinion regarding a nation's identity. As stated in Chapter 1, the moral component of world opinion deals with "*values* which relevant nations [are] supposed to share, where issues are discussed in terms of right and wrong behavior," thereby referencing the norms of the world community. The pragmatic component of world opinion deals with "*interests* which relevant nations were supposed to share, where issues are discussed in terms of practical costs and benefits" to the nations involved, thereby referencing the *interests* of the world community. Most of the activity concerning world opinion primarily includes leaders (and sometimes citizens) of the various nations involved in the negotiation of a country's identity in various world forums.

This chapter will test some of the hypotheses regarding the resurgence of nationalism in the post-Cold War era, and the resulting dynamics of the negotiation of national identity. The analysis focuses upon one of the most potent symbols of the fall of the Eastern bloc and the creation of national identity: the reunification of Germany. The following four hypotheses from our thesis will be tested:

Hypothesis 1: There exist feelings of *ressentiment*, or status anxiety, resulting from the direct and indirect effects of the Eastern bloc's collapse on Germany.

Hypothesis 2: This sentiment is reflected in a resurgent nationalism associated first with anomie, and leading to new assertions of national identity.

Hypothesis 3: A relationship exists between citizens' perceptions of their national consciousness and of their nations' international image.

Hypothesis 4: These individual-level negotiations between *Selbstbild* and *Fremdbild* parallel macro-level negotiations of German national identity carried out by political leaders, intellectual elites, and citizens, and directed toward a national and international audience through the media and other world forums.

Before proceeding with the analysis, however, it is necessary to put into operation several of the terms used thus far:

National Consciousness: This term includes citizens' affective reactions to national symbols such as the flag and the national anthem; it also includes opinions on what holds the nation together, and what constitutes national characteristics. This term is also referred to as *Selbstbild* or, literally, the self-image individuals have of their nation.

International Image: This term includes: (a) the affective reactions of other nations to the country in question (in this case, Germany); and (b) the reputation of the country in world opinion as perceived by the country's citizens. This term is also referred to as *Fremdbild* or, literally, the actual and perceived reputation of a nation in world opinion.

Ressentiment: This term, in the present usage, includes feelings of powerlessness and hopelessness which are linked to negative feelings about one's country, or to the country's standing in the world. Also included in this notion of international status deprivation are feelings of anomie which are linked to suspicion of outsiders, especially as they threaten the citizens' sense of national consciousness or the country's standing in world opinion.

NATION-BUILDING, STAGE I: THE FALL OF THE EASTERN BLOC AND THE LINKS TO *RESSENTIMENT*

Perhaps no nation carries with it more negative historical baggage regarding the assertion of national feeling than the German Federal Republic. Both within and outside of this country, assertions of German national pride are always viewed suspiciously through the lens of the Nazi experience. As such, the postwar history of the German nation has been marked, in part, by a search for a "masterable past," an interpretation of the Nazi era which would allow the expression of national consciousness freed from the spectre of a Nazi revival (Maier, 1988:49-50).

Despite these concerns, unification was initially greeted with increased optimism by German citizens; in 1989, 1990, and 1991 the percentage of German respondents stating they faced the new year "with hope" reached post-Cold War highs of 68%, 56%, and 56%, respectively. These results clearly linked to feelings about unification. In a 1991 survey, 61.2% of those who viewed unification "with joy" were hopeful about the coming year; by contrast, only 36.7% of those who viewed unification as a problem were hopeful about the coming year (Allensbach Survey 5055).

A closer examination of those individuals who were worried about the effects of unification (about 30% of the sample), reveals a link between these fears and classic measures of anomie. "Anomie," as defined in this case, refers to feelings of concern about the future, and helplessness and powerlessness regarding one's ability to affect government or society. The measures of anomie used here are the same or similar to those typically used to measure such feelings in survey research (see Smith, 1983:163-168; Davis and Smith, 1982). The following results illustrate the relationship between such feelings and concerns about German reunification. Individuals who were worried about reunification were more likely to believe that:

1. democracy could not solve the nation's problems (by a margin of 26.6% to 13.5%);

2. the government was run in the interests of the few (50.5% to 27.7%);

3. the government was run according to special interests (48.6% to 30.9%);

4. the politicians do not care what people like me think (71% to 56.9%);

5. people like me have no influence over what government does (60.1% to 49.5%); and that

6. one cannot trust most people (50.4% to 36.1%).

Negative feelings about unification were also linked to another factor traditionally associated with anomie: the citizens' views about the economic situation in the country; 57% of those who viewed unification with joy felt the economic situation in Germany was "very good" or "good," as compared with only 34.6% of those who viewed unification negatively (Allenbach Survey).

These measures of anomie are linked to misgivings about the new nation as constituted. Indeed, respondents who expressed concerns about unification tended to believe that most Germans still had a "wall in their head" separating the two nations by a margin of 63.2% to 40.7% (Allenbach Survey). This question measures the extent to which Germans felt their fellow citizens accepted the "idea" of a unified Germany, or whether they still thought of the country as two separate nations. Just over 53% of respondents agreed with the latter statement, indicating signficiant doubts among citizens about the newly constituted nation. Moreover, these doubts were also related to feelings of anomie similar to those measured previously.

Individuals who answered that German citizens still had the "wall in their head" separating the two countries were more likely to believe that:

1. democracy cannot solve the nation's problems (by a margin of 21.2% to 14.3%);

2. the government is run in the interests of the few (45.2% to 26.8%);

3. the government does not work in the interests of the people (44.8% to 30.6%);

4. politicians do not care what people like me think (67.7% to 51.8%);

5. politics is too complex for people like me to understand (57.4% to 47.9%); and

6. people like me have no influence over government (57.1% to 48.9%) (Allensbach Survey).

Finally, the lingering "wall" in German citizens' perceptions of their nation was also linked to their evaluations of the Federal Republic's economic state. Only 43.4% of respondents who felt this separation rated the economy as "very good" or "good," as compared with 56% of respondents who did not feel this continued separation.

The results suggest that negative feelings about the new nation, so constituted, were linked to feelings of anomie. This relationship suggests the presence of *ressentiment*, or a feeling of powerlessness that is linked to negative feelings about one's country. This relationship is confirmed by one more finding from the survey. The percentage of individuals who felt that a "wall still existed in Germans' heads separating East from West" increases from 43.7% for those who were "very proud" to be German, to 47.8% for those who were "somewhat proud," to 53.9% for those who were "not very proud," to 57.8% for those who were "not at all proud." This inverse relationship between national pride and the feeling that East and West were still distinct entities provides more evidence of the relationships between a lack of national pride, nonacceptance of the re-created nation, and anomie.

These feelings were especially evident in the former Eastern sectors of the nation. In spite of the celebrations after the wall came down, persons living in the East were more likely to believe the wall still existed "in the heads" of citizens than those living in the West, by a margin of 58.1% to 48.8%. It is not surprising that the separation should be especially acute in the former Eastern sector. Harry Pross notes the contrasting ideas about development that existed in the East and the West prior to the German Democratic Republic's collapse:

> As far as the loss of state unity was concerned, the GDR forecast its recovery once the final stage of true socialism envisioned by Marxist theory had been reached. Similarly, in a distant, more just world, material living conditions would also have improved. . . .
>
> On the other hand, the Western state declared itself a provisional construct from the start. . . . Here, unity was not associated with a distant vision of satisfied economic needs. The state's role was seen as that of policing the market and of trying to ensure the immediate and repeated satisfaction of contemporary needs (Pross, 1991:346).

The loss of identification with the Eastern model of development removed a source of pride which had formerly served as an alternative means of status. As Konrad Jarausch notes, in the wake of unification "toughest of all was psychological reconciliation. Easterners struggled with a loss of identity" (Jarausch, 1994:204). Jurek Becker links this loss of identity with the changed status of the former Eastern sector since unification:

> Almost every single East German standard was abolished, not because it proved in each individual case to be inferior, but because it had been in force on the wrong side of the border. . . . In a part of the world that called itself, with involuntary openness, the "Socialist camp," a proud idea has been so discredited that none of us will live to see an attempt to resurrect it (Becker, 1994:6).

Other evidence suggests that a significant gap in perceptions of the two systems existed even following unification. In 1990, for instance, citizens in the former Eastern sector overwhelmingly blamed poor leadership, rather than a general failure of socialism, for the collapse of the German Democratic Republic, by a margin of 67% to 20%; by contrast, citizens in the former Western sector split about evenly on this question (45% to 41%, respectively) (Noelle-Neumann and Kocher, 1993:554).

It is important to note, however, that there are few differences in the relationships between anomie and concerns about unification between the former Eastern and Western sectors. Where there are doubts about the effects of unification, this form of powerlessness is present. The reasons for *ressentiment* differed, though, for citizens in the two regions. Citizens in the former Eastern sector felt threatened by different changes than citizens in the former Western sector.

These concerns are reflected in the characteristics that correlated with national pride for the Eastern and Western sectors. In the former Eastern sector, decreased national pride tended to correlate with anomie; in the former Western sector, this relationship is much more ambiguous. Figures 3.2 and 3.3 show the

Figure 3.2. Anomie and National Pride: Eastern Sector

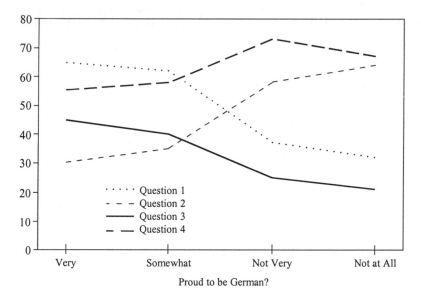

Figure 3.3. Anomie and National Pride: Western Sector

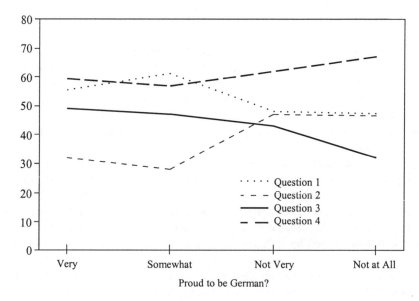

results of the following measures of anomie, broken down according to responses citizens' pride in being German:

Question 1: Do you face the coming year with hopes or fears? (Percentages indicate respondents who answered "with hopes".)

Question 2: Do you believe the government is run in the interests of the few? (Percentages indicate respondents who answered affirmatively.)

Question 3: Do you think the government acts in the interests of the whole population, or according to special interests? (Percentages indicate respondents who answered "in the interests of the whole population.")

Question 4: Agree or Disagree: "Politicians don't care what people like me think." (Percentages indicate respondents who agreed with this statement.)

For questions 1 and 3, a lower percentage indicates a higher level of anomie among respondents; for questions 2 and 4, a higher percentage indicates a higher level. Figure 3.2 shows the results for citizens living in the Eastern sector. For all four questions, anomie is inversely proportional to feelings of national pride; as national pride decreases, anomie increases. This finding supports the thesis that for many citizens of the former Eastern sector, reunification brought a form of disorientation and powerlessness that one associates with a diminished sense of national identity. Their weaker sense of national pride in the new setting correlates with increased pessimism and mistrust of government.

The results are different for the former Western sector, as shown in Figure 3.3. For questions 1 and 2, there are no clear patterns related to national pride; results increase or decrease and then converge. Questions 3 and 4 do follow somewhat the pattern one would expect if anomie and a lack of national pride correlated; however, these relationships are considerably less dramatic than shown in the Eastern sector's results. Citizens in the former Western sector understandably did not experience the sense of disorientation and powerlessness which citizens in the Eastern sector felt after unification.

However, another factor correlates more strongly with national pride in the former Western sector than in the former Eastern sector: the performance of the economy. Figure 3.4 shows the percentage of respondents from the former Eastern sector describing the Federal Republic's economic situation, and their own economic situations, as "Very Good" or "Good," broken down within categories of national pride. In both cases, the relationship between the two factors is questionable for respondents in the East; the percentage of respondents is almost as high among those who were "Somewhat Proud" to be German as among those who were "Not at All" proud to be German. By contrast, Figure 3.5 shows that in the Western sector, the lower the percentage of positive evaluations of the economy, the less pride citizens had in being German. For respondents in the former Western region, economic performance was more tied to national pride than for respondents in the former Eastern region.

This contrast is underscored by results from a 1990 survey, fielded just prior to reunification. East Germans who expressed worries about unification were more likely to doubt that the East and West had the same national

Figure 3.4. Percentage Saying Economy is "Very Good" or "Good" and National Pride: Eastern Sector

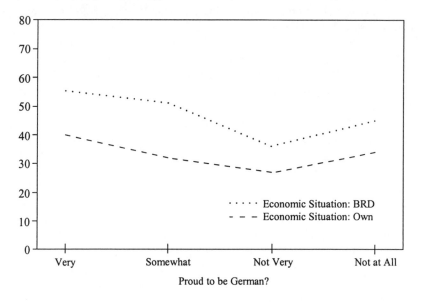

Figure 3.5. Percentage Saying Economy is "Very Good" or "Good" and National Pride: Western Sector

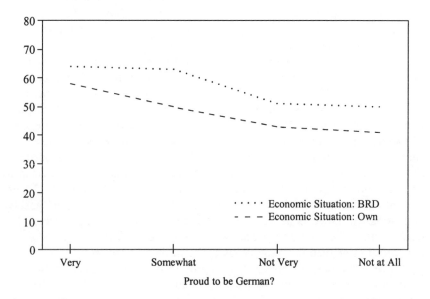

character than East Germans who expressed joy, by a margin of 51.3% to 25.6%. West Germans who expressed worries about unification were more likely not to view reunification and currency union as an achievement than West Germans who expressed joy, by a margin of 60.6% to 31.1% (Allensbach Survey 5040). Even prior to the formation of a newly unified Germany, East Germans were concerned about differences in national consciousness, while West Germans were concerned about the financial ramifications.

These results describe a situation where the economic dislocations caused by reunification threatened the status of former West German citizens. These individuals saw their nation's position as one of the preeminent economic powers possibly undermined by the costs of change. Not surprisingly, the economic results of unification were viewed much more positively in the former Eastern sector than in the West. A majority of citizens in West Germany in 1990 did feel that unification would have positive economic effects, by a margin of 55% to 27%; however, this expectation was more widely held in the East, by a margin of 78% to 10% (799).

The findings therefore suggest several relationships between the misgivings about a reunified Germany and feelings of anomie or a feared loss of economic status. These results indicate the presence of *ressentiment*, or feelings of helplessness which correlate with a negative image of one's nation. A weakened pride in being German correlated with anomie in the former Eastern sector; the same weakened pride correlated with economic concerns in the former Western sector. Status dislocations of different sorts in the two regions promote sentiments of *ressentiment* arising from reunification.

NATION-BUILDING, STAGE II:
THE CRISIS OF ANTI-IMMIGRANT SENTIMENTS IN GERMANY

One of the effects of *ressentiment*, according to our thesis, is an increase the (often negative) expressions of nationalism, as citizens attempt to reclaim the status they lost in the changing international order. Such horrors as ethnic cleansing in Bosnia are often cited as one grim consequence of these extreme forms of nationalism. Another commonly cited example was the anti-immigrant sentiment that often found violent expression in Germany following reunification. It follows from our thesis that anti-immigrant attitudes in Germany should have a relationship with both *ressentiment* and national pride from the 1991 survey, among citizens of both Eastern and Western regions, albeit for different reasons. This relationship should exist, even though the vast majority of Germans disapproved of the violent extremism associated with the anti-immigrant attacks.

As expected, a link exists between anti-immigrant sentiment and national pride that points to a protectionist nationalism existing in both sectors after unification. For this analysis, four questions were used to test the degree of anti-immigrant sentiment:

Question 1: Do you feel disturbed by the foreigners in Germany? (Percentages indicate respondents answering affirmatively.)

Question 2: Agree or disagree: "I have nothing against foreigners, but there are simply too many of them here." (Percentages indicate respondents agreeing with statement.)

Question 3: Should German family background be considered in asylum decisions? (Percentages indicate respondents answering affirmatively.)

Question 4: Should asylum laws be changed to make it more difficult to immigrate to Germany? (Percentages indicate respondents answering affirmatively.)

For each of the four questions, a higher percentage of positive responses indicates a higher level of anti-immigrant sentiment. Figures 3.6 and 3.7 break down responses on national pride, for the former Eastern and Western sectors, respectively. The results indicate that for both regions, national pride correlates directly with anti-immigrant sentiment; the more proud individuals were to be German, the more likely they were to agree with anti-immigrant statements.

We observe here an apparent transfer of sentiments between the 1990 and 1991 surveys. In 1990, anomie correlated negatively with national pride. In 1991, anomie correlated with anti-immigrant sentiment, which, in turn, correlated *positively* with national pride. The change suggests a *process* by which feelings of powerlessness came to be associated with negative feelings about those considered "outsiders" in the nation. These feelings then become associated with a sense of national pride, as one begins to define one's country by the definition, exclusion, and rejection of other outsiders. Particularly for those in the former Eastern sector, anti-immigrant sentiment seemed to allow citizens to project feelings of powerlessness as outsiders onto a different group in society, thereby regaining a sense—albeit a negative one—of identity and national pride.

The feelings of powerlessness or anomie measured above also correlated with anti-immigrant sentiments. Individuals who agreed with the statement "I have nothing against foreigners, but there are just too many of them here" were also more likely to answer that:

1. between elections there was no means by which one could influence government (by a margin of 59.8% to 44%);

2. many times politics is so complicated, you cannot tell what is going on (57.6% to 47.9%);

3. people like me have no influence over government (59% to 40%);

and less likely to answer that:

4. one can trust most people (45.5% to 33.8%).

Figure 3.6. Anti-Immigrant Sentiment and National Pride: Eastern Sector

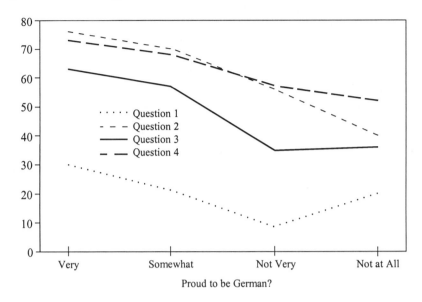

Figure 3.7. Anti-Immigrant Sentiment and National Pride: Western Sector

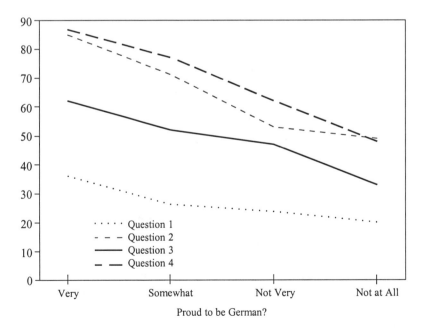

The results were similar when individuals were asked "when there are few jobs, should positions be taken from foreigners?" Respondents who agreed were also more likely to agree on Question 1 (by a margin of 58.3% to 50.3%), Question 2 (57.8% to 48.2%), and Question 3 (59.7% to 45.9%), and less likely to agree on Question 4 (41% to 34%).

The combination of national pride and ressentiment proved a volatile mixture for certain elements in German society. It is not surprising that these attitudes should converge. In a period of status dislocation, national identity becomes a path to regaining a lost position and a sense of one's place in the world. It also raises questions of "Who is German?", particularly in the wake of reunification. The analysis indicates this question is relevant in several of the forms discussed earlier. "Who is German" can be interpreted to mean "Who should be allowed to claim a national identification with this particular country, and the status that identification carries with it?" It can also be interpreted to mean "Who should reap the economic benefits of citizenship?" Both sets of questions become relevant after reunification, both relate to *ressentiment*, and both promoted some degree of hostility toward foreigners in Germany.

It is no surprise, then, that extremists in the society gave these sentiments violent expression. Anti-immigrant violence broke out, particularly in the Eastern sectors, in 1991 and 1992 following reunification. While it was clear that this violence was neither supported nor condoned by a majority of Germans, it did precipitate a crisis that the reunified state needed to meet—a crisis of identity, which had to be worked out according to the process of negotiation described above.

NATION-BUILDING, STAGE III: NATIONAL CONSCIOUSNESS, INTERNATIONAL IMAGE, AND THE CONSTRUCTION OF IDENTITY

In the September 1990 survey, 31.8% of West German respondents stated that they were worried about the effects of reunification. These citizens were far more likely to fear conditions in the Federal Republic would lead to unrest than those who faced unification with joy, by a margin of 69.1% to 26.2%. In East Germany, 26.2% of respondents expressed worries about reunification. These citizens were more likely to believe it was not a good thing for Germany to be an influential nation in the world than those who faced unification with joy, by a margin of 49.1% to 12.6% (Allensbach Survey 5040).[6]

By 1992 these concerns seemed preiscent; reunification had led to unrest and citizen concerns about Germany's status as a major nation in the world. Violence against immigrants exploded, often encouraged by neo-Nazi gangs. Not surprisingly, this violence tended to be concentrated in the former Eastern sector, although incidents occurred in the former Western sector as well. The former Eastern citizens, aware of their inferior economic position vis-à-vis the former West Germans, often reacted with violent expressions of their "rightful" German identity against foreigners. The new citizens' status dislocations arose due to their new political status as members of German society, coupled with their inferior economic status vis-à-vis West Germans and certain immigrant groups.

As a result, hopes about the future, which were closely linked to feelings about unification, faded significantly among German citizens. Respondents saying they faced the coming year "with hopes" had reached post-Cold War highs of 68%, 56%, and 56% in the years 1989, 1990, and 1991, respectively. This optimism faded by the end of 1992, however, due partially to anti-immigrant unrest; only 37% and 41% of respondents faced the new year with hope in 1992 and 1993, respectively (Allensbach Surveys, 1991, 1992, 1993). In this case, the assertion of Germany's national identity in unification had resulted in nightmarish reminders of the Third Reich.

Our analysis assumes that German citizens' sense of national consciousness and their perception of Germany's international image are linked. As such, the national crisis of anti-immigrant violence should have individual-level and macro-level effects on the manner in which Germans view and construct their national identities. We consider the individual-level effects first, by investigating whether a link exists between citizens' views of national consciousness (their *Selbstbild*, or the manner in which they view their nation) and their perception of Germany's international image (their *Fremdbild*, or their nation's reputation in world opinion). The evidence indicates just how much was at stake in citizens' negotiations of their national identity. Germans' perceptions of how other nations view their country are strongly related to how they feel about their nation and the tangible symbols of national consciousness.

In a survey conducted in the former Eastern sector in December 1990 through January 1991, just after reunification, the new citizens were asked a series of questions relating to national consciousness and their feelings about the newly constituted nation. One question directly addressed perceptions of Germany's international image, asking respondents whether they felt" Germans were "liked" or "disliked" by the rest of the world. While 49% felt Germans were liked, and 27% felt they were disliked, their opinions correlated consistently with other feelings about the country, as the following results indicate:

1. 79.6% of those who believed Germans were liked were "very proud" or "somewhat proud" to be German; only 48.6% who felt Germans were not liked were "very proud" or "somewhat proud" to be German;

2. 55.7% of those who felt Germans were liked faced the coming year, the first of a reunified Germany, "with hopes"; only 33.5% of those who felt Germans were not liked faced the year "with hopes";

3. 73.5% of those who felt Germans were liked were happy to see the German flag; only 43.2% of those felt Germans were not liked were happy to see the flag;

4. 79.3% of those who believed Germans were liked felt that "national consciousness" was a good thing; only 58.5% of those who believed Germans were not liked felt "national consciousness" was a good thing;

5. 56.5% of those who believed Germans were liked felt that East and West Germans had the same national character; only 39.7% of those who believed Germans were not liked felt that East and West Germans had the same national character;

6. 86.8% of those who believed Germans were liked felt that as a German one could feel as proud of their country as an American, French, or English citizen; only 60.3% of those who believed Germans were not liked felt the same;

7. 50.9% of those who believed Germans were liked ascribed to the slogan of reunification which proclaimed "We are one people"; only 27.1% of those who believed Germans were not liked felt the same; and

8. 49.5% of those who believed Germans were liked stated they were "very happy" to be German; only 22.5% of those who believed Germans were not liked stated they were "very happy" to be German.

These results constitute a response to perceived world opinion about Germany. Citizens from the former Eastern sector who believed Germans had a negative international image were less likely to associate themselves with the very idea of German national consciousness (Questions 4, 5, and 7) or with the symbols of the nation (Question 3). They were also less likely to have positive feelings about being German (Question 8), and to express feelings of national pride, individually (Question 1) or in relation to other nations in the world (Question 6).

These relationships illustrate a characteristic response to world opinion about a given nation. In Chapter 1, it was noted that the idea of "isolation" in world opinion was generally evident when citizens or leaders expressed a desire to avoid association with the isolated nation. In the international arena, such opinions are expressed by such actions as closing embassies, recalling diplomats, canceling state visits, boycotting a nation's trade, or barring a country from international sporting events such as the Olympics. The above results reflect the *individual-level* effects of international isolation, however. The feeling that their country is disliked by other nations promotes a desire within the individual to dissociate themselves from the symbols, pride, and very notion of their national consciousness. Such feelings are especially salient in a nation like Germany, where sensitivity about their international image has been heightened due to the Nazi past. Unless feelings of international isolation are resolved, the construction of national identity, and the legitimacy of the nation, are in doubt.

Of course, the causal ordering might also go in the opposite direction, so that individuals who have negative feelings about their country and its symbols project their attitudes upon the rest of the world. We would argue, however, that in the German case the causal relationship likely runs in both directions. Negative feelings about one's nation derive from somewhere, and one would be remiss in denying that Germany's image suffered from the historical judgment pronounced by other nations after the Second World War. As such, it seems likely that German citizens who perceive their country negatively tend to both project and absorb these attitudes as doubts about their national identity.

Such doubts are likely to intensify in a time of crisis—and 1992 was a year of crisis following reunification with a sharp rise in anti-immigrant violence and xenophobia in Germany. In a survey conducted in March of 1992, respondents were again asked if they regarded unification with joy or worries. Figures 3.8 through 3.11 show the relationships between responses to this question and other questions regarding German unification. Figure 3.8 shows that individuals who viewed unification "with joy" were more likely to believe Germans were liked; those who viewed unification "with worries" were more likely to believe Germans were disliked. Figure 3.9 shows that individuals who agreed there was "too much anxiety in German society" were more likely to believe Germans were disliked; those who disagreed were more likely to believe Germans were liked. Figure 3.10 shows that individuals who felt that period after unification was "happy" were more likely to believe Germans were liked; individuals who believed the period after unification was difficult were more likely to believe Germans were disliked. Finally, Figure 3.11 shows that individuals who felt unification made life better were more likely to believe Germans were liked; individuals who believed unification made life worse were more likely to believe Germans were disliked (Allensbach Survey 5062).

The findings indicate that when citizens perceived they had a negative image internationally, their feelings about unification suffered. Once again, a negative perception of Germany's image in world opinion was associated with a negative perception of German citizens' feelings about their country.

One may, of course, question whether a nation's citizens have an accurate perception of their country's international image. Certainly, Germans appear to have an inordinant sensitivity to their international image, even when other countries seem otherwise occupied. For instance, during the prewar Kuwaiti crisis between August 1, 1990, and January 15, 1991, the *Frankfurter Allgemeine Zeitung*, a German newspaper of record, contained almost as many references to world opinion on the upcoming German unification as references to world opinion on the Iraqi invasion. By contrast, neither *The New York Times* nor the *Times of India* even mentioned German unification in their references to world opinion during this period (Rusciano, 1992). By 1992, unification was a central aspect of German national consciousness, of how citizens viewed their nation.

Two responses address this issue. First, the relationship between perceived international image and national consciousness is sufficient to indicate that on an individual level, at least, citizens feel they must construct their sense of national identity from an internal negotiation between *Fremdbild* and *Selbstbild*, respectively. These findings confirm a major assumption of our thesis.

Second, the correspondence between a nation's actual image in world opinion and its citizens' perceptions of their international image is difficult to establish due to the lack of time-series international survey data. However, some comparative studies do suggest that, at least within various countries, citizens have a relatively accurate view of how their fellow countrymen view another nation. A survey was conducted in 1989 to measure Germany's image in eight

Figure 3.8. Opinions on Unification and Germany's Perceived International Image

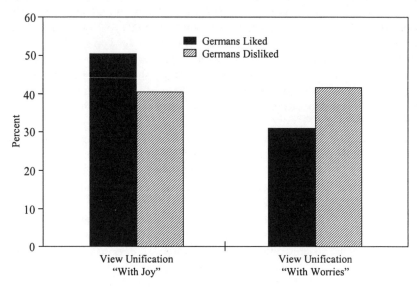

Figure 3.9. Respondents' Opinions Regarding Whether There Is "Too Much Anxiety in German Society" by Germany's Perceived International Image

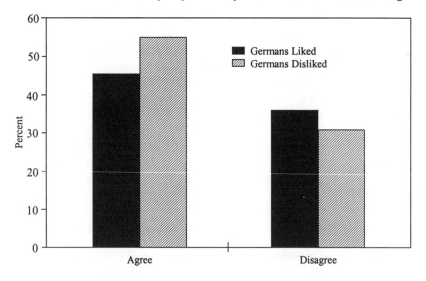

Figure 3.10. Feelings About Results of Reunification and Germany's Perceived International Image

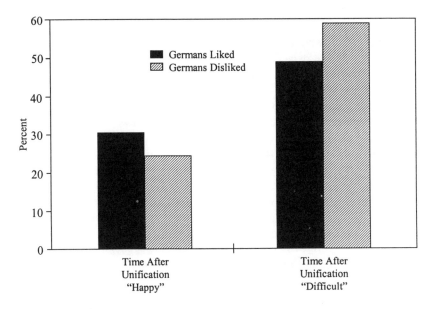

Figure 3.11. Feelings About Unification by Germany's Perceived International Image

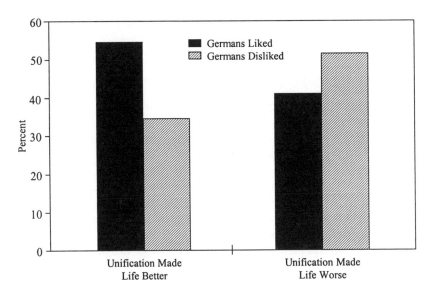

nations: France, Great Britain, Italy, Spain, the Netherlands, Sweden, the United States, and Japan. Respondents were asked two questions of relevance to this study: (1) "Do you like or dislike the Germans?" and (2) "Do most people in [your country] like or dislike the Germans?" Figure 3.12 shows the percentage of individuals in each nation who said "I like the Germans" graphed against the percentage in each nation who said "Most people in [my nation] like the Germans." The resulting product moment correlation between these measures was .8791, with a significance level less than .01. Similarly, Figure 3.13 shows the percentage of individuals in each nation who said "I do not like the Germans" graphed against the percentage in each nation who said "Most people in [my nation] do not like the Germans." The resulting product moment correlation between these measures was .9091, with a significance level less than .01.

In both cases, citizens' perceptions of Germany's image in each nation correlated very highly with the actual evaluation of this image on the national level. While these results represent only comparative opinions in different nations, they imply a strong association between perceived opinion about another country, and the actual evaluation of that country, within specific nations. As such, the results suggest that evaluations of world opinion regarding a given country are also generally known within nations, particularly the nation in question (assuming it is an open society like Germany).

Crises of public confidence that affect a nation's image in world opinion and citizens' national consciousness interfere with the negotiation and construction of national identity. It is no surprise, then, that the public reaction to these potentially harmful expressions of national identity was swift. In Germany, the individual-level connections between national consciousness and international image were paralleled by macro-level negotiations in international forums and the media, as assumed in our thesis.

MACRO-LEVEL EFFORTS TO NEGOTIATE NATIONAL IDENTITY

For German intellectuals and citizens, the negotiation of their new identity became a matter of concern that involved all levels of society, not just the political leadership. This negotiation was directed toward domestic audiences and the international media primarily in the beginning of 1993.

On the elite level, intellectuals joined a campaign to counteract the negative images being broadcast in the media. Several German academics involved in international exchange programs submitted a letter to a German newspaper, condemning the violence and stating that it was atypical of the nation's attitudes toward foreigners. Copies of this letter were circulated to academics in the United States who had participated in foreign exchange programs with German scholars. Poll results that indicated German tolerance for foreigners, and intolerance for right-wing extremism, were also publicized (*Allensbach Berichte*, 1993).

Figure 3.12. Evaluations of Germany's International Image in Eight Nations ("Like Germans")

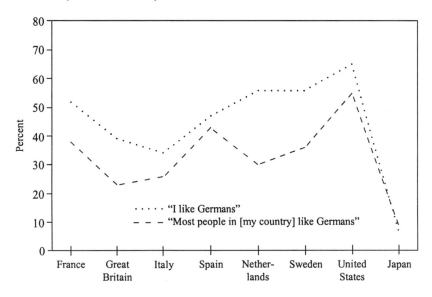

Figure 3.13. Evaluations of Germany's International Image in Eight Nations ("Dislike Germans")

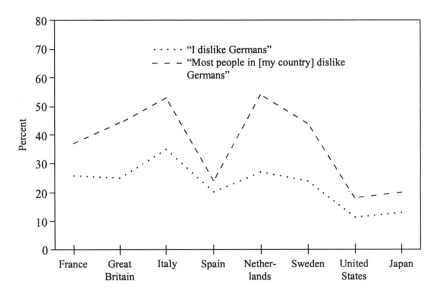

This publicity clearly illustrated the full significance of the confrontation between national consciousness and international image in the construction of a nation's identity. One press release from a noted survey research institute stated how "pictures and news stories were transmitted to every corner of the globe, creating the impression that a reunited Germany was on its way to becoming a hotbed of a new and dangerous right-wing extremism" (1). The report's authors attempted self-consciously to serve two purposes. They addressed the issue of German national consciousness by claiming to "show that right-wing rioters and hooligans, who until recently believed they were admired or at least tolerated by a silent majority of the German population, were operating under completely false assumptions" (5-6). They addressed the issue of Germany's international reputation by claiming a desire to "curb the damage inflicted on Germany's image abroad" with the survey results (5-6).

German citizens also became involved in the effort to assert a more benevolent view of their national consciousness, both domestically and in the international media. In January 1993, candlelight vigils were held in dozens of major German cities to protest the anti-immigrant violence. Originally conceived by four individuals in Berlin as a means by which "the country's 'silent majority' [could] break its silence and show its repudiation of these attacks," the movement grew to involve over 2 million German citizens, or approximately one in every 40 people in the country (Kinzer, 1993a:A4). As with the publicity campaigns described above, this movement served two purposes. An organizer claimed that it addressed questions about German national consciousness, as "it [showed] that a majority of Germans are not secretly hostile to foreigners or sympathetic to fascism." As a result, he claimed that "the climate in Germany" had changed regarding citizens' public reactions to the attacks (A4). Another observer stated that these efforts were directed toward an international audience: "Some people go out and hold candles because they want to improve Germany's image in the world" (Kinzer, 1993b:A4).

German government officials were quick to use this publicity to establish a link between the efforts of citizens and opinion leaders and a drop in anti-immigrant violence in the early part of 1993. On March 17, 1993, Cornelia Schmalz-Jacobsen, the government's advisor on matters dealing with foreigners in Germany, announced:

> A year ago, even six months ago, it seemed that our society was paralyzed by violence. . . . That has clearly changed. Our society and our political leaders have shown that this violence is something we do not want in our country (Kinzer, 1993c:A13).

Schmalz-Jacobsen then attributed the "change in attitude" in part to the candlelight vigils and to "countless smaller initiatives by individuals and social groups" (Kinzer, 1993c:A13). *The Week in Germany*, a newsletter published by the German Information Center, echoed the statistics regarding the drop in attacks on foreigners in its March 19, 1993, edition.

All of these efforts illustrate a determined effort on the part of German citizens, intellectuals, and government officials to identify their national consciousness with antifascist and antixenophobic sentiments, and to protect Germany's international image after unification. In part because these individuals used their influence over media sources so effectively, through careful public relations efforts, the negotiation appears to have been accomplished primarily in the nation's favor. Even as right-wing attacks increased again in the later months of 1993, analyses speculating about whether a resurgence of German nationalism was to blame did not reappear. Instead, these acts were interpreted as criminal behavior, and they were treated as such by the international press.

This change in emphasis is reflected in the analysis of headlines in American newspapers regarding Germany's immigration issues for 1992 and 1993. In 1992, five major American newspapers carried 31 stories and editorials dealing with the German immigrant problems.[7] Of these, 21 or 68% had headlines concerning violence against immigrants, while 10 or 32% dealt with the legal aspects of immigration policy in the Federal Republic. In 1993, coverage of the immigration issue not only dropped in absolute terms, to 21 total stories or editorials, but the emphases changed dramatically. Violence against immigrants was represented in only 3 or 14% of the headlines, whereas the legal issues surrounding immigration occupied 18 or 86% of the headlines.

The change in depiction of Germany in the foreign press paralleled changes in individual-level sentiments as well. The polls reflected increased optimism about the future among Germans after 1993. Among respondents in 1994, 58% said they faced the future with hope, up from 41% the previous year (Allensbach Surveys, 1993; 1994).

CONCLUSION

The German case study supports several of the central tenets of our thesis regarding the resurgence of nationalism in the post-Cold War era. The results support the following hypotheses from our analysis:

Hypothesis 1: There is clear evidence of *ressentiment*, or a status anxiety, resulting from the collapse of the Eastern bloc, and related to national identity, in both regions of the formerly divided nation.

Hypothesis 2: This sentiment is reflected in a resurgent natonalism associated with anomie and national identity.

Hypothesis 3: There exists a clear relationship between citizens' national consciousness (or the manner in which they view their nation, their *Selbstbild*) and their perception of Germany's international image in world opinion (or the manner in which other countries view their nation, their *Fremdbild*).

Hypothesis 4: The individual-level associations (and negotiations) of national identity were paralleled by macro-level negotiations carried out by political leaders, intellectual elites, and citizens who directed their concerns toward a national and international audience, by means of media and international scholarly contacts.

To what extent may one generalize these findings from Germany to other nations, however? Perhaps there are regions where citizens are not as conscious or concerned about their international image in world opinion. Bosnia comes to mind as an example, where atrocities were committed seemingly without regard for the reactions of the international community in the name of nation-building. However, even recent events in Bosnia suggest that these concerns were never as far from the relevant actors' minds as they might have appeared. Among certain Bosnian leaders, the need to reconcile one's national consciousness with their image in world opinion is evident in the following statement:

> Bosnian Serbs daily attack their self-styled president for . . . their *isolation in the world community.* . . . "Our main goal is to take these war criminals, like Karadizic, and put them on trial . . . otherwise, *in the eyes of the world we will bear the guilt for the atrocities* they *have committed in our name* . . . nationalist ideology will make our dream of becoming part of *the world community impossible*" (Hedges, 1996:A1-A8; emphases added).

One may also consider the negotiations which allowed the following statement by Isamil Ibrahim Abuyayy, a Palestinian speaking after the Israeli peace accords which allowed creation of a Palestinian state in 1993:

> For 40 years I have no identity. I am pushed from here to there. *I am shunned by the world.* . . . *But when I hear this news, I lift my head. Today I am a citizen from Gaza* (*The New York Times*, 1993:A26; emphases added).

These few sentences eloquently capture the feelings of *ressentiment* and the sense of international isolation which existed prior to nation-building. They also describe how one person's sense of national identity was affected by macro-level negotiations in the international arena.

The process of the construction of identity outlined in this case study defines an agenda for future research. This research must necessarily focus upon two variables: national consciousness, or how citizens conceive of their nation's boundaries, culture, historical heritage, and ethnic composition; and international image, or how other countries conceive of that nation's identity. The former variable may be measured, in part, by survey data from public opinion studies within the respective nation.[8] But such investigations must be expanded to include measures of the *ressentiment* or status deficiencies which form a critical impetus for the construction of national identity in the new order. The analysis regarding the effects of status deficiencies in this chapter suggests the usefulness of further elaboration.

The latter involves world opinion about the nation's identity, and defines different problems of measurement. Such tools as media content analyses, international surveys that study opinion on the subject within various nations, and studies of proceedings and records from the United Nations are useful in operationalizing this variable. Also, the degree of influence a nation has over the international media, as measured partly by the credibility and power of its own media outlets, is an important factor that must be considered in this negotiation.

Finally, further linkages must be established between the micro-level processes of nationalism and the macro-level negotiations that are aimed at the construction of national identity. Such research must include the individual-level associations between *Selbstbild* and perceived *Fremdbild*, as used in the preceding analysis. The next step could be to link these associations more directly with the macro-level negotiations, perhaps through a survey designed specifically for these purposes.

These issues, and the new role of political communication in the negotiation of identity, define a major arena of conflict in the post-Cold War era. Nations will struggle to establish their status in the new world order. Leaders will be driven to extreme or preventive actions by their citizens' psychological need for a sense of "dignity" to overcome new feelings of ressentiment or status deficiency generated by the collapse of one path to national pride. These questions of identity, and the negotiations that take place in the broadest of international forums, have their source in the psychic needs of individual citizens. The challenge in the post-Cold War era lies in reconciling these micro-level needs with the macro-level negotiations in the international mass media involved in satisfying them.

This challenge sensitizes the observer to the limits and possibilities of the power of world opinion. Some theorists have envisioned that international public opinion would restrain extreme nationalistic tendencies and the atrocities that so often accompany them. The reality is more sobering. World opinion actually plays a complex role in the resurgence of nationalism; it supplies the international status that *ressentiment*-prone individuals seek in their construction of national identity. As stated earlier, the "social value" of citizenship is measured by its capacity to grant status to individuals internationally. In principle, it should be possible for world opinion—guided by imaginative leadership and given the right circumstances—to compel nations to achieve international status from national identity without embracing virulent forms of nationalism. In practice, recent history counsels cautious skepticism in approaching optimistic scenarios.

NOTES

1. There is some controversy over which nations should be included in the second and third world categories. For instance, nations such as Vietnam or Albania could have been classified in either group, depending upon the analyst's purposes and orientation.

2. Eugene Rostow self-consciously proclaims his book *The Stages of Economic Growth* (1971), to be a "Non-Communist Manifesto" in its subtitle. Similarly, Daniel Bell's thesis (1973) on the emergence of postindustrial society necessarily includes an

extended critique of the shortcomings of the Marxist theory of development (Bell, 1973: 99-112).

3. Some authors, notably Hamid Mowlana and Laurie Wilson (1990:1-35) and Everett Rogers (1978) have argued that the major paradigms of development are of little use in analyzing nations in certain comparative contexts, and should be abandoned. However, they fail to outline a convincing alternative that has gained wide acceptance among social scientists and opinion leaders. See Bosah Ebo (1983) for a more detailed discussion.

4. Of course, the Communist nations also promised a higher standard of living to nonaligned third world countries. However, this appeal was based upon an interpretation of development which argued that the third world was subject to a permanently lower standard of living due to its economic arrangements with the Western nations, which included the acceptance of Western theories of development.

5. In this manner, this chapter uses A.A. Mazrui's commentary on the "social construction" of reality regarding Africa as just one critical resource from the third world literature which is relevant to the discussion of nationalist phenomena (Mazrui, 1986).

6. Unfortunately, this survey did not ask the same questions of East and West Germans; hence, it is not possible to compare responses from the two areas on these questions.

7. The newspapers surveyed included *The New York Times*, the *Los Angeles Times*, the *Washington Post*, the *Wall Street Journal*, and the *Christian Science Monitor*.

8. Attempts to define national consciousness solely in terms of the psychological dispositions of the citizens include Sidney Verba and Gabriel Almond (1965); David Conradt (1980); and William Bloom (1991).

4

World Opinion and the Global Market

Frank Louis Rusciano
and Sigfredo A. Hernandez

World opinion deals with cross-national attitudes that individuals share regarding such issues as human rights, the definition of aggression, and the legitimacy of governments; global consumer preferences deal with cross-national appetites individuals have for such products as Coca-Cola beverages, Mercedes automobiles, and Sony stereos. The world public exists as a theoretical construct with uncertain borders and questionable legitimacy; the global market exists as an acknowledged reality, shaping business decisions in a competitive international economy. But these contrasts are artificial—for global consumer preferences are but one form of world opinion, and the global market encompasses one nexus of relationships within the world public. Further, the parallels are vertical as well as horizontal. For just as the scope of world opinion defines the borders of the world public, so too does the scope of global consumer preferences define the borders of the global market. This is not to say that attitudes toward human rights, terrorism, or sovereignty are of equal "importance" with attitudes toward soda, cars, or electronic equipment. Rather, the overlap acknowledges that both reflect an underlying process of symbolic meaning which individuals comprehend across national borders.

It is no accident, then, that inquiries into "world opinion" and the "homogenization of global preferences" appeared within the same decade in their respective literatures. The first systematic analysis of media usages of world opinion appeared in 1990, while the germinal article on global consumer preferences appeared in 1983 (Levitt, 1983). A comparative study of the two concepts serves three purposes. It gives structure to the notion of international consumer behavior, describing its motivations. It gives a practical grounding to discussions of world opinion, which are too often given to utopian speculation. Finally, it illustrates the interaction of politics and markets in a manner that describes the potential for conflict and consensus in the emerging international order.

The following analysis is divided into four sections. The first section describes the parallel structures for world opinion and global consumer preferences as the two exist in their respective literatures. The second section describes the common criticisms both theories have encountered, and their common responses. The third section discusses the similar factors, including international communications and the spread of technology, which have made "world opinion" and "global preference structures" increasingly powerful forces. Finally, the fourth section describes how understanding global consumer preferences as a form of world opinion helps define the boundaries of the emerging global economic and political order.

"WORLD OPINION" AND "GLOBAL PREFERENCE STRUCTURES": COMPARATIVE CONCEPTUALIZATIONS

Synonymous Usages

The analogy between world opinion and global preference structures begins with similarities in the variety of synonyms used for each concept. Our analyses of media usages in American, German, and Indian newspapers revealed several explicit phrases referencing the term "world opinion" directly, including "world public opinion," "international opinion," and "international public opinion." Similarly, Theodore Levitt references global preferences explicitly in such phrases as the "global commonality of tastes" (Levitt, 1983:293). World opinion also tended to be referenced implicitly, as attitudes or preferences were attributed to the world or all nations considered together; such usages include "world support," "international outrage," "international prestige," and others. Levitt also references global consumer preferences implicitly, referring to a "commonality of preferences" internationally (293), "global homogenization" (296), a "homogenized world market" (296), and "fundamental underlying commonalities" in the world (303). Finally, implicit citations of world opinion were often dynamically constructed, as if "the world" were expressing an opinion: "observing," "forgetting," or "praising" some action or individual. In a similar fashion, Levitt notes how "the world's needs and desires have been irrevocably homogenized" (293).

Component Parts

Behind these linguistic usages lies a similarity in the structure of world opinion and international consumer preferences. World opinion involves a consensus that crosses national boundaries regarding moral and pragmatic issues. The moral component of world opinion refers to evaluations based upon values that relevant nations are assumed to share. Issues are discussed in terms of right or wrong patterns of behavior, as when one newspaper stated how sanctions against apartheid were useful as "moral gestures of foreign policy." The pragmatic component of world opinion refers to evaluations based upon interests which relevant nations are assumed to share. Issues are discussed in terms of practical costs and benefits, as when one newspaper stated how the Soviet Union deserved "credit for rational calculation of important international interests."

The moral component drives world opinion. It is more likely to be referenced than the pragmatic component and tends to override the pragmatic component in cases when the two elements clash, when the values and interests shared by nations do not coincide.

Levitt echoes this analysis when he discusses two vectors which shape the world's values and interests regarding global consumer preferences: "technology and globalization. The first helps determine human preferences; the second, economic realities" (Levitt, 1983:304). Technology affects values because

> reality is not a fixed paradigm, dominated by immemorial customs and derived attitudes, heedless of powerful and abundant new forces. *The world is becoming increasingly informed about the liberating and enhancing effects of modernity* (302; emphases added).

But values are often considered to be immutable, generated from derived attitudes, and transferred between generations according to immemorial customs. The transformation Levitt describes therefore inevitably affects values. Within global consumer preferences, values are considered a superstructure built upon "satisfying universal drives . . . [as] people are remarkably alike regarding love, hate, fear, and envy" (Simon-Miller, 1986:6). Values may be redirected or restructured in new ways by technology to fulfill these desires.

However, the analogy between the value component of global consumer preferences and the moral component of world opinion may appear a bit strained. One does not tend to discuss consumer preferences in terms of "right or wrong" behavior, or "moral or immoral" attitudes. Yet the moral component in world opinion depends upon the notion that values can be shared across national boundaries; global consumer preferences also imply shared values which cross national boundaries. Levitt notes how "everyone in the increasingly homogenized world market *wants exactly products and features that everyone else wants* (Levitt, 1983:296; emphases added). The result is often a disruption of previously held moral conceptions about "proper" behavior or desires: "Almost everyone wants all the things they have heard about, seen, or experienced via the new technologies . . . *even if those aren't what mother said was suitable, what immemorial custom said was right"* (292-296; emphases added).[1]

But are common values regarding products or fashions on the same level as common values regarding such issues as human rights or the difference between legitimate defense and aggression against another nation? Does equating the value component of global consumer preferences with the moral component of world opinion trivialize the latter? While some issues may be more important (by whatever standard one uses) than others, they are all reflective of an underlying process of symbolic meaning which goes into the creation of norms which bind societies or, in this case, cross-national borders. As Paul Herbig and

Joseph Miller note, "human societies create a hierarchy of codes for regulating human interaction. . . . Over a period of time, useful behaviors, values, and artifacts become institutionalized as part of the cultural traditions" (Herbig and Miller, 1992:78).

To the extent that cultures converge, at least partially, due to the forces described, they include both the seemingly trivial (such as fashions in hairstyles and clothing) and the important (such as standards defining human rights). It is undeniable that changes in fashions, eating habits, and other areas of social life affected by consumer choices have profound symbolic and moral implications. One observes how changes in women's clothing from the traditional Muslim garb to more Western clothing in certain nations have caused a considerable furor (and reactionary measures, as in Iran).

The pragmatic component is similarly reflected in the economic effects of globalization. Levitt notes how standardization of products serves the shared interests of worldwide customers, providing them with cheaper goods because of "aggressive low pricing." All respond to, and benefit from, such actions because the desire "to make one's money go as far as possible" is classified as a "universal need" by the author (Levitt, 1983:295).

The global standardization of tastes and products has still other benefits for international consumers. Companies may no longer sell older models or inferior versions of advanced products in less-developed countries; also, prices, margins, and profits will not necessarily be higher than in the domestic markets (295). The availability of these new goods "lighten(s) and enhance(s) work, raise(s) living standards, divert(s), and entertain(s)" (293), all results which define shared interests among international consumers, and which, taken together, define an equivalent to the pragmatic component of world opinion.

The relationship between the moral and pragmatic components of world opinion is reflected in their equivalents in global consumer preferences. Often, the two components do not coincide in their messages; what a nation views as morally right in world opinion might not be viewed as serving the interests of all nations. Prior to the Persian Gulf War, an editorial in the *Times of India* stated that world opinion granted Kuwait a "moral right to self defense." But the editorial also argued that action against Iraq was not in the pragmatic interests of all nations, since third world nations would be harmed the most in the event of a conflict.

Similar conflicts may also arise between the value component of global consumer preferences (which affects what consumers desire) and the interest component of global consumer preferences (which determines the price and benefits of these goods). First, as Yoram Wind notes, "some of the products viewed as global are fairly expensive—Cartier watches, Louis Vuitton handbags, or Canon cameras . . . [also] very often a standardized product will be over-designed for some countries and underdesigned for others; the same product then could be overpriced in some countries and underpriced in others"[2] (Wind, 1986:24). But higher prices or overdesigned products do not deter consumers from wanting the more universally respected goods; the value component dominates the interest component in the global market.

A similar phenomenon occurs when conflicts between the value and interest components of global preferences arise because of the vagaries of supply and demand. As global demand for products replaces national demand, supply could lag behind in the short run, resulting in increased prices for goods international consumers have begun to value. In the early 1970s, for example, an increased demand for blue jeans around the world raised the price of denim in the United States and other countries. However, the value judgment dominated; consumers paid the higher prices.

Power and the Threat of Isolation

The moral component of world opinion determines the power of the value component of global consumer preferences to enforce conformity across national borders. Both have the capacity to *isolate* citizens or consumers who do not conform to their dictates. The notion of isolation as a social force was originally derived from the public opinion literature. Noelle-Neumann references the threat of isolation regarding "fashion," a term which encompasses all aspects of shared social attitudes and behavior. This behavior includes, but goes beyond, "the height of heels or the shape of shirt collars," for fashion generally calls "attention to common characteristics" and is therefore an "excellent means of integration." Enforcing this integration is the threat of social isolation, which "is present wherever individual judgments become prevailing opinion"; as such, "along with Socrates, we may presume a connection between tastes in music and hairstyles and not miss the fact that, by this movement, laws may be overthrown" (Noelle-Neumann, 1993:118-119). "Fashion" connects such seemingly disparate phenomena as attitudes about moral and political issues, and tastes in clothing and other consumer goods. All carry with them a specific meaning and status, and all open the individual to the threat of isolation.

The threat of isolation was adapted to the research on world opinion as the force punishing nonconformity with attitudes or moral judgments which cross national borders. Here, isolation has two related meanings. It refers to disruption of tangible relationships of trade, diplomacy, and business; embassies may be closed, ambassadors recalled, or a nation's goods may be boycotted. But it also refers to a general feeling or message that citizens are unwelcome in foreign countries, that leaders are snubbed by other world leaders, and that the "isolated nation feels as a pariah to other nations." Certain countries may gain a negative international reputation that causes citizens to be ashamed of their national identity.

The threat of isolation may also cause a nation's leaders or citizens to seek out relationships with one side to avoid association with the target of international isolation. An editorial noted in the *Times of India*, for instance, that

Indian leaders had deliberately supported the coalition against Iraq during the Kuwaiti crisis in order to avoid association with the isolated nation.

The threat of isolation operates in the same way to further the spread of global consumer preferences. International consumers' desires are not only driven by the superior quality or potential savings which global marketing may offer them. They are also motivated by the desire to have what "everybody else wants" (Levitt, 1983:296), since "almost everyone wants all the things they have heard about, seen, or experienced via the new technology" (292). Technology has "made isolated places and impoverished people eager for modernity's allurements" (292). In the process, global consumers come to associate a lack of desire for the new products with isolation, backwardness, poverty, and low social status in the society or the world. This transformation is illustrated in the following description of Chinese consumers:

> When Chinese shoppers go to market now they are armed . . . with a highly refined sense of cachet. A hierarchy has developed, in fact, with imported goods the most coveted, followed by goods made in China at joint venture factories. A distant third are the home-grown products. . . . The foreign goods are from three to eight times more expensive as Chinese products, but that hardly seems to matter (Sterngold, 1992:5).

The "hierarchy" of preferences favors those products which are associated with status internationally—hence, the Chinese consumer's "highly refined sense of cachet."[3] The home-produced goods also carry a social significance: "Zhao Gurong, a salesman behind a counter full of Sony and Aiwa tape players, said that his shop did carry a few Chinese brands at low prices, *but that they were mostly for shoppers from the countryside who did not know any better*" (1; emphases added). The desire for global brands is associated with refined or sophisticated tastes; settling for home-grown brands is associated with the rough or noncosmopolitan tastes of the rural areas. Consumers who wish to avoid social isolation seek to associate themselves with the global products, to possess and display them. Their motivation is to acquire things which symbolize higher status across national boundaries. John Hill and Richard Still note that urban consumers in the third world, particularly middle-class and upscale consumers, generally wish to "keep up" with their counterparts in industrialized countries (Hill and Still, 1984).

A final note should be added regarding the threat of isolation. One might object that world opinion isolates "nations" while global consumer preferences isolate individuals (i.e., consumers). However, the isolation of nations is a shorthand description of the process. In practice, nations cannot be isolated; only individuals may be isolated. The isolation of a nation is expressed in terms of the isolation of individuals, in such acts as denying landing rights to aircraft, recalling ambassadors, boycotting trade, snubbing leaders, or making citizens feel unwelcome in foreign countries. Association with something held in low esteem internationally, be it something as tangible as a product or as intangible as national identity, lowers the targeted individual's status.

The threat of isolation inevitably raises questions about the entity from or within which the individual is isolated. In the literature on world opinion, isolation tends to occur within a described unit—"the world community," the "world public," or among "civilized nations." Similarly, global consumer preferences are transmitted within a world public, an international market which crosses national boundaries: "In contrast to multinational companies, global companies *view the world or its major regions as one entity instead of a collection* of national units" (Simon-Miller, 1986:6; emphases added). These commentaries assume that an international system, however loosely defined, exists within which world opinion and global consumer preferences are transmitted, displayed, and played out. But doubts about the existence of such a system have led to analogous criticisms of both concepts.

"WORLD OPINION" AND "GLOBAL CONSUMER PREFERENCES": COMPARATIVE CRITIQUES

Hamid Mowlana rejects the existence of world opinion as a system of shared meanings which cross national boundaries; as noted in Chapter 1, he argues that

> as the complexities of the modern world grew, it became fashionable in the literature to apply a variety of terms to the world stage as a whole, with phrases such as "international community" and "international system." It is, however, doubtful whether the aggregation of states alone possess the *common values and assumptions*, which are by definition the essential conditions of community, and whether or not the working of a world society is in some way analogous to a mechanical system. The result has been to emphasize the tangible, the formal, and the measurable (Mowlana, 1986:176; emphasis added).

Herbig and Miller similarly reject the existence of global consumer preferences as a system of shared cultural values which cross national boundaries:

> Culture means a system of communications that makes a human society possible. This system of communications is an all inclusive system which incorporates the biological and technical behavior of human beings with their verbal and non-verbal systems of expressive behavior. . . .
> One can have jet aircraft, faxes, personal computers, satellite dishes and yet not yield one's own culture . . . indeed a globalization of values is not occurring . . . the opposite seems to be taking place; cultures are diverging in their attitudes while still modernizing (Herbig and Miller, 1986:77-82).

The authors go on to argue that individuals react *against* the globalization of identity by asserting their differences in an increasingly integrated world:

it appears that in this age of global information and travel, a return to and deepening of ethnic awareness and values (hence cultures) provides the self-awareness and sought after identity to the problem of the ever increasing closer world: "I am not a man of the World; I am a Hawaiian (or German or Scotsman); a man of the Earth has no cultural history yet I do so I must be something" (82).

The manner in which the authors structure their criticisms invites its own response. Mowlana acknowledges the existence of a "world stage" upon which countries' citizens and leaders act, and are observed. Such a construction implies an open arena for international action, observation, and judgment by other actors. The "public" nature of world opinion does not derive here from association with a defined group, but rather from the individual's international exposure to others' approval or disapproval. This exposure, in turn, describes a condition—if not a "system"—of relations between nations and citizens.

In a similar fashion, Herbig and Miller define culture as a "system of communication"; they later acknowledge the existence of "global knowledge" transmitted within an "ever increasing closer world." If culture is communication, and knowledge is transmitted globally, one must see the beginnings of a global culture—if not a "system . . . of expressive behavior"—emerging between consumers of different nations.

Indeed, there is considerable anecdotal and empirical evidence supporting the existence of global markets within which preferences are disseminated. The anecdotal evidence includes instances of standardized products which are marketed successfully around the world with little or no modification; McDonald's fast food, Coca-Cola and Pepsi-Cola beverages, Rolex watches, Kodak film, Sony video and audio products, Honda cars, and Levi's blue jeans are but a few notable examples. The empirical evidence includes studies which indicate that the standardization of international marketing practices is high and growing (Boddewyn, Soehl, and Picard, 1986), and a study of consumers in six countries which demonstrated the existence of consumer segments for toothpaste and bath soap which transcend national boundaries (Yavas, Verhage, and Green, 1992).

The issue is not whether a state of relations exists between nations whereby values and preferences may be shared; the authors admit that it does. Their critiques demand further, though, that the result should be a complete convergence of values across national boundaries. As such, they juxtapose global and national values in an either/or configuration; according to Herbig and Miller, if national cultures (and identities) exist, global culture cannot. Similar criticisms have been addressed previously to the concept of world opinion. Hans Morgenthau (1962) and Leo Bogart (1966) argue that the diversity of cultures and ideologies existing among nations invalidates this concept.

But one need not accept the adversarial juxtaposition of international and national values to defend the validity and existence of world opinion or global consumer preferences. With reference to the former concept, it is common to refer to "public opinion" as pertaining to the opinions of individuals within specific national borders. That does not preclude public opinion researchers from describing "publics" within nations defined by such characteristics as race, ethnic background, social class, and such (see Hennessey, 1985:9-10; Yeric and Todd, 1983:2-4; and Childs, 1965:12 as examples). It follows that world opinion does not preclude the existence of "publics" defined by the borders of individual nations. National and subnational publics coexist regarding values and opinions; international and national publics may coexist in a similar manner.

With reference to global consumer preferences, it is common to refer to "national markets" as if they were entities sealed by a nation's borders (Kotler, 1986:14). This does not preclude market researchers from describing "market segments" or "intracountry segmentation" within nations defined by such characteristics as race, ethnic background, social class, and the like (Wind, 1986:23; Kotler, 1986:14; Stanton, Chandran, and Hernandez, 1982:126). As such, global consumer preferences need not preclude the existence of national markets, any more than national markets preclude the existence of intracountry market segments. Indeed, the coexistence of universal preferences and country-specific ones is a well established "fact" in the international marketing area (Simon-Miller, 1986); country market segments exist alongside global market segments (Yavas, Verhage, and Green, 1992). As above, national and subnational market segments may coexist regarding customer preferences; international and national market segments may coexist in a similar manner.

These insights promote similar calculations among policymakers and marketing strategists concerned with world opinion and global consumer preferences, respectively. Both sets of actors must balance global and national values when choosing tactics. For national leaders, options might include limiting the single-minded pursuit of their country's interests if the alternative is to risk isolation and the disruption of economic, political, and diplomatic ties to other nations. When Chinese leaders brutally suppressed the prodemocracy movement in Tiananmen Square, they clearly opted to ignore world opinion and were condemned by other nations. However, some analysts argue that world reaction to this event caused the Soviet Union to take a more cautious approach to the prodemocracy movements in the former Eastern bloc nations. Similarly, the threat of international isolation was not sufficient to remove Saddam Hussein from Kuwait, but it was sufficient to prevent other nations from breaking the embargo on goods to Iraq, and to promote the military coalition that eventually drove Hussein out of Kuwait. World opinion does not remove consideration of public opinion from leaders' calculations; instead, it helps define a "middle strategy," balancing international values with national ones.

Marketing strategists must also weigh the forces of globalization of preferences against the diversity of national tastes and values when deciding how to sell products. Neither force will always dominate, and the existence of one does not negate the existence of the other. Hence, "the internationalization of marketing activities" has become "a multidimensional decision process. . . . 'All or nothing' scenarios are inappropriate for the decade of the 1990s and beyond:

each company must weigh the pros and cons of standardized marketing practices along a number of marketing activities" (Sandler and Shani, 1992:27-28). The result is "a resolution to the futile standardization versus customization debate" (Baalbaki and Malhotra, 1993:40); a "middle strategy" develops in which marketing planners balance global preferences with local variations in approaching consumers. This strategy considers heterogeneity among countries as well as the homogeneity across cross-national segments in international marketing (Ohmae, 1985; Quelch and Hoff, 1986; Wind, 1986; Whitelock, 1987; Hite and Frazier, 1988; Sandler and Shani, 1992; Yavas, Verhage, and Green, 1992). As part of world opinion, global consumer preferences affect the calculations of relevant actors concerned with them.

The Challenge of Regionalism

Perhaps the most direct challenge to the notion of a world public comes from Samuel Huntington's argument about the "clash of civilizations." According to this thesis, "the great divisions among humankind and the dominating source of conflict will be cultural . . . the principal conflicts of global politics will be between nations and groups of different civilizations" (Huntington, 1993a:22). This argument dismisses the existence of a "world public" or a "world community" as "euphemistic collective noun(s) (replacing 'the Free World') to give global legitimacy to actions reflecting the interests of the United States and other Western powers" (39). The notion of a "global market" is similarly dismissed as a collection of regional markets organized among nations who share "basic values, attitudes, [and] behavioral patterns." As such, even though the economic issues between the United States and Japan are comparable to those between the United States and Europe, the former have a greater "political saliency and emotional intensity" because greater cultural differences separate America from Japan than from Europe (34). Instead of values disseminating across borders, cultural values form the new borders; and instead of trade leading to global consumer preferences, it merely emphasizes the different tastes and business behaviors of various cultural groups.

Huntington's argument suffers from many of the same flawed assumptions as earlier critiques of world opinion and the global public. He begins with the premise that "civilizations" are a "cultural grouping of people and the broadest level of cultural identity short of that which distinguishes humans from other species" (24). Even though "people have levels of identity," so that a resident of Rome is at once "a Roman, an Italian, a Catholic, a Christian, a European, a Westerner," the civilization remains the highest level of abstraction. But there is no reason why this "cultural grouping of people" needs to be the "broadest level of cultural identity." Because a global public has emerged displaying particular cultural, social, and consumer behavior, a cultural grouping exists at a higher level of abstraction than the "civilization." Indeed, Huntington's thesis actually counters the argument that the differences between nations are so pronounced that world opinion cannot exist.

However, he replaces this criticism with the thesis that the differences between "civilizations" are so diverse that a global culture cannot exist,[4] giving three counterarguments to the emergence of world opinion and a global public. First, he argues that with the demise of Communism, the entire world has not taken up the values of liberal democracy; hence, "globalism must equal liberalism." Second, he argues that while increased interaction may produce a common culture, it may also produce conflict; hence, "globalism must equal the absence of conflict." Finally, he argues that technology has not necessarily produced a common modern culture resembling that of the West; hence, "globalism must equal Westernism."

Each of these arguments is a straw man. None of the preceding analyses of world opinion and the global market rests upon these assumptions. The notion of world opinion assumes that all nations have the potential for input into decisions where an international consensus might form. The moral or pragmatic judgments involved in world opinion may affect, as well as be affected by, such "civilization" or "national" values as liberalism or Western culture. There is no reason to assume the interaction runs only one way, so that world opinion becomes another name for Western hegemony. The emergence of world opinion or a global market also does not mean the end of conflict; instead, conflicts will occur in a manner different from the Cold War era, when world opinion was the object of semantic battles between defined ideologies with different definitions.

Huntington's assumption that "civilizations" are the highest cultural grouping transforms discussions of world opinion into discussions over which civilization will dominate the global public. Once one acknowledges a global public exists above the level of the "civilization," then no one nation or group of nations need claim such hegemony.

The author's objections are easily restated with reference to the global market. Must global consumer behavior necessarily reflect liberalism? Must a global market necessarily preclude, or even reduce, international conflicts? Finally, must a global market necessarily be a market defined by Western hegemony? Even those analysts who tout regional markets as important parts of the global economy would reject these assumptions.

Huntington assumes open markets produce open political systems. But a more complex relationship exists between markets and liberalism. Liberal regimes are all market systems, but not all market systems are liberal regimes (Lindblom, 1978:161-166). Markets are necessary but not sufficient to assure a liberal system. In a similar way, open global markets need not signal a worldwide acceptance of liberalism.

A global market need not reduce conflict, either. As consumer values converge and individuals desire the same things, they might understand and tolerate each other more. But they will also surely suffer from differential abilities to possess universally desired goods. The result could be more conflict, particularly between the citizens of richer and poorer nations.

Finally, analysts do commonly use examples of Western products dominating the global market. This habit is not a measure of Western hegemony as much as an indicator of the examples most familiar to them. Indeed, Kenichi Ohmae notes how the emerging global market invariably combines tastes from all three of the "Triad powers": the United States, Europe, and Japan (Ohmae, 1985). The inclusion of Japan violates the assumed borders of Huntington's "civilizations"—and it is not only Western values which determine the international market: "In his dark blue suit . . . frequenting a *sushi* bar for lunch, and commuting in a Celica, the typical New York businessman would not draw a second glance on the streets of Dusseldorf or Tokyo" (12; see also Hormats, 1994:98).

Huntington assumes regional markets reflect the borders of "civilizations" in their trade and related activities; values again define the barriers between "civilizations" and a global public. However, the same forces and values direct companies toward regional *and* global markets. Successful regional market integration requires favorable economic, political, and geographic conditions (Cateora, 1993). Economic factors include the need to reach larger markets with reduced internal barriers. As regional markets are partially exhausted due to competition and product saturation, global markets are the next logical development: "as barriers come down and multicountry markets [regions] truly are treated as one common market, a global market will be one notch closer to reality" (289).

Political factors are often cited as barriers to the global market on national and regional levels; but once regional barriers are removed global barriers tend to follow. Acceptance of the General Agreement on Tariffs and Trade (GATT), which reduced tariffs from an average of 40% in 1945 to 5% today (Keegan, 1995), was no doubt made easier by the earlier approval of the North American Free Trade Agreement (NAFTA) in the U.S. Congress (see also Bergsten, 1994: 20-21).

Finally, geographic considerations once limited markets to manageable national units. Recently, technological advances in communication and transportation have stimulated the growth of regional markets. This trend will continue, encouraging the growth of global markets: "The rise of regional trading blocs has led many companies to reassess the anticipated rise of globalization. Increasingly, regionalization is being viewed by managers as a stepping stone to more effective global competition" (Keegan, 1995:733).

Regional markets grow toward global markets, increasing the influence of world opinion and international consumer tastes. Values need not separate regional consumers from global markets, or members of different "civilizations" from the global public. The convergence of values need not occur on all levels nor wipe away all national or regional differences to exist.

The global market exists within a global public, and the parallel structures of world opinion and global consumer preferences are illustrated on three levels in Figure 4.1. On the level of individual preferences which cross national boundaries, an international consensus emerges on moral and pragmatic issues in world opinion; similarly, a homogenization of global preferences emerges regarding consumer goods. On the level of a "public" that crosses national boundaries, "world opinion" comes to be expressed in international forums such as the media and the United Nations; similarly, "global preference structures" come to be expressed in the demand for, and awareness of, those products which confer status internationally. Finally, on the systemic level, world opinion results in a loosely defined international community, or in some collective effort to a generally accepted end; similarly, global consumer preferences result in a world market in which goods are advertised and distributed with little regard for national borders. In both cases, the individual preferences made public result in a loosely defined or institutionalized system of relations—an international community or a global market.

The concurrent growth of these complementary forces does not end with analogous structures. The changes in dissemination and communication of individual attitudes that increased the importance of world opinion had a similar effect on global consumer preferences.

Figure 4.1. Comparative Structures of World Opinion and Global Consumer Preferences

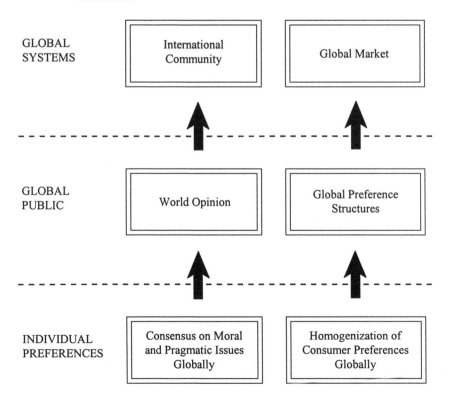

| GLOBAL SYSTEMS | International Community | Global Market |

| GLOBAL PUBLIC | World Opinion | Global Preference Structures |

| INDIVIDUAL PREFERENCES | Consensus on Moral and Pragmatic Issues Globally | Homogenization of Consumer Preferences Globally |

WORLD OPINION AND GLOBAL CONSUMER PREFERENCES: DISSEMINATION AND COMMUNICATION

There are several forces which encourage the global homogenization of attitudes: technology, increasing global interdependence, the globalization of mass media, the urbanization of the world, the globalization of labor, and the collapse of the Soviet Union and the end of the Cold War.

Technology

According to Levitt, the key force driving world markets "toward a converging commonality" is technology (Levitt, 1983). Developments in worldwide communications and the increased availability of rapid transport and travel have contributed to the rapid diffusion of a global consumer lifestyle. Technology creates its own markets, according to Levitt, by developing tastes for new goods and needs which had not theretofore existed. Technology thereby has a twofold effect upon global consumer preferences: it generates new products which consumers come to crave, and it creates a market for these products by facilitating contacts between consumers.

Technology plays a similar key role in the diffusion of world opinion. As citizens have increased mobility across national borders, they come to realize the manner in which other nations' citizens perceive them and their country. It has been noted that nations are very conscious of the image they project to others; indeed, the feedback which communications and travel provide regarding a nation's image in the world becomes a critical factor in the negotiation of that country's national identity. Finally, by increasing the contacts between nations, technology has increased the threat of isolation, since contacts made can also be contacts withdrawn as punishment.

One may also see the role of technology in the increased use of the Internet and the World Wide Web for disseminating political and consumer information. Indeed, a recent survey of users of the World Wide Web showed that while most individuals used the system for information or entertainment, shopping through the system was expected to increase by 85% in the near future (Gupta, 1995). The dual usage of these technologies, which facilitate global communication at low cost, illustrates the mutual growth of a global market within an expanding global public.

Global Interdependence

Global economic interdependence clearly promotes the existence of a global market for goods; economic ties must preexist the advertisement and dissemination of products among nations. But the market ties between nations are by nature porous; one cannot allow trade on one product and easily restrict it on others. Once ties are established with nations that had formerly been isolated economically, the forces toward globalization of preferences also enter. As an illustration, the removal of trade barriers as a solution to world economic problems tends to facilitate product standardization, since trade barriers limit the global availability of products and often require a variety of product and market adaptations (Douglas and Wind, 1987).

Increased global interdependence on the cultural, economic, political, and ecological levels has also increased the awareness that solutions to certain problems are not to be found at the national level. Since national-level problems require some degree of national consensus for a solution, global problems, where they are addressed, must also require some degree of international consensus for solution. Ironically, it is with regard to such problems that the concept of world opinion is commonly misinterpreted. Analysts attempting to "disprove" the existence of international opinion are often quick to point to cases where it was unable to compel nations to address global problems; halting the carnage in Bosnia is one case usually cited. Such logic confuses a fragmented world opinion with its nonexistence. In cases where international opinion has been united, such as in the Persian Gulf War, its power has proven effective; indeed, in the few instances where world opinion has reacted consistently against events in Bosnia the parties involved have responded. As such, analysts attempting to use examples of fragmented world opinion to prove the concept does not exist ignore the near impossibility of united international action without an external authority (see Jervis, 1970; Schelling, 1958; and Snidal, 1985, for examples); those cases where world opinion can compel collective global action are important exceptions which run counter to this logic.

Global interdependence also increases the potential power of the threat of isolation; the more nations have economic and cultural ties, the more likely their leaders and citizens will feel the effects of the disruption of relations. Finally, world opinion can also facilitate the opening of global markets by underscoring issues of global interdependence. The growing concern about ecological issues, for example, could facilitate product standardization and international demand for "environmentally friendly" products.

The Globalization of Mass Media

The globalization of the media industry exerts a potentially homogenizing effect upon ideas, images, and preferences. A significant number of media companies have merged globally since 1988. Most of these mergers involve foreign acquisition of American media outlets, for a variety of reasons: (1) the United States has had long experience in developing film and television programs that enjoy worldwide audiences; (2) the American market offers high profit potential because of its huge size; (3) the United States is a lead market, so that popular programs in America can be sold easily in other parts of the world; and (4) American technology and experienced personnel are desired in television and film production (Terpstra and Sarathy, 1994). In addition, the new broadcast technologies have made it possible for American music in its MTV format to be broadcast around the world, creating a market defined by the "global teenager" (Hassan and Katsanis, 1991). The Cable News Network (CNN) sells condensed versions of its news production in 83 countries (*Business Week*, 1989). Other nations are involved in this business as well: Germany's satellite channel signals may be picked up by central Europe, half of France, nearly all of Italy, the eastern United Kingdom, and Southern Norway and Sweden (Terpstra and Sarathy, 1994).

Anthony J.F. O'Reilly, chief executive officer of the H.J. Heinz company, notes that the communications revolutions in satellite and cable television "have set the stage for truly global marketing." He predicts that the globalization of the media will have the same effect on the homogenization of international preferences as the advent of national television had on the homogenization of national preferences in the United States. Consumers will not only be increasingly exposed to global brands through television; they will also be exposed to "advertisements for different life-styles." As such, "Television will further homogenize the cultures of the developed world. It will in turn generate the cosmopolitan aspirations satisfied by global brands" (O'Reilly, 1991).

The globalization of media has a similarly profound effect upon world opinion. Some critics have argued that American (or Western) control of the media causes all international news to have a pro-Western slant. Such criticisms ignore the reciprocal relationships which media have with public opinion in general. For news outlets not only transmit images, they seek audiences. Therefore, the globalization of the American media does imply that American images may dominate images from other nations' media outlets; but it also implies that the American-based media will be forced to become more international in focus, given the extended market they wish to reach.

Our studies support these conclusions. The first chapter's study of the usages of the concept of "world opinion" in American and German newspapers found a surprising correspondence in the manner in which the term was used, and in the *agenda* for world opinion described in the newspapers. The second chapter also indicated that the correspondence between the American and Indian newspapers on the Kuwaiti crisis was reflected in discussions of Kuwaiti sanctions in the United Nations, once the timing of references to this issue in world opinion converged between the two papers. These studies indicate that the global media are critical, not only as a means of disseminating their perspectives on world opinion, but also as a possible means of generating a "world public" defined as a new arena of discourse in which issues of international concern may be discussed.

The Urbanization of the World

The world population is increasingly an urban population. By the end of this century, one half of the world's inhabitants will reside in large cities. As such, these populations experience a change in venue and perspective. A nation's communications media are developed and concentrated in its cities; information contributes to the city dweller's sophistication as consumer and citizen (Terpstra and Sarathy, 1994). Cities are more connected to the rest of the world than rural areas. Hence, urbanites tend to be more exposed to foreign products and less tradition-oriented than rural dwellers. There is also a stronger demonstration effect of new products and consumption patterns in urban areas (Hill and Still, 1984). These factors provide fertile ground for the growth of global consumer preferences in the growing urban population. Indeed, one recalls the earlier note about the Chinese consumers, who are characterized as urban or rural (and, thus, sophisticated or unsophisticated) by the choice between global or local products, respectively. Urbanization is associated with globalization of preferences—and as the former increases, the latter is likely to do so also.

One of the criticisms often directed toward the concept of world opinion is that it, too, appears to be a construct restricted to urban areas. As one student on the subject noted, "What do Africans in a remote village, or Bedoins in the desert know, or care, of world opinion?" This argument merely acknowledges that those areas that are physically isolated from outside contact tend not to be probable publics for world opinion. Conversely, the more urbanized a society becomes, the more likely it is to be threatened by the disruption of these contacts, since urbanization carries with it citizen demands for goods and information. Recall that one article on South Africa, written during apartheid in 1986, noted how the nation would often allow in forbidden international broadcast signals out of a "fear of isolation." Populations tend to become less physically isolated as they move into cities. As such, they are more likely to feel the effects of international social and economic isolation than before. The growth of world opinion as a power increases accordingly.

The Globalization of Labor

A study of world workforce trends predicted that during the 1990s the flow of workers across international borders would accelerate, creating a world market for labor (Johnston, 1991). Several factors have made it practically inevitable that more workers will cross national borders during the 1990s. First, the cost of international travel is likely to drop in the coming years. Second, the barriers that governments place on immigration and emigration have broken down. Third, employers in the aging, slow-growing industrialized nations are hungry for talent, while the developing world is educating more workers than it can employ productively (Johnston, 1991).

The increased flow of workers across international borders augments cultural contacts between nations, particularly between first and third world countries. Third world people working in industrialized countries are likely to become agents of social change as they transmit consumer preferences and values back to their countries of origin. The earnings sent home from many of these individuals might also help finance purchases of global brands that would not otherwise be affordable. Return migration brings workers to their homelands with tastes acquired for global brands, and values acquired from first world nations, furthering the acculturation process toward modernization.

The globalization of the labor market will also further the creation and dissemination of world opinion. Johnston notes:

> As labor gradually becomes international, some national differences will fade. Needs and concerns will become more universal, and personnel policies and practices will standardize. As developing nations absorb women into the workforce, for example, they are likely to share the industrialized world's concern about child care and demand conveniences (Johnston, 1991:126).

To the extent that such issues as working conditions and the role of women become subjects for international opinion, the globalization of the workforce will affect world opinion. Indeed, in the recent past, the power of world opinion has been shown as boycotts of specific products crossed national borders as a result of unsafe or unfair working conditions in the nation of manufacture.

The Collapse of the Soviet Union and the End of the Cold War

The end of the Cold War and the collapse of the Soviet Union opened markets that had heretofore been limited for the West, notably those in Eastern Europe and China. As an example, the opening of the Moscow McDonald's was a social and cultural event of international proportions (O'Reilly, 1991); indeed, it quickly outpaced Lenin's tomb as an attraction for visitors to Moscow. Similarly, consumer awareness of global brands is spreading quickly through Eastern Europe. A consumer survey conducted by A. C. Nielsen in 1989 concluded that East German consumers knew some important global brands better than brands of their own country (O'Reilly, 1991).

Consumers in the former Communist nations also often wish to enjoy the "good life" as defined by the consumption lifestyles of individuals in the Western industrialized nations and Japan. As their transition to market-based economies are advanced further, more global marketers will seek part of that market. Indeed, it has been suggested that the collapse of the Eastern bloc was as much an economic as a political phenomenon, that citizens were driven almost as much by a desire for Western products as for democratic rights.

The end of the Cold War also created conditions making world opinion a more evident and cohesive force. International consensus is unlikely when the world is divided into two major, and several minor, competing ideologies. A common language is difficult to establish when one nation's "freedom fighters" are another nation's "terrorists." The collapse of the Eastern bloc and the refutation of Soviet interpretations of Marxism increase the possibility of shared discourse on issues of international concern. Indeed, if the "post-Cold War order" is to have any meaning beyond the demise of the Soviet Union, it must include consideration of the enhanced power of world opinion.

Conclusions and Suggestions for Further Research

The parallels discussed in this chapter show global consumer preferences to be a function of world opinion. This finding allows one to advance a preliminary definition of such preferences, beginning with a definition of world opinion from Chapter 1:

> World opinion refers to the moral judgments of observers which actors must heed in the international arena, or risk isolation as a nation.

A similar definition of global consumer preferences follows:

> Global consumer preferences refer to the tastes and behavior one must observe in the global market, or risk isolation and association with lower social status.

This definition does not assume that individuals will necessarily be isolated by citizens of other nations, although that is possible given the transmission of images in the international media and the image visitors take with them, or bring, as they cross national borders. The definition does assume, though, that the tastes and behavior which define status and the avoidance of social isolation in a given society now often cross national borders. The comparison between world opinion and global consumer preferences thus allows us to note that cultures need not converge completely for global preferences to exist. Instead, it is when tastes cross national boundaries and become a standard within different societies that the globalization of tastes is occurring.

The empirical study of global consumer preferences also allows the researcher to address nagging problems about world opinion. For instance, a commonly asked question is "Who is the audience for world opinion?" We take up this question in the next chapter. However, some progress has been made in reaching an answer regarding global consumer preferences. Studies indicate that cosmopolitan consumers who have greater exposure to world communications are more likely to be subject to the homogenizing influences of global markets than their noncosmopolitan compatriots. A study of multinational corporations conducted by Hill and Still (1984) found that products targeted for urban markets in third world nations needed few changes from products targeted for urban markets in industrialized countries. The authors conclude that "modern products fit into the life-styles of urban consumers wherever they are." As such, urban consumers seem more likely to belong to global market segments than rural consumers.

Social class also appears to be a factor in defining the global consumer. According to Ernst Dichter (1962) the creation of the "world consumer" was prompted by the growth of the middle class around the world. Ugur Yavas, Bronislaw Verhage, and Robert Green (1992) identify the existence of consumer segments for toothpaste and bath soap which transcend national boundaries; the sample for this study consisted of middle- and upper-income women residing in major urban areas in six different countries. Similarly, Philip Cateora notes in another study how the "preferences of consumers in midtown Manhattan are more similar to those in central Milan than the Bronx. . . . Yuppies in New York need the same dishwashers as Yuppies in Paris" (Cateora, 1993:373).

If urban, middle-class, and upscale constituencies define the "global consumer," these individuals are also more likely to define the global "opinion leaders" in the public for world opinion. These persons seem more connected to world communications and world events. In turn, they seem more likely to hold opinions about world events and, perhaps, to be aware of world opinion, at least as it is communicated by the national and international media.[5]

Understanding the global market as part of an emerging public for world opinion helps define a paradigm for conflict and consensus in the emerging international system. First, on a basic level, global corporations, like nations, may find themselves the subject of international isolation and boycotts when the dysfunctional consequences of marketing activities to world societies become so critical as to create outrage among global consumers. A famous case involved Nestlé's marketing of infant formula to mothers in third world nations. Touted as an upscale alternative to breast-feeding, the formula precipitated a crisis of monumental proportions, as mothers abandoned the traditional breast-feeding practices in favor of bottle feeding. The result was that powdered formula was often mixed with polluted water, or diluted because the families could not afford sufficient amounts of the product. The crisis, and Nestlé's poor handling of the problem, led to a consumer boycott of Nestlé's products among middle-class consumers in developed nations (Laczniak and Murphy, 1985). Similarly, an informal boycott of Exxon products by environmentally conscious consumers occurred after the *Exxon Valdez* oil spill in Alaska. More recently, Shell Oil was the subject of a boycott in 1995 because of its plans to sink an oil platform off the North Sea coast of Great Britain; international consumer reactions were so strong that the plan was abandoned. Future boycotts may also target cigarette companies that are marketing their products in third world nations as smoking declines in the more developed countries.

A second area of overlap concerns the effects of the spread of global markets and world opinion. In one sense, the globalization of consumer preferences may reduce other potential conflicts between nations. As consumer desires converge globally, certain commonalities in customs and mores might result, creating means of cultural communication where few had existed before. Also, since satisfying these consumer desires requires the maintenance of trade relations between nations, countries can no longer "go their own way" as easily, and they risk disrupting the means of meeting their citizens' material demands. The working contacts between nations, and the threat of isolation, would thereby increase accordingly.

However, analysts often make the mistake that a convergence of material desires necessarily leads to a lessening of hostilities; in effect, "as countries become more like us, they will like us more." In fact, the opposite may be true.

As citizens come to desire the same products internationally, their different capacities to satisfy these desires will become more evident. These circumstances create a situation in which, as Z. Brzezinski notes, one finds "individual and collective expectations rising rapidly, especially as the world's rich want more of everything and the poor desire what the rich already have" (Brzezinski, 1993:24). Indeed, as Chapter 3 argues, the recent rise of nationalistic movements in the world is prompted partly by a desire within certain nations to gain a respect in world opinion which they are denied because of their relative status deprivation economically—a deprivation which has become more evident since the collapse of the alternative Soviet model of development. As such, nationalism need not be interpreted as a rebuke to world opinion, as much as an effort to gain respect in a newly emerging system which includes a global public and a global market.

These hypotheses give lie to Benjamin R. Barber's thesis, in *Jihad vs. McWorld*, that the deep-rooted ethnic consciousness of the Jihad necessarily unfolds dialectically against the seemingly more superficial world of global consumer preferences (Barber, 1995:155-183). If superficiality adequately described the latter, then simple juxtaposition would be sufficient to explain the ongoing resistance to any sort of global integration. However, the globalization of consumer preferences is but one (very salient) manifestation of the emergence of world opinion as a force separate from the "public opinions" which feed nationalistic tendencies within societies or groups. Furthermore, the two need not exist in some dialectic confrontation wending itself toward resolution or apocalyptic showdown. Instead, like public opinion and the opinions of "publics" within a given society, the two forces conflict, coincide, or merely coexist as circumstances dictate. The results may not be as utopian as Woodrow Wilson envisioned, when he proclaimed that world opinion would restrain the differences and conflicts between nations (see Davison, 1973). Relations between the emerging systems will involve both the cooperative and zero-sum features that characterize economic exchanges. The problem is to understand these relations as the sense of "public" emerges more forcefully on a new, global level.

NOTES

1. Such new "moral imperatives" can be adapted to the most traditional (and stereotypical) relationships, as when Levitt describes how husbands can be made to feel a "sense of obligation" to provide certain goods, such as vacuum cleaners for their wives (Levitt, 1983:300; 1990).

2. Wind offers this observation as a counterargument to Levitt's thesis; however, conflicts between the value and interest components of global preferences do not contradict Levitt's argument.

3. The discussion of a hierarchy of preferences among goods echoes, in many ways, Abraham Maslow's discussion of the hierarchy of needs which require fulfillment (Maslow, 1962). This is not surprising, since one's material needs must be satisfied before considerations of social cachet become salient. Ronald Ingelhart makes a similar

point in his discussions of postindustrial society, arguing that at this stage, consumer preferences tend to be driven by postmaterialist considerations, since a basic level of subsistence is guaranteed to all (Inglehart, 1977:41-71).

4. He states that "the argument that a universal culture or civilization is now emerging takes various forms, none of which withstands even passing scrutiny" (Huntington, 1993b:191).

5. These conjectures allow us to make some preliminary suggestions for means to measure world opinion, following the models used to measure global consumer preferences (see the methodological note in Appendix II).

5

Does an "Attentive Public" Exist for World Opinion?

*Frank Louis Rusciano
and John Crothers Pollock*

In his germinal article on "International and World Opinion," published in 1973, W. Phillips Davison noted that the development of communications technologies would be a major force in the development of world opinion. Such changes "make it increasingly possible for people everywhere to focus their attention on the same issues and to engage in an exchange of ideas about them" (Davison, 1973:882). However, "for world opinion to grow relative to national opinion, communication and coordination mechanisms must expand their capabilities at a rate that will more than keep pace with the growth of politically attentive publics" (884).

Two decades ago few could have foreseen the scope and speed with which communications technologies would grow. Few could also have foreseen the extent to which these technologies would "decentralize" the reception and communication of ideas, by means of electronic mail and news reportage which presents even the most isolated areas with access to world events. A driving force in the evolution of these technologies has been the development of markets for the information and attitudes they transmit. These markets represent both the "politically attentive" and those who are interested for financial and social reasons. The changes have increased the potential size of the "attentive public" for world opinion beyond the small communities of scientists and international private organizations that Davison described as the beginning of this public two decades ago.

The potential increase in size is so great as to be daunting when one attempts to define the populace involved in the creation and dissemination of international opinion. In theory, all individuals who have access to CNN or even to the Internet are part of this public; hence, the potential membership begins to approximate the sum of all audiences for public opinion within the individual nations. However, having access to information about world events does not automatically engender interest in these events—one may ignore them, or observe without feeling that international issues have any salience to one's life. The audience for world opinion is likely guided by an "attentive public," one with enough interest and involvement in international issues to develop an opinion about them.

Finding these individuals is a difficult task using traditional survey research methods, since there are few international institutions to which individuals connect to express their opinions about issues. In societies like the United States, for instance, researchers can measure an individual's involvement with a political issue by the extent to which it motivates participation in politics by voting, joining voluntary organizations, or other activities for the display and exchange of opinions. The means by which world opinion develops and is disseminated among individuals is difficult to define in the absence of such institutions.[1] One may use traditional survey methods to poll within different nations, but aggregating these results and calling them "world opinion," even if one includes only those individuals to whom the issues are salient, is suspect as an approach. We have no means of distinguishing if we are merely adding responses within specific nations into an artificial construct, or if we are tapping into an actual "world opinion" which individuals share across national borders.

This chapter attempts to deal with this problem through a two-part research strategy. First, we assume that information and perspectives on world opinion are a commodity which members of an interested public will seek out. Therefore, one means of defining members of this public is by the media they use to acquire this commodity. We utilize content analyses of four newspapers to test for the presence of each of the six components of world opinion. We then perform a factor analysis on these components to derive the principal factors involved in their discussion of world opinion. We discover that all six components represent unique elements that are grouped into two factors: a *Pragmatism Factor* and an *Idealism Factor*. Both of these factors taken together constitute a *Cumulative Index of World Opinion*, designed to measure the depth of coverage world opinion receives in each newspaper. We then correlate the readership characteristics of the various newspapers with the Cumulative Index to discover the profile of individuals reading newspapers with the most in-depth discussion of world opinion. The section concludes with the derivation of four characteristics of this audience.

In the second portion of the analysis, we hypothesize that individuals who share the profile most associated with in-depth coverage of world opinion might define an "attentive public" of like-minded persons that crosses national boundaries. To test this assumption, we construct five scales regarding attitudes toward social inequality, from the 1992 International Social Survey. We then test whether the variance among responses from different nations decreases within groups defined by one or more of the profile characteristics. We discover that the more of these features individuals share, the more they concur on the survey questions. We conclude by discussing the ramifications of these findings for the possible existence of an "attentive public" for world opinion that crosses national borders.

METHODOLOGY

We begin by assuming that stories or editorials in a particular newspaper are written with a specific audience in mind; this audience is defined by the readership of the newspaper in question. It is not assumed that reporters or editors consciously choose material based upon market demographics. Instead, newspaper content is assumed to be directed toward stories that the readership would find "of interest." As such, the unit of analysis for this study is all individual stories or editorials which reference world opinion in four news-papers: the *International Herald Tribune*, the *Frankfurter Allgemeine Zeitung*, *The New York Times*, and the *Times of India*. The first two newspapers were studied for the months of February, March, and April 1986; the third newspaper was studied for the months of August 1990 through January 1991; and the fourth newspaper was studied for both periods. The newspapers and dates were chosen to give as broad a range for analysis as possible within the boundaries of a single study. All four are quality newspapers of record. One newspaper is pub-lished out of Zurich, but is considered "international" in audience (the *International Herald Tribune*). The other three newspapers represent an American newspaper (*The New York Times*), a European newspaper (the *Zeitung*), and an Asian, third world newspaper (the *Times of India*). The sample's diversity serves the purposes of the study well. With so much variation present, any consistent, coherent findings in the search for a working measure of the depth of coverage for world opinion are by definition compelling.

Because of the different periods and regions covered, the number of stories or editorials that referenced world opinion varied according to the dates in-cluded. Hence, depth of coverage could not be measured by the number of references to the concept. Similarly, the agenda for world opinion also varied by date and nation of origin; hence, depth of coverage could also not be measured by diversity of subject matter.

The saliency of world opinion for the newspapers' readers was measured according to the manner in which the subject was covered, as reflected by the content of the articles and editorials. Previous analyses by Pollock and Guidette (1980) and Pollock et al. (1995, 1997) use the characteristics of a newspaper's potential audience to explain their coverage of certain events. The present analysis applies this method to the *approach* used to cover world opinion, rather than to the specific subjects covered as part of an agenda for world opinion.

For this study, the depth of coverage of world opinion, as measured by the presence of the concept's major components in its analysis, was used as a depen-dent variable. It was assumed that those stories and editorials that gave the most in-depth analyses of world opinion were directed toward an audience which had a particular interest in the concept. The deeper and more detailed the coverage, the more likely the newspaper's readership profile would define the audience for world opinion.

The measure for depth of coverage for world opinion uses the six components of world opinion identified in Chapter 1. We attempted to derive the primary and peripheral elements that would be included in the coverage of the concept. Since not all components tend to be mentioned in every reference to international opinion, an "ideal" form of the concept might embrace fewer than six of these elements. To address this possibility, we ran a principal component factor analysis on all references to world opinion in the four newspapers, using the six elements of world opinion: the moral component, the pragmatic component, the threat of international isolation, and references to a nation's image, the power of world opinion, and the world as a unit. The general importance of all the elements was reflected in the result that all of the components appear in the model, with positive loadings, organized into two factors. These results are shown in Table 5.1.

The first factor emphasizes the common values nations share, and the means by which nations enforce these moral decisions; it was composed of the moral component, the power of world opinion, whether the world was referenced as a unit, and the threat of isolation. The analysis in Chapter 1 indicated that when these four elements correlate, the moral component is driving the relationship, defining the attitudes and behavior that invite international isolation. An index was derived by assigning the presence of each of these components a value of 1, and their absence a value of 0; these values were then weighted according to the factor loadings in the previous analysis, and summed to form an additive scale. This index was designated the *Idealism Scale.*

The second factor emphasized the common interests nations shared, and the manner in which they calculated their place in the formation of these shared interests; it was composed of the pragmatic component and the nation's image. Again, drawing from previous chapters, we note that a nation must balance

Table 5.1. Factor Analyses Using All Components of World Opinion

Factor Name	Components	Loading
Idealism Scale	Isolation	.68373
	Power of World Opinion	.65353
	World Referenced as a Unit	.57782
	Moral Component	.56271
Pragmatism Scale	Nation's Image	.81077
	Pragmatic Component	.73589

considerations of its own interests with world opinion in many cases. In certain instances, national leaders may find it difficult to dissent from general statements about the "interests of all nations," while preserving their nation's image as a reasonable international actor. Both of these components, then, relate to the various pragmatic considerations which a nation brings to the discussion of world opinion—the perceived interests nations are supposed to share, the country's own interests, and its stake in protecting its international image. An index was derived by assigning the presence of each of these components a value of 1, and their absence a value of 0. The values were then weighted according to the factor loadings in the previous analysis, and summed to form an additive scale, designated as the *Pragmatism Scale*. Taken together, the Idealism and Pragmatism Scales form a *Cumulative Index of World Opinion* which measures the depth of coverage the concept receives in a given newspaper article or editorial.

This study correlates characteristics drawn from the readership profiles of the newspapers in the project with the "scores" which the different newspapers accumulated on each of these indexes. The independent variable in this analysis was the readership profile, not the newspaper; in cases where newspapers had the same readership profile for a given characteristic, they were grouped together into one category. Focusing on the readership level is innovative for cross-national research on news reporting because it utilizes an explanatory proposition common in global marketing but new to the cross-national reporting of political issues.

This proposition argues that measures of world opinion do not just form coherent patterns regardless of nation, region, or time of origin; they also reflect certain readerships or readership markets, regardless of nation, region, or time period. Hence, it is possible that a relatively homogeneous "global market" exists for information on "world opinion." This market for news on international opinion would be expected to behave like other traditional economic and media markets. The market, defined by the readership demographics of certain newspapers, could affect the product or service itself (conceived here as the treatment of world opinion). At the same time, readership demographics may be a product which media sell to advertisers. In that case, the treatment of world opinion would be crafted to attract the demographic profile of individuals the newspaper was trying to reach. Newspaper demographics therefore would be expected to affect, and be affected by, the treatment and coverage of world opinion.

The analysis is thus guided by five hypotheses regarding the relationship between newspaper demographics and coverage of world opinion, as they relate to the definition of an "attentive public" for information on this subject:

Hypothesis 1: "Marketing" perspectives used to sell and move products abroad suggest that major newspapers should link up services or products with specific readership "markets." It is therefore reasonable and prudent to examine the relationship to be viewed as between newspaper coverage of "world opinion" and the newspaper markets exposed to that concept.

Hypothesis 2: The concept of "world opinion" may be reduced to some set of finite measures which can be empirically defined and replicated in different circumstances, regions, and times.

Hypothesis 3: World opinion is a coherent, yet multidimensional, concept. Its dimensions can be measured by systematic testing.

Hypothesis 4: Certain "audience" or "market" characteristics can be specified and tested to discover those associated with a richer treatment of world opinion. The demographic profile of this audience is assumed to define partially the market, or *"attentive public"* for world opinion.

Hypothesis 5: Evidence of the existence of this "attentive public" can be found in the cross-national consistencies of opinion among groups that share this public's characteristics. By using public opinion data from an international survey, it should be possible to show that individuals who fit the readership profile associated with in-depth coverage of world opinion are more similar in their attitudes than those who do not fit this profile. Such a finding would support the assumption that these individuals do indeed define a "public" in world opinion that crosses national borders.

RESULTS

Four readership characteristics were used in the attempt to identify the public for world opinion. Their descriptions, and the readership profile they

Table 5.2. Correlations of Independent Variables with Idealism Scale

Variable	Eta	(n)
Age	.4293	(327)
Education	.3163	(327)
Income	.4293	(327)
Gender*	.5454	(213)

*Data not available for *Times of India*.

Table 5.3. Correlations of Independent Variables with Pragmatism Scale

Variable	Eta	(n)
Age	.5169	(336)
Education	.2777	(336)
Income	.5169	(336)
Gender*	.5982	(222)

*Data not available for *Times of India*.

define, are described below. Tables 5.2 and 5.3 show the eta values for the relationships between the profile characteristics and the *Cumulative Index of World Opinion* scales. Figures 5.1 through 5.8 show the distributions of means values on the *Index* scales according to readership characteristics.

Age: This variable was defined as the median age of readers for each of the newspapers in the sample. The values for the variable were 30, 43, 47, and 49. The results indicate that the relationship between age and both scales was significant and nonlinear. The median readership age correlated with the Idealism Scale with an eta of .429, and with the Pragmatism Scale with an eta of .517. The distributions of mean values, shown in the displayed graphs, however, indicate that both scales' means peak at a median readership age of 43. The downward slopes of the distributions on either side of this point suggest that these means approximate a normal distribution, with age 43 as the peak for the values measured.

Education: This variable was defined as the median education level of readers for the newspapers in the sample, and had three categories: high school, college, and graduate school. The results indicate the relationship between education and both scales was significant and nonlinear. The median education for readers correlated with the Idealism Scale with an eta of .316, and with the Pragmatism Scale with an eta of .278. The means of both scales peak at a college education. The downward slopes of the distributions on either side of this point suggest that these means approximate a normal distribution, with a college education as the peak for the values measured.

Income: This variable was defined as the median income of readers of the four newspapers, adjusted for the per capita income of the nation of origin. To derive this measure, the median household income for each newspaper's readers was divided by the per capita income of the country in which it was published, yielding four values: 2.1, 3, 4, and 5.7. The relationships between the income measure and both scales were significant and nonlinear. The median income measure correlated with the Idealism Scale with an eta of .429, and with the Pragmatism Scale with an eta of .517. The means of both scales peak at a median income measure of three times the median income of the nation of origin. The downward slopes on either side of this point approximate a normal distribution for these means, with 3 as the peak for the values measured.

Gender: This variable was measured as the percentage of males in the readership, and had three values: 49, 60, and 79; the *Times of India* was not included in this analysis because the information on gender was not available for its readership. The relationship between this variable and the two scales was significant and linear, peaking at the almost even gender split of 49% male readership. The gender measure correlated with the Idealism Scale with an eta of .545 (and an r of .498), and with the Pragmatism Scale with an eta of .598 (and an r of .444). The results indicate that the closer the readership approximates an even split between males and females, the higher the scores on these two scales. As one moves away from the 49% value, the mean scores on both scales decline.

Figure 5.1. Idealism Peaks at Median Readership Age of 43

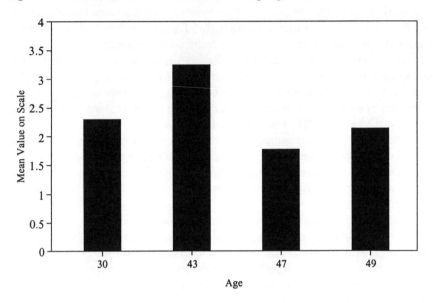

Figure 5.2. Pragmatism Scale Peaks at Median Readership Age of 43

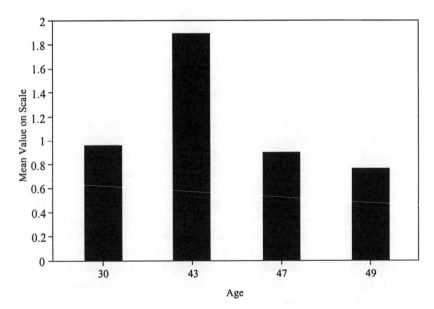

Figure 5.3. Idealism Scale Peaks at College Education Level for Readership

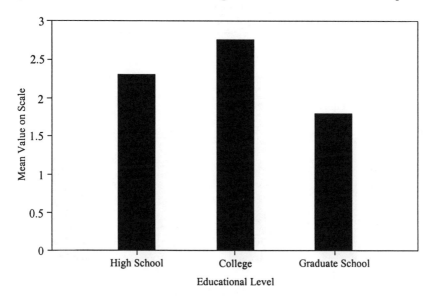

Figure 5.4. Pragmatism Scale Peaks at College Education Level for Readership

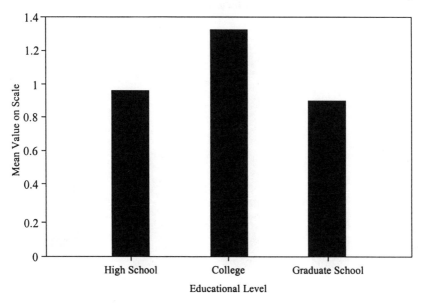

**Figure 5.5. Idealism Scale Peaks at Income Level Three Times
the Median Per Capita Income of the Nation of Origin**

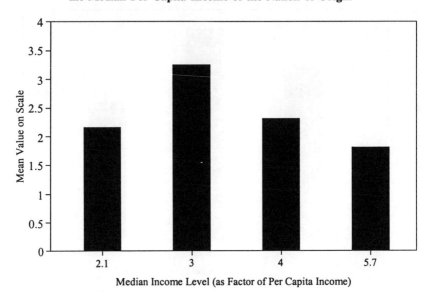

Median Income Level (as Factor of Per Capita Income)

**Figure 5.6. Pragmatism Scale Peaks at Income Level Three Times
the Median Per Capita Income of the Nation of Origin**

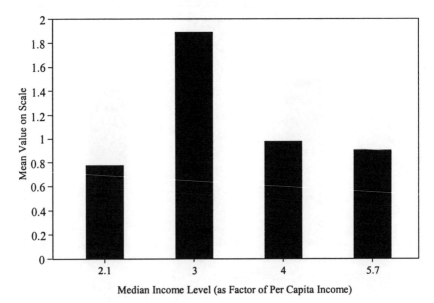

Median Income Level (as Factor of Per Capita Income)

Figure 5.7. Idealism Scale Peaks at Readership Evenly Divided by Gender

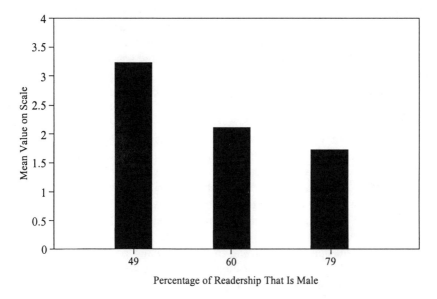

Percentage of Readership That Is Male

Figure 5.8. Pragmatism Scale Peaks at Readership Evenly Divided by Gender

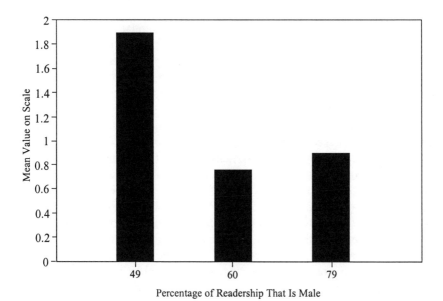

Percentage of Readership That Is Male

A discriminant analysis was performed to test the usefulness of all four variables in predicting scores on the Idealism and Pragmatism Scales. For the purposes of this analysis, the two scales were split at their respective medians for the sample, and coded into two categories. Because inclusion of the gender variable eliminated cases from the *Times of India*, the analysis was run twice, once excluding gender and once including it. The results are similar for all of the analyses. The three variable analysis of Age, Education, and Income correctly classified values on the *Idealism Scale* in 63.9% of the cases; the three variables correctly classified values on the *Pragmatism Scale* in 66.1% of cases. Similarly, the four variable analyses of Age, Education, Income, and Gender correctly classified values on the *Idealism Scale* in 63.9% of cases; the four variables correctly classified cases on the *Pragmatism Scale* in 60.7% of cases. These results suggest that this set of variables describing the readership profiles of the four newspapers has high discriminatory power with respect to the measures of world opinion. The results are summarized in Tables 5.4 and 5.5.

The initial results of this research therefore suggest that the "attentive public" for world opinion, according to the readership profile analysis, has a median age of 43, a median education level of a college degree, a median income three times the nation's per capita income, and is as likely to be female as male. This conclusion parallels the profiles of individuals who are likely consumers in a "global market" for other goods, as described in Chapter 4. Indeed, the multinational marketing studies cited in the previous chapter have shown that products targeted for upper-middle-class markets in third world nations required few changes from products marketed among the same groups in industrialized countries (Hill and Still, 1984). Similarly, Dichter notes that the creation of "world consumers"—individuals with similar tastes across countries—was prompted by the growth of this class around the world (Dichter, 1962). One recalls Cateora's observation that "the preferences of consumers in midtown Manhattan are more similar to those in central Milan than in the Bronx. . . . Yuppies in New York need the same dishwashers as Yuppies in Paris" (Cateora, 1993:373).

It is no surprise that the public for world opinion would appear similar to this public for global consumer goods, for three reasons. First, global consumers must obtain information about those goods that define status cross-nationally; hence, these consumers tend to be connected to the same media sources that disseminate world opinion. Second, information about world opinion is a commodity that is marketed globally, as shown by the study of the four newspapers in this analysis. It is no accident that the customers in this market for information are similar to the customers for other products in the international market. Finally, since global consumer preferences are but another form of world opinion, individuals who are interested in global products seem likely to have a passing interest in, and experience with, world opinion.

Table 5.4. Percentage Cases Correctly Placed for Two Scales Split at the Median (Discriminant Analyses)

Scale	Variables	Percentage of Cases Placed
Idealism Scale	Education Age Income	63.9%
Pragmatism Scale	Education Age Income	66.1%

Table 5.5. Percentage Cases Correctly Placed for Two Scales Split at the Median (Discriminant Analyses)*

Scale	Variables	Percentage of Cases Placed
Idealism Scale	Education Age Income Gender	63.9%
Pragmatism Scale	Education Age Income Gender	60.7%

*Does not include *Times of India*, for which gender data were not available.

The common characteristics shared by those in a potential global market for information on world opinion, as well as other goods, however, do not prove the existence of an attentive public with like attitudes which crosses national borders. It does imply that if customers with this profile have similar tastes in consumer goods, there are some networks of communication which are promoting complementary tastes internationally. The question is whether these similarities transfer to attitudes other than the tastes in clothes or electronic equipment described in Chapter 4.

SEARCHING FOR "ATTENTIVE OPINION PUBLICS" INTERNATIONALLY

The next step in the analysis assumes that if opinion publics do cross national boundaries, they should be identifiable according to the same demographic characteristics that defined the market for global consumer goods and information on world opinion. This "attentive opinion public" would need to exist regardless of the differential status these characteristics confer upon individuals in their respective nations. For instance, an individual with a college education in the United States is part of a subgroup that constitutes approximately 25% of the population. In a nation like Slovenia, however, the percentage of persons with a college education will necessarily define a much smaller portion of the total population. Hence, the individual in the latter society would probably be part of a more privileged class than the individual in the former society. If the preceding analysis is correct, however, these national differences should make little difference in defining the attentive opinion public globally. It may be that individuals in this public represent a smaller or more privileged group in one nation than in others, but these national differences should not suppress attitudinal similarities on an international level if our approach is useful.

To test the demographic model for this attentive public, the analysis used data from the International Social Survey from 1992. First, we defined the independent variables in the model, which were derived from the previous analysis. These included age, income, and education. The Age category included all individuals in the nation who were 43 years of age, or fell within one standard deviation of that age for that nation's population. Similarly, the Income category included all individuals with an income within one standard deviation of three times the nation's income. Finally, the Education category was simply defined as all individuals who had received an undergraduate degree only. We recognize that these measures, as they are defined, are somewhat "rough and ready" with reference to the age and income categories. The decision to include all cases one standard deviation above and below the values for age and income being investigated was made in order to secure a sufficient number of cases. In nearly all instances, however, these categories corresponded with the categories into which data were grouped in the survey itself.

In order to test whether these characteristics did indeed define an "attentive public" with similar attitudes that crossed national borders, we defined five opinion scales pertaining to the International Survey's subject of Economic Inequality. These measures dealt with the equity and causes of the distribution of wealth in various societies, and were particularly suited to testing similarities of opinion in the groups defined by readership characteristics. By definition, the Income and Education factors in our analysis define a privileged class within each society; however, this class was clearly more privileged in some nations than in others. A college education, for instance, is a somewhat common achievement in a country like the United States, but it is less common in a country like Russia.

Similarly, separating out those individuals with incomes three times the median in a given country will define groups in different positions in the economic hierarchy, depending on the distribution of incomes in the nation. In a nation with a large percentage of poor people and a few rich individuals, the median income can be quite low, and three times the median defines the middle class. In a nation where income is more or less evenly distributed, an income three times the media would almost certainly place an individual in the upper class.

As a result, it is difficult to argue that any similarities in attitudes toward economic inequality occur because we are studying individuals in the same social class within their respective nations. Social class, which we would expect to have a strong influence on questions of economic inequality, is not comparable as a concept across the different groups defined in this study.

In order to construct the attitudinal scales for the study, a principal factor analysis was performed on ten questions from the International Social Survey. The factor analysis produced five significant factors, which formed the basis for the indices used: (1) *Income Distribution Factor* I; (2) *Capitalism Factor*; (3) *Provincialism Factor*; (4) *Income Distribution Factor II*; and (5) *Meritocracy Factor*. The questions making up the components of each factor are defined below. The factor loadings for each component are included in Table 5.6.

Income Distribution Factor I: This factor dealt with economic equity and reasons for inequality in the society, and included the following questions:

Income inequality continues to exist because it benefits the rich and powerful. (Responses: Strongly Agree, Agree, Neither Agree nor Disagree, Disagree, Strongly Disagree.)

Inequality continues to exist because ordinary people don't join together to get rid of it. (Responses: Strongly Agree, Agree, Neither Agree nor Disagree, Disagree, Strongly Disagree.)

Do you think that people with high incomes should pay a larger share of their income in taxes than those with low incomes, the same share, or a lower share? (Responses: Much Larger Share, Larger Share, The Same Share, Small Share, Much Smaller, Share.)

Capitalism Factor: This factor dealt with whether prosperity depended upon income differences and the ability of businesses to accrue substantial profits.

Large differences in income are necessary for [respondent's country's] prosperity. (Responses: Strongly Agree, Agree, Neither Agree nor Disagree, Disagree, Strongly Disagree.)

Allowing business to make good profits is the best way to improve everybody's standard of living. (Responses: Strongly Agree, Agree, Neither Agree nor Disagree, Disagree, Strongly Disagree.)

Provincialism Factor: This factor dealt with perceptions of regional or gender advantages in economic advancement.

The part of the country a person comes from, how important is it (for getting ahead)? (Responses: Essential, Very Important, Fairly Important, Not Very Important, Not Important At All.)

Being born a man or a woman, how important is that (for getting ahead)? (Responses: Essential, Very Important, Fairly Important, Not Very Important, Not Important At All.)

Income Distribution Factor II: This factor dealt with perceptions of taxation rates for middle and lower income groups.

For those with middle incomes, are taxes . . . (Responses: Much Too High, Too High, About Right, Too Low, Much Too Low.)

For those with low incomes, are taxes . . . (Responses: Much Too High, Too High, About Right, Too Low, Much Too Low.)

Meritocracy Factor: This factor dealt with the importance of education for advancement in the society.

How important is having a good education yourself (for getting ahead)? (Responses: Essential, Very Important, Fairly Important, Not Very Important, Not Important At All.)

Since each of the components in the factors had positive loadings of approximately the same magnitudes, they were converted into attitudinal scales by a simple additive formula. The responses to each question were recoded to 0 for values below the sample median, and 1 for values at or above the sample

Table 5.6. Factor Loadings for Indices from International Social Survey

Index	Factors	Loading
Income Distribution I	Inequality benefits rich	.62291
	Ordinary people don't battle inequality	.62060
	Rich pay higher taxes	.65436
Capitalism	Income differences for prosperity	.78002
	Business profits raise living standards	.77915
Provincialism	Region important for success	.77105
	Gender important for success	.78853
Income Distribution II	Evaluate middle income taxes	.85210
	Evaluate low income taxes	.54040
Meritocracy	Good education important for success	.77892

median. The responses were then added together, yielding five scales: an *Income Distribution Scale I*, with a range of 0 to 3; a *Capitalism Scale*, with a range of 0 to 2; a *Provincialism Scale,* with a range of 0 to 2; an *Income Distribution Scale II*, with a range of 0 to 2; and a *Meritocracy Scale*, with a range of 0 to 1. These measures were used in the analysis of opinion differences on economic inequality among the nations studied.

OPINION CONTINUITIES ACROSS NATIONAL BORDERS

The study compared the number of significant differences in opinions on the five measures within the demographic groups defined by the readership survey, for eight nations: the German Federal Republic, Slovenia, Austria, Russia, Canada, Norway, the United States, and New Zealand.[2] We divided the sample according to the number of "attentive public" readership characteristics individuals shared from the previous analysis; four groups resulted, ranging from those who shared none of the characteristics to those who shared all three of the characteristics. We then performed a multiple range analysis on the attitudinal scales within categories of the assumed "attentive public" characteristics. The results are presented in Figures 5.9 and 5.10. Figure 5.9 shows the results for the raw scores on each of the individual scales. For Figure 5.10, each attitudinal scale was recoded at the median for the entire population.

The figures indicate that the more characteristics of the hypothesized "attentive public" respondents shared, the more similar their opinions tended to be. As shown on Figure 5.9, significant differences in attitudes among respondents from different nations declined as one moved from the group sharing none of these characteristics to the group sharing all three of these characteristics. These changes ranged from 15 to 1 on the Income I Scale, 18 to 4 on the Capitalism Scale, 24 to 1 on the Provincialism Scale, 29 to 0 on the Income II Scale, and 32 to 3 on the Meritocracy Scale. The recoded values used for Figure 5.10 show similar declines.

The results suggest a convergence of attitudes across national borders among those who form the most likely audience for in-depth information about world opinion. This potential linkage between information dissemination and opinion convergence suggests important lessons for the theoretical and empirical analysis of world opinion.

CONCLUSION: MEDIA, INFORMATION FLOWS, AND THE DISSEMINATION OF WORLD OPINION

The preceding results underscore the prescience of Davison's vision of world opinion from his 1973 article. As noted in the introduction to this chapter, Davison linked the growth of world opinion to "communication and coordination mechanisms" that would need to develop alongside of "politically attentive publics" for international attitudes (Davison, 1973:884). Since that time,

Figure 5.9. Number of Significant Differences Among Nine Nations on Attitudinal Scales, by Readership Characteristics

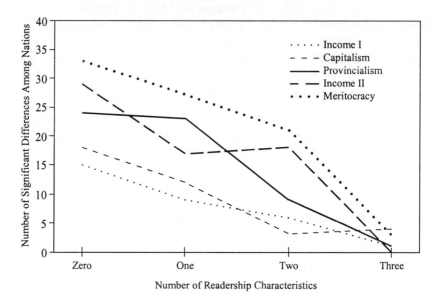

Number of Readership Characteristics

Figure 5.10. Number of Significant Differences Among Nine Nations on Recoded Attitudinal Scales, by Readership Characteristics

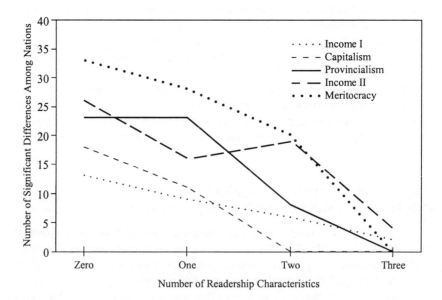

Number of Readership Characteristics

the "attentive public" for world opinion has grown beyond the privileged elite of scientists and diplomats with special access to the international flow of information. The development of global communications and the interest accorded world opinion in different media outlets have made media perspectives on world opinion accessible to a broader audience.

The preceding research suggests that this group is still an elite within their respective nations; certainly an undergraduate degree and an income three times the nation's median describes a group of individuals who occupy the upper socioeconomic categories in their respective countries. But this group is different from the audiences Davison described for world opinion in 1973 in two critical ways. First, Davison's groups consisted of the few diplomats and scientists who had the power or international reputation to overcome national and ideological barriers, and to establish regular contact with individuals from other nations. These individuals were a tiny elite from within the upper socioeconomic groups in their nations. Second, there is little indication that this smaller elite interacted with individuals outside of their groups, particularly regarding the content or direction of world opinion. Indeed, examples such as the effort by scientists to limit the threat of nuclear weapons were the exception rather than the rule, and were either ignored or greeted with hostility by their nations' governments.

Our research suggests that the potential "attentive public" for world opinion has grown far beyond the boundaries of a tiny elite of politicians and intellectuals, to a broader based mass of opinion leaders—individuals whose primary occupations do not necessarily bring them in contact with the smaller elite groups which had previously formed the audience for world opinion. This new "attentive public" for world opinion can draw much of its information from media sources which commonly reference the concept. Additionally, this group likely has links to the general public through other forms of everyday contact and opinion leadership. Consider that the profile of this attentive public also fits the profile of those individuals most likely to participate in politics, particularly in the United States. As such, the attentive public could provide a critical bridge between the governmental and intellectual elites who participate directly in the leadership of world opinion, and the mass of citizens in individual nations who are affected by it.

This insight addresses one criticism of the content analysis approach to studying world opinion. Wilcox et al. have argued that "journalistic usage refers to an agreement among world elites and leaders that may or may not imply agreement among the citizenry" (Wilcox et al., 1993:71). The results described in Chapter 3, however, suggest that the general citizenry in a least one country had definite perceptions of world opinion regarding their international image. Moreover, these perceptions related strongly to how they perceived their own national identity. The causal ordering in this relationship is unclear: perceptions of world opinion may affect perceptions of national identity, perceptions of national identity may affect perceptions of world opinion, or the relationship could run both ways. But world opinion was clearly involved in the construction

of identity among the nation's citizens. Hence, some perception of world opinion, however flawed, appears to filter down to the mass of citizens.

If world opinion were a conversation limited to elites and journalists, this
flow of information would not occur. The preceding analysis, when combined
with the results in Chapter 3, thus suggests a three-step process in the creation
and dissemination of world opinion. In the first step, a nation's or leader's
actions attract international attention, creating some effect regarding the nation's
international reputation. This step is often expressed in the realm of discourse
described in Chapter 1 as the "international arena." Media necessarily play a
critical role in defining this realm, by disseminating perceived impressions of
world opinion to the next step in the process, the attentive public. Indeed,
Wilcox et al. also note, referencing Page and Shapiro (1983), that the "public
forms rational opinions *given the information available*," and that a primary
source of information on international events is the mass media (Wilcox et al.,
1993:71).[3]

The individuals in the proposed "attentive public" define a group that seeks
out the most in-depth information on world opinion; this group also shares opinions on critical issues across national borders to a greater extent than individuals
who are outside of the group. One can speculate that the attentive public serves
somewhat of a "filtering" function, sorting through various interpretations of
world opinion, and settling upon certain issues which may allow agreement
across national borders. This group also may serve as a conduit to the general
citizenry, through various forms of opinion leadership, so that citizens who are
not commonly consumers of the media which discuss world opinion have some
knowledge of it. Indeed, it is noteworthy in the German case described in Chapter 3 that concern over the nation's international image prompted *mass political
demonstrations*, eventually involving 1 in 40 Germans in such activities as
candlelight vigils to protest anti-immigrant violence. Similarly, it is significant
that these efforts, which filtered down to the mass citizenry, were begun by
intellectuals and political elites who initiated international letter-writing
campaigns and other actions to express their outrage at the violence.

A hypothetical map of the three-step dissemination of world opinion is
illustrated in Figure 5.11. International elites operating in the international arena
gain a reputation for their nation that is communicated in certain media of
record. This reputation, and other indications of world opinion, are internalized
by an attentive public sensitive to, and interested in, world opinion. As a result,
this group possesses attitudes that converge across national borders more than
the attitudes of other citizens. This group also links to the mass of citizens,
however, through various forms of opinion leadership, to convey messages about
world opinion. It is probable that the effects of world opinion and the global
public upon individual identities increases the more closely involved the person
or group is in the initial actions which stimulated world opinion. Such effects are
likely strongest among the elites involved in the first step, less strong among the
attentive public, and weakest among the mass of citizens who receive filtered

Figure 5.11. The Three-Stage Dissemination of World Opinion

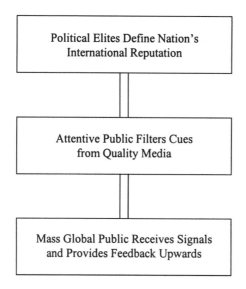

messages about international public opinion. However, the global opinion processes which affect identity are apparently present at each level, as suggested by the opinion convergences among the attentive public, and the relationship between world opinion and national identity among the mass of citizens in Chapter 3.

The analysis suggests several propositions for further research. First, the model must be refined further, using more newspapers for the content analyses; also, whenever available, other variables describing readership demographics must be added into the model. Second, this model must be tested further using cross-national survey data on other issues, to discover whether: (1) individuals in this group had more consistency on the agenda of issues for world opinion than other groups in their respective societies, and (2) these individuals share similar other views on topics relevant to world opinion across national borders. In this manner, one might discover details about the "attentive public" world opinion can be expected to reach.

Finally, audience-focused approaches suggest that a "media marketing" analysis of the communication of world opinion reveals a major role for prominent newspapers. Publishers may search for foreign affairs audiences, in the same way that other providers of goods and services search for the most lucrative, responsive markets in which to sell. Hence, one has somewhere to begin in searching out the public for issues on the agenda for international public opinion. Adopting a "marketing approach" helps researchers adapt the tools and assumptions of international business and foreign affairs research to the study of political communication.

The four-newspaper cross-national analysis also has significance beyond its hypotheses regarding information flows and world opinion. Two dimensions of world opinion were proposed, tested, and confirmed in the *Cumulative Index of World Opinion*; across different nations of origin, regions, and time periods, the two dimensions of Idealism and Realism emerged from the combination of the papers' stories and editorials referencing world opinion. Moreover, these dimensions included all six components of world opinion which have formed the basis for this book's analysis. The results provide evidence of a transnational, "global" concept of world opinion that transcends time and place, and suggests a common discourse in the combination of the four newspapers. However, this insight is partially challenged in the next chapter, which describes permutations in the construction of world opinion which occur across different regions and historical eras.

NOTES

1. Although it should be noted that recent developments suggest the growth of international nongovernmental institutions (NGOs) which do connect individuals across national borders regarding such issues as the environment, women's rights, and so on. As such organizations continue to develop, they will provide ample grist for the study of world opinion processes and their effects upon international collective action and governmental response.

2. Nations were included in the analysis solely on the basis of available data; any nation from which there were sufficient responses on the survey questions was included in the analysis.

3. Goldmann also concentrates primarily on this level in his analysis of world opinion (see Goldmann, 1993).

6

"Imagined Communities" in the Cold War and Post-Cold War Eras

Frank Louis Rusciano

It could be said that Africa invented Man, that the Semites invented God and that Europe invented the world, or rather the *concept* of the world . . . it even imposed its form of that concept on the outlook of peoples in other continents. . . .

Is Europe *north* of Africa? Is Europe *up* and Africa *down* in geographical location, as well as in income, power, and global status? Of course, the maps say Europe is north of Africa (and therefore *up*). But that decision was arbitrary and made primarily by European mapmakers . . . there is no reason, from an astronautical or cosmonautical point of view, why the South Pole should not be the North Pole and vice versa.

A.A. Mazrui, 1986:23

The "foreign policies" of nation states are based on what have been shown to be representational practices through which various forms of global otherness have been created. For example, to refer to "Latin America" is not just to refer to an area on the globe; it is to help reproduce an institutionalized form of dominance, one in which the minority, Hispanic part of populations in the region control the original indigenous groups. Even the use of the name of a recognized nation is a political gesture.

M.J. Shapiro, 1989:15

To construct the world is the mapmaker's privilege. The naming and placing of nations and regions have profound effects upon the composition and status of people living in those areas. This power accrues to the mapmaker independent of whether this work consists of graphic representations or linguistic constructs which group regions into nations, and nations into continents or some other form of supranational entity. The exercise becomes more important when the individual drawing the map tries to convince others that the representation is a "true" or "accurate" picture of the world, for "the separation of the world into kinds of space" is a significant means for establishing "the systems of intelligibility" which make global politics comprehensible (Shapiro, 1989:12). "Once we attempt to articulate *what* there is [in the 'world out there'] we enter the world of discourse. At that moment the process of construction begins," and the map moves from individual to "social construction," is shared, and ultimately accepted or rejected, by others (Gergen, 1992:171).

Acceptance depends in part upon "various reality-making scripts one inherits or acquires from one's surrounding cultural/linguistic condition" (Shapiro, 1989:11). Changes in the power structures and relations underlying cultural and linguistic conventions may thereby alter the map. In the most obvious sense, nations may be divided, absorbed, or created. In a more subtle way, the manner in which entities are constructed may be altered.

To use the concept "world opinion" is to construct a map. Certain nations are placed within a consensual public—a loosely defined "international community"—while other nations are isolated from it. This chapter studies the social construction of world opinion as it was practiced in first and third world newspapers in 1986 during the Cold War era and in 1990-1991, during the post-Cold War era. The comparisons illustrate the conflicting national and international forces which affect the way the media construct reality. This conflict affects the presentation of "world opinion" across different historical eras and in different regions of the world. But the study of world opinion is not used solely for illustrative purposes. Rather, world opinion is taken to be the means of constructing "maps" of a global community such as affect the placement and status of individual nations.

Drawing a map by means of various forms of descriptive discourse involves creating what Benedict Anderson calls an "imagined community." Once boundaries are sketched out and disseminated through the media, "imagined communities" are transformed into entities, such as nations, with recognized boundaries that have profound effects upon individuals' lives. Anderson argues that this process was facilitated by the development of print media in the sixteenth century, affecting the manner in which individuals perceived their position both within their society and beyond it, since "the very possibility of imagining the nation only arose historically when, and where, three fundamental cultural conceptions, all of great antiquity, lost their grip on men's minds." These conceptions were: (1) that a script, or written language, offered privileged access to ontological truth, and was considered an inseparable part of that truth; (2) that society was naturally organized on a hierarchical basis, founded upon a cosmological order which granted certain individuals special privileges; and (3) that history was no more than an explication of this cosmology, making the origins of the world and the origins of man identical (Anderson, 1995:89). According to Anderson, these conceptions lost their grip upon philosophical thinking as the print media became more accessible to mass audiences, thereby promoting the dissemination of a common language and the beginnings of nationalism. In short, print media transformed public opinion into a "social skin" (to use Noelle-Neumann's phrase) which would give form to a hitherto imagined national community (Noelle-Neumann, 1992).

It is a short analytical leap to apply Anderson's thesis to a later stage in the development of media: the globalization of communications. His analysis can be used to argue that the same processes which operated to transform "imagined communities" into nations in the early stages of print capitalism operate to transform an "imagined community" of nations into a loosely defined "global community," bound by shared conceptions of world opinion. First, once global communication systems gave individuals all over the world immediate access to news, the privilege of national leaders to isolate their citizens by controlling the information they received about the outside world diminished accordingly. Second, it followed that the special privileges granted to certain leaders based upon their control of access to knowledge would diminish once citizens had greater access to outside information. It is no accident that the movement toward democracy in nations such as South Africa and the former Eastern bloc occurred in tandem with the development of global media. Finally, access to global media helped weaken the notion that the history of a "people" and the history of their "nation" were one and the same—an idea invented, in part, to maintain social control over a nation's citizens by sharply distinguishing the origins of the "self" and the "other" as defined by national borders. It is in this way that global media transform world opinion into a "social skin" which would give form to a hitherto "imagined global community." Our very sense of what constitutes a community determines our allocation of resources, facilitating our response to, and anticipation of, a global community.

Recent history provides numerous examples of how access and reference to global media and world opinion have dramatically altered the power structures of nations in dramatic ways. The fall of the Marcos regime in the Philippines and the demise of apartheid in South Africa are but two instances of such changes. The latter case is especially significant, since it not only involved a change of regime, but also a fundamental reconstruction of a power structure that had been based upon an imagined hierarchy of races.

However, it would be naive to assume that the globalization of media and the invocation of world opinion will loosen the grip of the nation-state upon individuals' imaginations. Just as nationalism has often lacked the power to erase tribal loyalties within nations, so too world opinion may lack the power to erase national loyalties. The locus of power over most individuals' lives still resides in the nation-state. Moreover, nations still retain the power to affect the media content of their newspapers; consequently, they can "filter" discussions of world opinion and modulate them in formats compatible with national and dominant private interests. Herman and Chomsky discuss such processes, which run counter to the transformation of world opinion discussed previously. They argue that newspapers in certain nations "manufacture consent" by such "filtering." Factors contributing to this include the concentrated ownership of mass media, media dependence on advertising revenues, media reliance on government and corporate sources of information, criticisms of media objectivity as a means of disciplining the media, and anti-Communism as an accepted ideology (Herman and Chomsky, 1988:2).

Through the exploitation of such channels, a nation's dominant private and government interests can affect the manner in which they describe and create national "consensus," and similar arguments are applicable to the description of consensus in world opinion. It is no surprise, therefore, that governments and private interests adjust their perspective on international consensus to suit national concerns. An illustration of this tendency appears in *The New York Times* regarding the downing of the Korean jetliner by a Soviet fighter plane in 1983. The American government's point of view clearly slants the statement that "*worldwide criticism* of the Soviet handling of the crisis has strengthened the United States in its relations with Moscow" (quoted in Herman and Chomsky, 1988:32). It is questionable whether all or even most foreign newspapers echoed this "worldwide criticism."

The upshot is a meeting of two conflicting forces. The globalization of media disseminates world opinion, and weakens the grip of national governments upon their citizens' conceptions of community, while national "filtering" of the media imposes slanted interpretations of world opinion to support the dominant interests and regime of the country. The former force makes discussion of world opinion in a nation's major newspapers inevitable, while the latter force limits the integrating effects of world opinion to the degree that they conflict with national interests. Two hypotheses follow. First, while major newspapers will discuss world opinion, they will do so in a manner that reflects their nation's position and interests in the international power structure. Second, should that power structure change, as in the transition from the Cold War to the post-Cold war era, the discussion of world opinion may be expected to change accordingly. This chapter studies the conflict of two forces affecting discourse on world opinion: that which *protects* the "imagined national community" and that which *advances* the "imagined world community." Comparisons of the respective media illustrate this conflict, and our sense of what constitutes a community develops out of the confrontation.

What follows falls into three parts. The first part is analytical and separates the concept "world opinion" into its component parts, and compares the way they were employed in first and third world newspapers, and during the Cold War and post-Cold War eras. The second part is taxonomic, and in it the concept will be reconstructed for each of these categories, and the principal factors defining their usage will be analyzed and explained according to their classification. The final part is comparative. The differences in the construction of world opinion will be described in terms of the roles the concept plays in the "map" of the different categories. It will be argued that the comparison between first and third world newspapers reveals differences in usage from that between the two historical eras.

These differences are explained in light of the Herman/Chomsky and Anderson theses. First those between the way first and third world newspapers deal with world opinion reflect the dominant forces and "national interests" at play in the respective nations' media outlets. Here, one detects the operation of the forces described by Herman and Chomsky. Second, the differences between Cold War and post-Cold War newspaper evaluations of world opinion reflect different stages in the development and general acceptance of an "imagined community" of nations. Here, one detects the operation of the forces described by Anderson, updated to show how the globalization of media served as both cause and effect of the collapse of Cold War barriers.

THE SAMPLE AND THE STUDY DESIGN

The source material for this analysis includes all references to "world opinion" in the *International Herald Tribune* and the *Times of India* during February, March, and April 1986, and in *The New York Times* and the *Times of India* during August through January 1990-1991. The two Western dailies represent first world newspapers; the latter represents a third world newspaper. The notion of "representation" must be construed correctly here. The analysis is directed toward understanding the usage of the concept in terms of the geographic and historical identity of the newspapers. It is not claimed that any of the papers is "representative" of a group of nations or their media; rather the status of the nation of origin confers a perspective on references which helps to explain their construction.

It is reasonable to use the *Tribune* and *The New York Times* as similar examples of Western newspapers for this analysis. The *International Herald Tribune*, published out of Zurich, shares reporters, editors, sources, and a reputation as a quality paper aimed at a Western audience with *The New York Times*. Doubts about comparability were resolved methodologically; since the nation and date of origin are both independent variables in this analysis, the two Western newspapers could be isolated for separate study as warranted. The results support grouping the two together as first world newspapers for comparison with the *Times of India*.

A content analysis was applied to all news stories and editorials referencing world opinion, in implicit and explicit terms, for the newspapers and dates described. In the *International Herald Tribune*, the concept was referenced 103 times during the three-month period in 1986; in the *Times of India*, the concept was referenced 50 times in 1986. In *The New York Times*, the concept was referenced 67 times in the five-month period in 1990-1991; in the *Times of India*, the concept was referenced 65 times in 1990-1991. References to world opinion were content analyzed using the predesigned instrument from our previous analysis.[1]

R.L. Doty notes how a "Discursive Practices approach" to intertextual analysis allows one to discover a "controlling or dominant" discourse for constructing the world in international relations (Doty, 1993:308). If "the same kinds of subjects, objects, and relations are found to exist in different texts, this is indicative of a particular logic at work . . . if differences are constructed according to the same logic in a variety of texts, we can reasonably suggest that there is a dominant discourse" (308-309).

The present study disaggregates the components of world opinion. It then elaborates the relationships between the various components for first and third world, and Cold War and post-Cold War newspapers as a step toward describing the "dominant discourses" which exist within the two comparative categories. However, the project's structure demands analysis beyond what Doty describes. The very classifications of "first world/third world" and "Cold War/post-Cold War" are themselves social constructions. Consequently, interrelationships between the textual analyses must be considered. The issue does not arise due to the methodological division of the same sample along two different matrices. It arises because the very meanings of "first world" and "third world" change with the transition from the Cold War era to the post-Cold War era. Similarly, the phrases "Cold War" and "post-Cold War" have different meanings for first and third world countries. One must study the intertextual relationships *within* comparative categories, and the intratextual relationships *between* comparative categories.

DISAGGREGATING WORLD OPINION: THE BASIC ELEMENTS

All references to world opinion were studied according to their uses and combinations of six key components of world opinion: the moral component, the pragmatic component, the threat of international isolation, and references to the power of world opinion, the nation's image, and the world as a unit. First, newspapers were compared according to the frequency with which they referenced each of the components. Figure 6.1 shows a comparison between first and third world newspapers combined for both historical periods. In most cases, there is no significant difference between the percentage of references to each of the components by newspaper; both sets of newspapers were equally likely to reference isolation, the power of world opinion, the moral component, and the pragmatic component.[2] References to the nation's image were more likely to appear in first world newspapers than in third world newspapers (by a margin of 64.7% to 41.7%) as were references to the world as a unit (by a margin of 56.1% to 42.6%).[3]

There are significant differences in the percentage of references to all elements of world opinion between the Cold War and post-Cold War eras, as shown in Figure 6.2. Isolation, the power of world opinion, the nation's image, the moral component, the pragmatic component, and the references to the world as a unit were all more likely to appear in stories and editorials on world opinion after the end of the Cold War.[4] The post-Cold War era newspapers generally portray a richer picture of world opinion than the Cold War newspapers.

Figure 6.1. Components of World Opinion, by First and Third World Newspapers

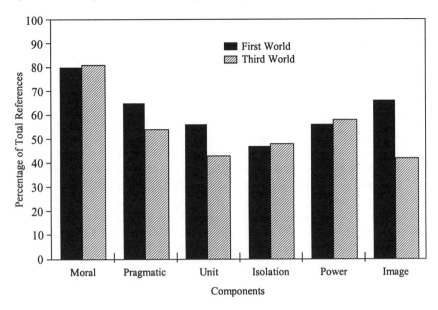

Figure 6.2. Components of World Opinion, by Cold War and Post-Cold War Newspapers

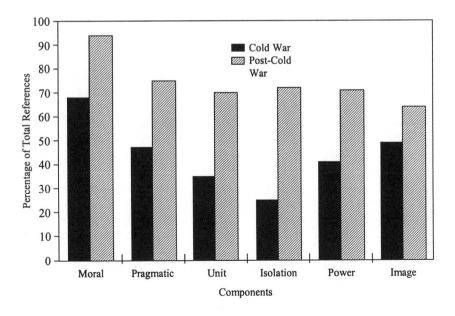

Interpreting the significance of these quantitative differences requires that we recall the original project: to describe how the comparative usage of world opinion provides for different "maps" of the world. A critical aspect of this analysis involves discovering how the concepts of "self" and "other" are defined in the construction: "Universalism [in this case, the description of a universal or "world" opinion] subjugates the particularity of the other to its own particular code" (Connelly, 1989:327).

For discourse on world opinion, a simple typology defining the self and the other exists among the components: regarding the former, those elements which describe "shared" attributes such as values, interests, or membership in a world community are defined as *integrative* components; regarding the latter, those elements which describe attributes dividing countries from the world community such as threats of isolation or concerns about an individual nation's image are defined as *discriminating* components. References to the moral and pragmatic components of world opinion and the world as a unit fit into the former category. References to isolation and a nation's image fit into the latter category.[5]

The "dominant discourse" for defining the "self" (i.e., those who are part of the public for world opinion) and the "other" (i.e., those who are isolated from the public for world opinion) in first world newspapers includes more references to a nation's image and the world as a unit than in third world newspapers. The dominant discourse in post-Cold War newspapers includes more references to all the components of world opinion than in Cold War newspapers. Interpreting these differences requires that one examine the interrelationships between the measures of "self" and "other" regarding world opinion. To this end, an index was constructed by summing the number of references made to integrative components of world opinion to define an Integrative Index with a range from 0 to 3; similarly, an index was constructed by summing the number of references to discriminating components to define a Discriminant Index with a range from 0 to 2. The mean values of the Integrative Index within categories of the Discriminant Index are shown for first and third world countries, and for Cold War and post-Cold War newspapers, respectively, in Figures 6.3 and 6.4.

The relationship between these two indexes is significant for first world references to world opinion ($r = .5421$, $p = .000$) and insignificant for third world references to world opinion ($r = .1073$, $p = .498$). These results indicate that inclusion of Integrative elements tended to be matched by inclusion of Discriminant elements in first world newspapers; defining the "self" in world opinion was given a similar priority to defining the "other"—as more of one measure was included, the other measure tended to increase accordingly. Such balance indicates a clearly defined sense of a nation's location in the "map" of world opinion. The division lines of "self" and "other" are consistently defined and emphasized together. Complementary references make for clearer borders between an international public and those isolated from it. By contrast, third world newspapers' references to world opinion include Integrative and Discriminant elements in a manner independent of each other. Such independence indicates

**Figure 6.3. Mean Integrative Scores by Discriminant Scores for
First and Third World Newspapers**

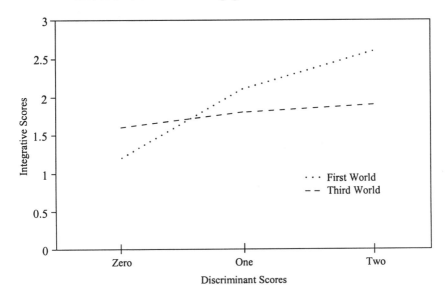

**Figure 6.4. Mean Integrative Scores by Discriminant Scores for
Cold War and Post-Cold War Newspapers**

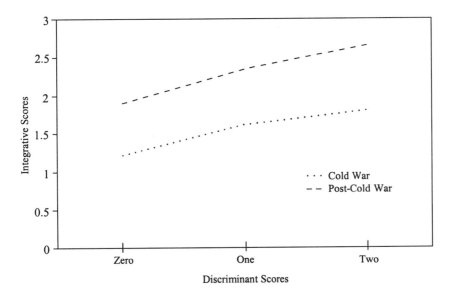

ambiguities in a nation's location in the "map" of world opinion. The division lines of "self" and "other" are not consistently defined or emphasized together, blurring the borders where the international public ends and the isolated nation or nations begin.

The relationship between the two indexes is significant for both Cold War references to world opinion ($r = .2494$, $p = .0073$) and post-Cold War references to world opinion ($r = .2893$, $p = .0039$). Defining the "self" and the "other" appears to have been of equal priority in both sets of newspapers. However, Figure 6.4 also reflects the more frequent occurrence of the components of the Integrative Index in the post-Cold War era; mean scores on this index are clearly higher in the second period than in the first.[6] These findings suggest that the delineation of the "self" and the "other" requires more elaboration, in terms of the separate elements, in the post-Cold War era than in the Cold War era. Defining the borders between the international public and the isolated nation or nations commands a similar priority in the two eras. But for some reason this enterprise is more complex in the second era than in the first.

The preceding analyses present two challenges: to discover why the "borders" of self and other in world opinion are more ambiguously defined in third world newspapers than in first world newspapers; and to discover why the definition of self and other in world opinion has become a more elaborate process in the post-Cold War era than in the Cold War era.

FIRST AND THIRD WORLD NEWSPAPERS: LOCATIONS IN THE "MAP" OF WORLD OPINION

In order to derive the significant components of world opinion for first and third world newspapers, a factor analysis was conducted for the six elements referenced above in the two categories. For first world newspapers, the six elements were reduced to one factor, composed of the moral component, the pragmatic component, and the nation's image. For third world newspapers, the six elements were reduced to two factors; the first was composed of the moral component, the threat of isolation, and the power of world opinion, while the second was composed of just the pragmatic component (see Tables 6.1 and 6.2).

For first world newspapers, the concept of world opinion is used as a means of evaluating a nation's image according to the shared values and interests among nations. The one principal factor can be referred to as an Image Evaluative factor, since it assesses a nation's international image according to that country's acceptance or rejection of world opinion. A nation's or leader's placement on one or the other side of this ledger defines the status of the subject in the world.

A close textual analysis of two examples from first world newspapers underscores their emphasis on image in descriptions of world opinion. When the South African government banned reporting of unrest during the anti-apartheid

Table 6.1. Factor Analyses of Components of World Opinion

Factor 1	Loading	Factor 2	Loading	Factor 3	Loading
		First World			
Image	.74717				
Pragmatic	.74334				
Moral	.72329				
		Third World			
Power	.70698	Pragmatic	.87675		
Isolation	.67176				
Moral	.66079				
		Cold War			
Moral	.72953	Isolation	.61788	Unit	.82996
Power	.61770				
		Post-Cold War			
Pragmatic	.76733	Isolation	.70543	Power	.81248
		Moral	-.66077		

Table 6.2. Factor Clusters of Components of World Opinion

Factor 1	Cluster	Factor 2	Cluster	Factor 3	Cluster
		First World: Image evaluation			
Image	Image				
Pragmatic	Evaluative				
Moral					
		Third World: Power and interest evaluation			
Power	Power	Pragmatic	Interest		
Isolation	Evaluative		Evaluative		
Moral					
		Cold War: Ideological definition of world public			
Moral	Ideology	Isolation	Isolative	Unit	Unit
Power	Evaluative	Moral			Definition
		Post-Cold War: Power of moral and pragmatic consensus			
Pragmatic	Interest	Isolation	Moral	Power	Power
	Integrative	Moral	Integrative		Definition

movement in 1986, the following editorial appeared in the *International Herald Tribune*:

> Three months after it was promulgated, South Africa's emergency press ban has helped the white minority government get pictures of unrest off both the air and the front page. The television images that dominated the nightly news last summer and helped crystallize Western anger against South Africa have all but disappeared. . . .
>
> The result has not reduced the level of violence in South Africa . . . but it has helped give South Africa something of a respite from the *intense world attention and opprobrium* it incurred last year, and officials seem satisfied as a result. . . .
>
> Although the ban contributes to an *image of South Africa as a closed society* that seeks to tightly control information, many in the country believe it is a price worth paying (*IHT*, 3/4/86, p. 6; emphases added).

One observes no ambiguities in the moral condemnation of South Africa; the nation's choice is between damaging its image by allowing journalists to report the violence, or damaging its image by suppressing these reports. The editorial later acknowledges that the South African strategy lessened international interest in apartheid, thereby reducing the pragmatic component's power. However, the strategy of the editorial is to put South Africa's image at risk due to the stories not being reported. Even without specific or graphic illustration, the lines between the international public and South Africa are made clear.

In a more recent example, George Bush's justification for increasing American forces in the Persian Gulf in November 1990 shows a similar concern for the image of the United States as an actor on the international stage:

> Secretary Baker has been consulting with our key partners in the coalition. He has met with the Emirs of Bahrain and Kuwait, King Fahd, President Mubarak, as well as the Chinese Foreign Minister, President Ozal, Foreign Minister Shevardnadze, President Gorbachev. He also will be meeting with Prime Minister Thatcher and President Mitterrand. I have been heartened by Jim's appraisal of the strong *international solidarity and determination* to insure that Iraq's aggression does not stand and is not rewarded. But right now Kuwait is struggling for survival. And along with many other nations, we've been called upon to help. The consequences of our not doing so would be incalculable; because Iraq's aggression is not just a challenge to the security of Kuwait and other gulf nations, but to the better world we all have hoped to build in the wake of the cold war. . . . The state of Kuwait must be restored, or no nation will be safe and the promising future we anticipate would indeed be jeopardized (*NYT*, 11/9/90, p. A16; emphasis added).

In this case, the important goal for the United States was to prove that it was not an independent actor in sending troops to the Gulf; instead, it was acting as part of a "coalition," and after consultation with an extensive litany of world leaders.

Bush emphasizes that *"along with many other nations* we've been called to help" and refers to "the better world we *all* hoped to build." Later, he states that it was a major "success" to have "world opinion totally on our side" because the United Nations condemned Iraq's actions. The pragmatic component is present in the stated interests of all nations to protect the principle of sovereignty; the moral component is present in the desire to build a "better world." The thrust of this statement, though, is to present an image of the United States as a leader in a broad-based coalition, even though the Gulf force, which contained mostly Americans, had just been increased by 200,000 U.S. troops.

It is not surprising that first world newspapers should emphasize a nation's image as their primary concern. As nations sitting atop an international hierarchy in terms of power and wealth, their stakes in preserving their status are quite high. Careful consideration of world opinion is one means of monitoring the standing of nations, as well as keeping track of their location in the "map" of world opinion. This does not imply that first world nations are only interested in their images, or the images of the major nations. Rather, it implies that the protection of international image is a primary lens through which these nations evaluate world opinion.

For third world newspapers, the concept of world opinion is used as a means of evaluating the power of nations to enforce their values, and as a means of evaluating whether nations like India necessarily share the same interests as the major nations in world opinion. The first factor, including the threat of isolation, the power of world opinion, and the moral component, may be defined as a Power Evaluative measure; it assesses the power of world opinion (and one of its expressions in isolation) as a means to enforce shared values. The second factor, including the pragmatic component, may be defined as an Interest Evaluative measure; it assesses whether the supposed shared interests of "all nations" actually describe the interests of India and other third world nations. Between these two factors, a possible tension may arise, as the newspapers acknowledge the power behind the moral force of world opinion, but remain unsure of the pragmatic ramifications for third world nations. No such conflict appears to exist for references in the first world nations.

This analysis allows one to address the issue raised by the previous section's results. The definitions of the "self" and the "other" in world opinion are more difficult for the *Times of India* to assess because the values espoused and advanced in world opinion do not always correspond to interests shared by India or other third world nations. While the newspaper references may accept the moral component of world opinion, they may take issue with the pragmatic component, particularly when these components are being defined with reference to conflicts in which the Western powers are involved. If the actions of a nation are morally abhorrent, but actions taken against them may set precedents or produce results which conflict with third world interests, the dividing line between the international public and the isolated nation becomes blurred. The location of third world nations like India in the "map" of world opinion becomes ambiguous with reference to "shared interests" with "all" other nations. As nations more to the periphery of world affairs, concerns for their interests must necessarily dominate concerns for their image. These differences show starkly the effects which Herman and Chomsky describe. Stories and editorials in first and third world newspapers reflect the dominant interests of their societies and political regimes in their usage and construction of world opinion.

Textual examples serve to underscore this concern in the *Times of India*. In an editorial critiquing the US bombing of Libya in 1986, the writer discusses the ramifications if world opinion condoned such actions to decrease terrorism:

> It is necessary . . . to put into some historical perspective, the present day claims of the U.S. government that by bombing Libya it is acting as a *moral champion of sorts in the war against international terrorism.* . . .
>
> On the domestic front, Mr. Reagan has achieved a grand success. Leading Democrats have applauded his action. Opinion polls show overwhelming public support for what he has done. Mr. Reagan, the great communicator, has successfully sold a number of his ideas to the public.
>
> From its point of view [Libya] is truly a "maverick" regime under a leader with undoubtedly grandiose pretensions who is prepared to support and finance subversive and terrorist actions on a scale more commonly associated with what the superpowers do.
>
> Many commentators have pointed out that American action against Libya has helped to increase *worldwide sympathy* and therefore enhance the legitimacy of Col. Gaddafi's Libya. . . . But the U.S. action has set a most dangerous precedent if it is not adequately condemned and countered. If terrorism can be used as an excuse for militarily assaulting and overriding the sovereignty of nations, then this is tantamount to *giving a blank check to America to wage war against rebellious third world nations* whenever it wishes and for whatever flimsy reasons it may wish to give (*TOI*, 4/23/86, p. 6; emphases added).

Here, one sees the portrayal of Gaddafi as an isolated "maverick" according to the United States, and America as a "moral champion" in the international struggle against terrorism. It also demonstrates the power of world opinion in the anticipated results which would occur if the United States is not restrained from actions of this type. It is on the interests of all nations generally that the *Times of India* explicitly challenges the American version, though. The action will not restrain Muammar Gaddafi's ventures or topple him; instead, the counterproductive strike will increase "worldwide sympathy" for the leader, creating the opposite effect in world opinion.

More telling is the fear of a precedent being set by the United States; if America could claim a moral and pragmatic legitimacy in world opinion for the attack on Libya, then no third world country without sufficient power to resist would be secure from similar attacks. On one side one finds the moral claims of the United States, its power in world opinion, and its claim of Libya's isolation; on the other side the third world newspaper disputes the claim that the pragmatic interests of all nations, particularly third world nations, are served by this attack.

A similar conundrum arises in an editorial from the *Times of India* in the period just before the Persian Gulf War:

> India fully endorses the U.N. Security Council's resolutions calling upon Iraq to vacate its occupation of Kuwait. . . . India has refrained from any criticism, even indirectly, of the large forces deployed against Iraq around its borders . . . it recognizes that each state has an *inherent right of self-defense and to take measures it considers necessary towards this end* . . . India is urging Iraq, a friend of long standing, to pull back its troops to clear the way for the redress of grievances against Kuwait. . . . If Iraq refuses to accept the peaceful alternative, *the onus will be on it for the consequences that may follow will be disastrous not only for Iraq but for countries like India* (*TOI*, 1/7/91; emphases added).

This editorial indicates the triad of the power of world opinion, the moral component, and the threat of isolation as one factor in the construction of world opinion. The power of world opinion is suggested in India's endorsement of the United Nations' resolutions. The moral component is present in its recognition of Kuwait's "inherent right" to self-defense. The threat of isolation for Iraq is present in the claim that "the onus will be on it" if war breaks out. On the other side of the ledger, though, representing the pragmatic component of world opinion, is the break with the nations in the Security Council; a war would be "disastrous" for "countries like India" (i.e., third world nations). The combination of power, morality, and isolation from the rest of the world was sufficient justification for the newspaper to refrain from criticizing the military buildup. Yet the newspaper's different view regarding interests shared—or not shared—by all nations separates the discussion of the pragmatic component from the others in the construction of world opinion.

The evidence suggests that first world newspapers were more likely to assume that one could evaluate all nations' images according to a fixed set of (supposedly) common values and interests. The third world newspapers were less likely to accept such a unified standard. They acknowledge the moral component of world opinion may carry power and the threat of isolation with it. But that does not imply that shared values for "nations like India" will necessarily correspond with a single standard for judging a nation's image in the world. Where the Western newspapers may perceive clearly "shared international interests" (such as in Iraq's invasion of Kuwait), the Indian newspaper considers such interests a separate factor to be evaluated.

One cannot conclude from this analysis that world opinion is therefore predominantly a Western construct, serving Western interests. Instead, one must acknowledge that the textual relationships of the concept of world opinion could be nationally or regionally dependent. "Identities are the basis of interests" (Wendt, 1992:398). The West has no more "claim" to use the phrase "world opinion" even though its identity may demand that it locate "shared interests" in a different position than the third world newspapers. As Herman and Chomsky make clear, both areas construct world opinion according to their dominant interests.

COLD WAR AND POST-COLD WAR NEWSPAPERS: CREATING THE "MAP" FOR WORLD OPINION

In order to derive the significant factors in the definition of world opinion during the Cold War and post-Cold War eras, a factor analysis was applied to the six elements above. The analysis isolated three significant factors for newspapers in each era, as was shown in Tables 6.1 and 6.2.

For the first era, the first factor included the moral component and the power of world opinion, the second factor included the threat of isolation, and the third factor included the world as a unit. The first factor is defined as the Ideological Evaluative factor. Ideologies assume shared values as the basis for power: "Ideology is the conversion of ideas into social levers. . . . [It] fuses these energies and channels them into politics" (Bell, 1962:400). In this construct, the power of world opinion is indistinguishable from the values it espouses. The second factor is defined as the Isolative factor; it functions to define those outside of the particular ideological evaluation present in the interpretation of world opinion. Finally, the third factor is defined as the Unit Definition factor; it functions to define those nations included in the "world" or public of world opinion.

The union of these three factors constructs an ideological standard to define the "public" for world opinion in the Cold War era. Those nations within, or isolated from, the unit (be it an "international community" or some other entity) were defined according to the conflict between East and West. Both sides attempted to assert that theirs was the "proper" definition of the world in international opinion, and that the other side was in violation of generally shared values. The pragmatic component, which indicates shared interests among nations, is notable in its absence here. If the purpose of world opinion is to define the world ideologically, then "shared interests" will have a different meaning depending upon the side one takes; as noted in Chapter 1, when one nation's "freedom fighters" become another nation's "terrorists," general international support for freedom or against terrorism becomes unlikely. As Connelly notes:

> One cannot rethink the category of terrorism, for instance, without thinking how the ideas of state, war, sovereignty, and international system become consolidated into a mutually reinforcing pattern within the discourse of inter-"national" relations. The coalescence of this discursive network creates terrorism as the other that is both indispensable to its self-definition and a covert sign of its fragility as a system of representation (Connelly, 1989:334).

Similarly, terrorism as an activity abhorred by the world community becomes an activity associated with an ideologically defined "other" in the Cold War conflict. The evidence suggests that defining the "other" as either the West or the East was the major theme in Cold War constructions of world opinion.

Textual examples illustrate this theme in both the *International Herald Tribune* and the *Times of India* in the Cold War era. The former newspaper described Soviet reactions to American attacks on Libya over maneuvers in the Gulf of Sidra:

> Mikhail S. Gorbachev, harshly criticizing the U.S. military strikes against Libya, offered Wednesday to withdraw the Soviet fleet from the Mediterranean if the United States would do likewise.
>
> The Soviet leader . . . said that the States had shown its "imperial bandit face" in its armed clashes with Libya.
>
> Mr. Gorbachev said the Soviet Union had to base ships permanently in the Mediterranean only because the United States did so. He questioned the American presence in the region, noting that it was far away from the United States.
>
> Before announcing the proposal, Mr. Gorbachev accused the United States of aggression against Libya and said its actions were a "challenge to the world public" (*IHT*, 3/27/86, p. 1).

In his words, Gorbachev mixes geographic and rhetorical imagery to locate the United States outside of a "world public" which clearly includes the Soviet Union. The geographic imagery describes America as intruding upon areas where it has no clear interests. In the "map" of world opinion, each nation has a legitimate area of influence defined by its own interests; to move beyond that area damages its image, and isolates it from the rest of the world. Putting U.S. forces in the Mediterranean, an area "far away" from the nation, upsets the "map" of world opinion in which each nation tacitly agrees to a "location" defined by its own legitimate interests. Hence, taking such action displays the "bandit imperial face" of the United States. Gorbachev then avoids having the same accusation leveled against his country by stating that Soviet forces were in the area only in response to the American presence. The components of values and power, isolation, and the world as a unit combine in an ideological "map" of world opinion in which the United States is excluded from the world public because of its actions.

A more explicit statement was made in this vein by Libya and Cuba after the U.S. bombing of Tripoli, as reported in the *Times of India*:

> The Libyan foreign minister, Mr. Kamal Hassan al Mansour . . . took the floor after the external affairs minister, Mr. B.R. Bhagat, called for breaking off diplomatic and economic relations with the U.S. . . .
>
> He said the U.S. having violated the U.N. charter, has *no right to remain a member of the security council or any other civilized world forum* after its bombing of the civilian targets in his country. . . .

Cuba in its characteristic language said the attack on Libya confirmed that Washington was the international headquarters of state terrorism against free nations and Mr. Ronald Reagan was the ringleader (*TOI*, 4/16/86, p. 1; emphasis added).

The elements of isolation are stated in an explicit manner here, with the Libyan foreign minister urging other nations to break off diplomatic and economic ties with the United States. Also present is the redefinition of America outside of the realm of the "civilized world," with no rights to participate in its forums after the raid. Finally, the Cuban representative adds an ideological interpretation to these claims: the United States becomes the leader of "state terrorism against free nations" (i.e., those supported by the East). World opinion again serves as a means to define the world public in ideological terms; excluding the United States from the forums of the civilized world is equivalent to denying the legitimacy of its voice in world opinion.

It is useful to note the use of terminology that underscores the absence of the pragmatic component of world opinion. In the first quotation, the United States shows its "bandit imperial face" by its actions and its presence in the Mediterranean; however, the Soviet presence in the region is merely in response to the American presence. Similarly, the American attack on Libya is evidence of "terrorism" according to Cuba; ironically, the United States cited Libyan support of terrorism as justification for the raid. These observations are not intended to defend the position of either side; rather, they illustrate the difficulty of reaching a common language about shared interests across ideological differences. When East and West justify similar actions by accusing the other side of "imperialism" or "terrorism," the pragmatic component of world opinion becomes nearly impossible to define. What remain are moral statements given justification by claiming the power of world opinion on the side of Eastern or Western ideological values.

In the post-Cold War period, the factors underlying world opinion differ sharply from the previous era. The first factor includes the pragmatic component of world opinion, the second factor includes the moral component of world opinion (with a negative factor loading) and the threat of isolation, and the third factor includes the power of world opinion. The first factor is defined as the Interest Integrative factor; unlike the previous period's newspapers, the post-Cold War newspapers include shared interests in their construction of world opinion. The second factor is defined as the Moral Integrative factor; because the moral component has a negative loading, its interpretation is negative, thereby defining a value integration running opposite to the isolation component, which has a positive loading. The third factor is defined as the Power Definition factor; its purpose is to define the power of world opinion in given situations in combination with statements of shared interests and values across nations. In contrast to the previous era when world opinion was used as an ideological construct, world opinion in the post-Cold War era is constructed when a moral and interest consensus among nations allows them to manifest the power of world opinion, without regard to ideological direction.

There is no attempt here to define a fixed unit, a "legitimate public" for world opinion ideologically, because the "map" of world opinion is no longer being defined or divided along the previous ideological lines. Instead, the presence of world opinion is evidenced by the power it manifests in a variety of situations. The result is a more free-floating concept, which may remake publics for world opinion more easily than when it was constrained by fixed ideological borders. The end of the Cold War advanced the elaboration of an "imagined global community," to borrow Anderson's terminology, which ceased to be a claim of ideological legitimacy in the global media's discourse and instead became a work in progress, a construction still in the making.

Textual examples from *The New York Times* and the *Times of India* illustrate the changed themes in references to world opinion. An article from the former newspaper describes Bush's justifications for action against Iraq after the invasion of Kuwait:

> We are in the gulf *because the world must not and cannot reward aggression.* . . . We're dealing with a dangerous dictator all too willing to use force . . . and who desires to control one of the world's key resources— *all at a time in history when the rules of the post-cold war world are being written.*
>
> Forces of 26 other nations are standing shoulder-to-shoulder with our troops in the gulf. *The fact is it is not the United States against Iraq, but Iraq against the world.* And there's never been a clearer demonstration of a world united against appeasement and aggression.
>
> Yesterday's United Nations Security Council Resolution was historic. . . . Until yesterday, *Saddam may not have understood what he was up against in terms of world opinion.* And I'm hopeful that now he will realize that he must leave Kuwait immediately (*NYT*, 12/1/90, p. A8; emphases added).

The rhetorical use of world opinion here outlines each of the factors described above for the post-Cold War era. The Moral Integrative and Interest Integrative factors are collapsed into one statement: "the world *must not* and *cannot* reward aggression." What one must do implies a moral imperative; what one can do implies what one's capabilities and interests will allow. The careful use of isolation in this statement underscores the process of Moral Integration; "it is not just Iraq against the United States . . . it is Iraq against the world." This reference also underscores the change from the Cold War era, when defining "the world" meant emphasizing American or Soviet ideology and excluding the other. Here, the disclaimer defines the conflict in terms of Iraq versus all other nations, not American versus Eastern values. Finally, the Power Definition factor is evident in the assertion that a new condition exists for world opinion in the post-Cold War era. As such, "there has never been a clearer demonstration of a world united" and the United Nations Security Council vote is described as "historic."

The statements describe a self-conscious break with the Cold War era. World opinion becomes instrumental in generating "new rules" for international conduct. The United States plays the role of coalition member voicing world opinion, rather than ideological advocate defining world opinion. The reference to "26 other countries" joining the effort in the Gulf avoids defining a specific, legitimate public for world opinion, other than to note a plurality of nations involved, and Iraq's isolation from them. In this new era, the moral and pragmatic components of world opinion become manifest in the power they have to influence world events; the stated assumption is that once Hussein realized his position in world opinion, he might conform to its dictates. An "imagined global community" has been defined, in this case, and the question is left open as to which nations will become members by accepting its judgment.

An article from the *Times of India* on the Kuwaiti crisis echoes this theme regarding the changing role of world opinion:

> With the U.S. President, Mr. George Bush, announcing that he would meet the Soviet President, Mr. Mikhail Gorbachev, in Helsinki on Sunday, *international efforts to end the standoff between Iraq and the rest of the world moved into new ground.*
>
> The leaders of the U.S. and the Soviet Union, for the first time since the end of the last World War would put their heads together in an attempt to fashion a strategy by which the two could move in co-ordination in efforts to make the Iraqi President, Mr. Saddam Hussein, back down.
>
> Mr. Gorbachev would want to demonstrate his sincerity in wanting to join the *international effort* against Iraq *so that the Soviet Union's "membership" in the Western community is not jeopardized.* . . . It is now up to Moscow and Washington to show that the cold war has indeed ended and that they are in a position today to deal with regional conflagrations in a framework of genuine international co-operation (*TOI*, 9/3/90, p. 11; emphases added).

The meaning of the "standoff between Iraq and the rest of the world" is articulated clearly in this article. The public from which Hussein is isolated specifically includes the United States and the Soviet Union in the post-Cold War era. Instead of offering an ideological alternative to the Western "map" of the world public, the Soviet Union wishes "'membership' in the Western community" of nations. The proof of this change in the role for world opinion will be measured according to the superpowers' success in creating a "framework for genuine international co-operation."

The existence of world opinion is once again evidenced in its *power* to alter events, and indeed, the entire structure of the emerging order. One witnesses the collapse of the same types of beliefs which Anderson argues lost their influence over individuals in the creation of the imagined national community (Anderson, 1995:89). First, information no longer offers privileged access to ontological truth; once control over information began to shift from national to global influences after the Cold War, national and ideological constructions had less influence over individuals' ideas of community. Second, this information lessens the influence of formerly powerful elites who had controlled access to information by "filtering" it through the interests of one particular regime or nation. Finally, the ideological views of the inevitability of the nation as the highest level of community, based upon an interpretation of cosmology and history that served dominant national interests, also lose sway over men's imaginations. The national or ideological idea of community does not disappear; instead, it shares discursive space with an emerging "imagined global community."

These results allow for an explanation of earlier findings regarding references to world opinion in the post-Cold War era. First, the definition of world opinion in the second period is more elaborate than in the first because the procedure no longer moves along fixed ideological categories. When the purpose was to describe the "map" of the world included in international opinion according to well-known, predefined groupings, there was less need for elaboration regarding the self and the other. When the purpose is to describe the power of world opinion, under circumstances when the "map" of the world public can change with the issue, the process becomes more complex and requires greater elaboration and detail.[7] The use of world opinion to advance one nation's interests in politics requires little elaboration, since the audience for such discourse tends to be limited to one's own citizens. The use of world opinion to define an "imagined global community," by contrast, is more complex, as it involves constructing a new order to organize human affairs. What is unfamiliar necessarily needs more detailed definition than categories that are customary for observers.

Such explanation suggests that *intratextual* relationships exist alongside of *intertextual* relationships in the dominant discourse between first and third world newspapers, and Cold War and post-Cold War newspapers. These relationships require brief exploration.

INTRATEXTUAL MEANINGS: THE SOCIAL CONSTRUCTION OF "WORLDS" AND "ERAS"

One must begin by collecting the various usages of world opinion within first world and third world, and Cold War and post-Cold War, categories. For first world newspapers, the concept serves as a means of image evaluation; conformity with world opinion is necessary to maintain one's status in the world. For third world nations, the concept serves as a means of evaluating the power of nations behind world opinion and discerning whether they represent shared interests with the underdeveloped nations. For Cold War newspapers, the concept serves as a means of defining which nations may be properly defined within the "world public"; this determination is made according to ideological criteria. For post-Cold War newspapers, the concept serves as a means of evaluating the degree of consensus on world opinion and, hence, its power to enforce its dictates on particular issues.

The samples for these results overlap. First world newspapers and third world newspapers group together stories and editorials from the Cold War and post-Cold War eras. Similarly, Cold War newspapers and post-Cold War newspapers group together stories and editorials from first and third world newspapers. More important, though, each of these terms, as social constructions, takes on a different textual meaning within each grouping; these different meanings affect the interpretation of usages of world opinion.

First, as noted in Chapter 3, the distinction between first and third world nations undergoes a fundamental change after the collapse of the Eastern bloc. Prior to this economic and ideological change, analysts tended to divide the world into three parts: first world nations (the major industrial powers), second world nations (the Communist nations such as the Soviet Union, the Warsaw pact countries, and China),[8] and third world nations (the less developed nations of Latin America, Africa, the Middle East, and Asia) (Best, Rai, and Walsh, 1986). In terms of economic development, though, where nations are classified as preindustrial, industrial, and postindustrial, the categories overlap. First world nations could be industrial or postindustrial, second world nations could be industrial or preindustrial, and third world nations tend to be preindustrial. This overlap occurs because a second, ideological dimension was introduced into the classification of regimes. Second world nations differ from first world nations because of the Communist ideology they embrace, which denies the sole use of economic position as a standard for defining a nation's developmental status. Instead, developmental status could also be defined by ranking nations according to their progress to the ultimate end of historical and material development—that is, the Communist society (see Talmon's distinction between liberal and "messianistic" interpretations of systems, 1960:1-2).

With the collapse of the Eastern bloc, the second world virtually disappears, and the classification of nations' statuses falls back solely upon the standard of economic development. As a result, the first and third world nation categories become more "compressed," as a single hierarchy based upon a nation's stage of economic development emerges. In this context, one would expect that the first world's concerns with world opinion as a means of image evaluation would become more pronounced. Without the alternative means of status based upon ideological categories, the highest status nations must guard their positions in the world even more carefully than before. Conversely, third world nations would be expected to focus more concern on world opinion as a means of evaluating their actual interests, and their capacity to pursue them. When the world was divided into two major competing ideologies, "shared interests" could be defined in at least two different ways, depending upon the bloc with which one associated oneself. In the post-Cold War era, the situation becomes more fluid, and the definition of "shared interests" must constantly be reevaluated for a third world nation. The concept of world opinion no longer easily lends itself to alternative definitions associated with a predefined bloc of nations.

In the post-Cold War era, "first world" and "third world" are different social constructions than in the Cold War era. The collapse of the second world alters the construction of the "map" of world opinion; the "positions" of first and third worlds are different without a second world to provide an alternative grouping for nations. Indeed, the very meanings of the "first" and "third" worlds, as qualitative groupings, are altered with this change and replaced with a single hierarchy of nations ranked according to their economic development. Without these set groupings, the concept of world opinion takes on a greater fluidity than when it was constrained within defined power blocs and ideological constraints.

Second, "Cold War" and "post-Cold War" have different meanings for first and third world nations. For first world nations, the transition from Cold War to post-Cold War eras represents a triumph of liberal philosophy, and a movement from an ideological to a more pluralistic view of the world. For third world nations, the transition from Cold War to post-Cold War represents a change in their positions. They are no longer possible allies to be recruited in an ideological war, but rather become nations expected to participate in an emerging international consensus. Whether the position in the world of a nation like India is advanced by this change is difficult to say. For both sets of nations, the concept of world opinion changes from a means of advancing one's ideology to a means of assembling a consensus among competing values and interests among nations. In the Cold War era, the first world nations may have defined the ideological "map" of world opinion, but the third world nations could place themselves within alternative definitions of the world. In the post-Cold war era, first world nations have less capacity for defining the "map" of world opinion, but third world nations may have less capacity for placing themselves in this "map" in terms of values *and* interests they share with other nations.

CONCLUSION: STUDYING THE "DOMINANT DISCOURSES" ON WORLD OPINION

The preceding observations raise fundamental issues about the meaning of "world opinion" in the discourse of the various newspapers discussed. There are changes in the "dominant discourse" regarding world opinion depending upon the historical and regional venue one assumes. Such differences would seem to undermine the notion of "world opinion." For if the concept acquires different linguistic usages, and hence meanings, depending upon the source, can there be anything approaching a "world opinion" representing attitudes or beliefs generally shared among nations? Put another way, which of these usages of world opinion is the "true" one? Liisa Malkki addresses these questions by noting the dual existence, and interpretations, of internationally shared values in world opinion:

> Key forms in the political imagination of international order may be globally, transnationally shared and yet may have profoundly different significances and uses in specific, local sociopolitical contexts. . . . On the one hand, internationalism is a transnational cultural form—a mobile set of representations and practices that has globally translateable currency and that is *supra-local* in its significance. . . . On the other hand, internationalism is also an intensely *local* phenomenon and is likely to vary in form and meaning from place to place (Malkki, 1994:42-61).

Malkki's statement disputes the assumption that world opinion has some existence outside of linguistic usages, or, more specifically, that it must have such existence to be a concept worthy of serious consideration. To assume one can or must separate the social construction of a concept from its actual existence is questionable. Concepts like "world opinion" require translation into social construction before we can communicate and share them, and, as such, the question of whether or not they "really" exist "out there" becomes irrelevant. If concepts exist and we cannot construct them, we will not know them; if they do not exist and we construct them, then they exist to the extent that they structure our thinking (see Gergen, 1992:176-177). As Michel Foucault states,

> To analyze a discursive formation is to weigh the "value of statements," a value that is not defined by their truth, that is not gauged by a secret content, but which characterizes their place, their capacity for circulation and exchange, their possibility for transformation, not only in the economy of discourse, but more generally in the administration of scarce resources (Foucault, 1972:120).

This insight underscores the power of Anderson's thesis; indeed, Foucault's quotation could easily describe the Andersonian analysis of the spread of "print capitalism" and the growth of imagined national communities. The "value of statements" described by Foucault takes on added weight when one considers the linguistic exchanges and transformations which were cause and effect of the transition of "imagined communities" into nations in Anderson's historical analysis. It is difficult to conceive of a sentiment in the twentieth century stronger than nationalism in determining the "administration of scarce resources" among countries and peoples. So, too, then would one expect that the "value of statements" regarding world opinion will change as the dynamics of their usage become more universal (due to media globalization and a wider dissemination of a common symbolic language internationally). It becomes possible to conceive of circumstances when the "imagined community" of nations, constructed from common linguistic usages, becomes integral to the "administration of scarce resources" beyond the nation-state. At that moment, a community defined by world opinion, however fleeting, could be said to exist.

These linguistic usages, and the forces affecting them, thus hold special meaning for the study of politics and communications. In the international realm, where so little is assumed to be structured, the study of linguistic usages and the search for a dominant discourse become all the more important. The common accusation that "world opinion" is merely a construct created by the most powerful nations to serve their own interests underscores the need for such analysis. If "world opinion" is to have any use as an organizing principle in world affairs, it must make the transition from an idea which has power because it is dominant (or, in this case, embraced by a dominant power bloc of nations) to an idea which is dominant because it has power (in this case, the power to explain the dominant discourse in different regional and historical venues). An important beginning is to understand the assumptions and practices of various nations using the same terminology to different ends. Here, Anderson's analysis points us toward the possible emergence of a new "imagined community," while Herman and Chomsky caution us regarding the staying power of the national idea. The researcher's task is to distinguish a universal discourse from its variations which are merely dominant in specific venues—and if, as is likely, no universal discourse emerges, to define the necessary steps toward discovering or creating one.

NOTES

1. The author, in all cases, reviewed each of the content analyses and coded the results to insure intercoder reliability.

2. The Pearson's r values for these references are .019 (p. = 748), .023 (p. = 690), .011 (p. = 866), and .105 (p. = 079).

3. The Pearson's r values for these references are -.227 (p. = 000) and .132 (p. = 027), respectively.

4. The Pearson's r values for these relationships are .471 (p. = 000), .139 (p. = 019), .324 (p. = 000), .276 (p. = 000), and .356 (p. = 000), respectively.

5. The power of world opinion is not classified in either category, since the location of power in the construction of world opinion is considered as a separate issue. Doty notes how the significant meaning of power in this textual analysis is "power that is productive of meanings, subject identities, their interrelationships, and a range of imaginable conduct" (Doty, 1993:299). As such, the manner in which references to the power of world opinion are used in combination with the other elements helps define their meanings in each of the comparative categories. However, it should be noted that the "power" which these linguistic usages represent go beyond just the explicit and implicit references attached to the concept.

6. Although the result is not represented graphically here, mean scores on the Discriminant Index are also higher within categories of the Integrative Index.

7. Once again, note how carefully Bush articulates the number and variety of nations involved in the Persian Gulf effort in this quotation.

8. There was considerable controversy over which nations were properly included in the second and third world categories. For instance, nations such as Vietnam and Albania could be classified in either group, depending upon the analyst's purposes and orientation.

Conclusion

Frank Louis Rusciano

The search for a "universal discourse" for world opinion has its roots in the Western philosophical tradition, whose thinkers were occupied, perhaps more than those of any other region, with eliminating contradictions and distilling truth down to its "essence." The contemplation of, for instance, the mysteries of Zen were not for them a means to wisdom, but rather a game, a puzzle to be either solved or ignored as irrelevant. When discussing the paradox of the town barber who shaves all and only those men who do not shave themselves, Russell Hardin dismisses the question of who shaves the barber by arguing that since no such barber can exist, the problem is of little interest (Hardin, 1982:139).

Plato pursues the Ideal of justice in *The Republic*, in opposition to Thrasymachus, who argued that justice was regime-specific. St. Augustine searches for the idealized *City of God* amid the chaos of the city of man. The Western tradition is marked by a yearning to define universals for all mankind, to separate the wheat of truth from the chaff of relativism. Never mind that each effort has been frustrated by some counterexample which contradicts our vision of the "true" nature of man, that our most "scientific" generalizations about race, gender, and biology are often turned on their heads by new anthropological or historical evidence. Like Jay Gatsby pursuing the "green light, the brilliant orgiastic future that year by year recedes before us," we tell ourselves that this truth eluded our grasp this time, but we need only run a little harder, hone our methods a little more, and it will be ours.

For this reason, when our methods fail to reveal these universals, we seek solace in history. Perhaps we as individuals are making imperceptible progress toward the truth, but as a people and a tradition, our movement is evident. In the fullness of time, the contradictions will be resolved, and we will be left with complete self-consciousness, the vision of who we are that allows no contradiction. Herein lies the promise of the Hegelian dialectic of thesis/antithesis/

synthesis laid out in the Introduction; we encounter "the Other," a synthesis occurs, and at some final end of history, we conclude with principles which all men accept, and which no man can deny. Because the end result sounds so much like "world opinion," it would seem that a closer look at the Hegelian schema might provide some insight into the "universal discourse" of world opinion.

RETHINKING IDENTITY IN THE GLOBAL CONTEXT: REFLECTIONS ON WORLD OPINION AND THE "END OF HISTORY"

The Hegelian dialectic has both abstract and concrete referents. In the abstract, the paradigm describes the interaction of ideas with their opposites, producing a constant state of becoming which is resolved only at the end of history. In the concrete, the paradigm maps the development of historical consciousness as traced by the identities individuals accrue through the clash of past cultures with their counterparts. Carl Friedrich analyzes this dichotomy, and the relationship of the abstract and the concrete, by noting how Hegel's *Phenomenology of the Spirit* concludes that "knowledge is spirit, and . . . the way to arrive at such knowledge is to recall the spirits (of the successive stages in the development of the spirit)." One may accumulate this knowledge because these spirits are preserved in two ways, "[in] history and the philosophical mastery of the organizations or patterns it produces or what Friedrich Hegel calls comprehended history (*begriffene Geshichte*)." From this means, individuals are able to recall the "absolute spirit, the reality, the truth" in history (Friedrich, 1954:xix).

Friedrich also provides a useful interpretation of the dialectic which underlies the "philosophic mastery of the organizations and patterns" of history:

> Hegel dialectically resolves . . . the antithetical paradox by suggesting that both being and non-being—or rather nothingness—are superceded by the higher synthesis of becoming (*Werden*). The truth of both being and non-being is to be found in their actual coexistence in "becoming" which constitutes "the identity of their identity and their non-identity." As Hegel puts it in the *Logic*, the truth is "each immediately disappears in its opposite" (xlii).

Hegel's notion of historical movement allows one to concretize his dialectical process in the contact between the various "publics" which generate human identities. The "Self" manifests itself in human consciousness as Being, and "the Other" as Non-Being, that which is the opposite and negation of the Self. It is for this reason that the contacts between the two have often been so brutal in the course of human history. Yet such conflicts are ultimately resolved in a "synthesis" of a new identity, combining in various degrees aspects of the thesis and the antithesis. A new "Self" and a new thesis emerge to encounter a new "Other" and a new antithesis. History, as such, is always in the state of becoming.

Further, according to Hegel, these steps in the development of human consciousness contribute to the creation of a "world spirit": "culture (*Bildung*) can at every stage of the configurations of the spirit emerge, grow, and flourish—indeed not only can but must do so. At such a stage a state will be developed and upon this basis of civilization the development will go forward to rational reflection and thus to laws and other forms of generality" (Hegel, 1954:32). The state becomes the rational manifestation of successive encounters with "the Other" and the historical "truth" that results from them. The "end of history" marks the completion of this process. In the Hegelian schema, history progresses toward a final rationality, a sort of ultimate synthesis, a thesis with no antithesis. "Being" becomes pure and is recognized in the realization of the "world spirit." At this moment, "the Other" ceases to exist.

It is tempting to equate "world opinion" with Hegel's "world spirit." In such a comparison, an apparent international consensus on certain issues, especially those dealing with the proper arrangements of the state, would be equivalent to a final realization of the "world spirit." This would seem to suggest that the end of history has arrived. This, in fact, was the essence of Fukuyama's argument in *The End of History and the Last Man*, where he "returns to a very old question: Whether at the end of the twentieth century, it makes sense for us once again to speak of a coherent and directional History of mankind that will eventually lead the greater part of humanity to liberal democracy?" He justifies a positive response on two grounds: "liberal democracy remains the only coherent political aspiration that spans different regions and cultures around the globe," and "liberal principles of economics—the 'free market' have spread and succeeded in producing unprecedented levels of material prosperity" (Fukuyama, 1992:xii-xiii).

Taken together, these twin realizations constitute a solution to the cultural relativism invented by Europeans to deal with their contact with non-European cultures (338). As such, a change in consciousness may be in the offing: "It is possible that if events continue to unfold as they have done over the past few decades, the idea of a universal and directional history leading up to liberal democracy may become more plausible to people, and that the relativist impasse of modern thought will in a sense solve itself" (338). A "world spirit" of democratic thinking may reveal itself universally, and "the Other," which prompted so much confusion in the early European encounters with non-European cultures, will disappear in this final rationality. The thesis with no antithesis becomes manifest in the democratic state and society.

Fukuyama may be describing an actual trend in world opinion in the democratization of more of the world's governments. It is certainly an encouraging development that more than half the nations in the world now embrace some form of democratic arrangement. But the analysis of world opinion suggests that equating this international consensus with the Hegelian "world spirit" is fundamentally incorrect. The differences between the two depose not only Fukuyama's analogy, but the very notion of directional history.

The very instability of *any* international consensus makes the emergence of democracy and liberal economies questionable as a permanent trend.

Fukuyama acknowledges this problem himself (339). However, it is not the content, so much as the process of world opinion which undermines his analysis. The notion of a global public, with its ability to influence nations' actions by the threat of international isolation, suggests the continuing existence of some "Other" warranting punishment due to their estrangement from the international community at any given time.

For Fukuyama, the emergence of a "global public" for world opinion heralds the disappearance of "the Other." This change provides one justification for the oft-cited observation that democracies generally do not make war upon other democracies, as if wars were motivated solely by difference, and not by an appetite for similar scarce resources. Because there is no higher level of abstraction than the global community, all nations and their citizens must belong to it. The problem just becomes one of consciousness, of realizing the common place we have all reached (339). In effect, because the international community encompasses the globe, we run out of "space"—real and metaphorical—where "the Other," or the antithesis to world opinion, may lurk.

Here, Fukuyama misinterprets how opinion publics operate to create identity, and how communities exist as a result. As Henri Zukier observes,

> the dominant group may use the outsider to reaffirm fundamental values by *casting the outsider's violations as a moral scandal, in punishing them, and in mobilizing members against the "enemy."* The outsider helps achieve clarity by producing, through his mere presence, a worldview of simple binary oppositions, through which he represents the polar opposite of the values of society. The outsider is word and values fleshed out. *He delineates sharply the boundaries of group identity by embodying its limits and beyond* (Zukier 1996:1118; emphases added).

A vague sense of group identity exists in the international community. This vagueness arises because a world community emerges only through discourse, and because the construction of identity occurs through a process of negotiation among different "opinion publics." Hence, the common (and continued) existence of "the Other" is necessary on the global level. "The Other" becomes the nations or individuals isolated from the international community. The world community exists by acknowledging and confronting such conflicts, at least until a new issue once again separates nations, and redefines its borders and the identities of "Self" and "Other" in the global schema.

Hence, the emergence of a "global public" does not herald the disappearance of "the Other" and an end to history due to the overarching nature of this reference group. The global public has no higher level of public to legitimize it, or recognize it as a foil for negotiation of identity. Hence, its borders are defined through the division of members into "Self" and "Other" through internal discourse carried out in the media and international forums. The ambiguous nature of the global public demands that the international community be defined partially by those isolated from it.

RETHINKING IDENTITY, DISCOURSE, AND HISTORY

World opinion affects identity and history in successive steps, as the ripple effects of introducing a "global public" sphere transform our sense of who we are and where we are going. The appearance of a "global public" prompts new encounters with "the Other." The construction of identity occurs in a similar fashion within the global public as within other opinion publics, but the former's overarching nature and fluid boundaries affect the stability of identity and history in unexpected ways.

Consider the changes in worldview paralleling the development of world opinion and the global public. The *discourse* of Cold War ideologies that defined the previous international order has yielded to that centering on the content of world opinion in a variety of issue areas. It is a truism to say that the "international order" is less stable than before; but this instability follows predictable—and indeed, mappable—patterns. By examining the discourse on world opinion from a variety of media and other sources, we find clues to the status of the global community at any given time. The community's boundaries emerge (and change) according to who is in conformity with its norms, and who has violated them.

A second change occurs in the construction of *national identity*. This no longer occurs primarily within a country's borders, in isolation from other nations. The shift in international discourse marked a refutation of Marxist models of development, and the collapse of a critical path to international prestige. Changes in the language of international development require new means of achieving status in world opinion, alongside such older means as nationalism. A nation's global standing now depends upon a variety of factors, including its international reputation. The country's international image must be reconciled with its citizens' self-perceptions before its identity is recognized by the rest of the world. These negotiations between *Fremdbild* and *Selbstbild* reflect the mutability of the emerging international order. Nations must acknowledge the judgments of world opinion in order to earn international respect. The construction of a "usable" national identity falls subject to the vagaries of international public opinion.

Finally, the very concept of world opinion is subject to variations in usage, as media tend to construct it with an eye to dominant national interests. As such, the emergence of a global public is not just a *quantitative change*, which adds a potential source of identity to the human experience. It is also a *qualitative change*, as the public that has such sway over human identity is defined differently, depending upon the origin and historical context of the source one studies.

This book began with a discussion of the way a person's identity is constructed primarily through encounters with "the Other." History itself is partly defined by the individual's or group's accumulation of "opinion publics"—be they familial, ethnic, state, or national. A global public of world opinion changes the *effects* of these encounters, even as the process of identity formation through negotiation remains the same. Our view of history is transformed as a result.

A comparison between the emergence of a global opinion public and national opinion publics, or nations, serves as an illustration. The transition from imagined to actual national communities, hinged on the general acceptance of two ideas. First, individuals residing within particular borders had to believe that a specific entity, a particular *nation*, should command their loyalty and support. At this historical moment, the "national public" came into being. Second, individuals had to accept generally the concept of a nation as a legitimate entity for grouping not just themselves, but other people. Nations were recognized both as a new means of identifying and dividing individuals, and as potential actors on the world stage. The concept of a nation, like Malkki's notion of internationalism, has both local and global referents (Malkki, 1994:61), and the first genuine "world opinion" may have been the consensus among countries that nation-states were legitimate groupings for the organization of human activities.

By contrast, no overarching agreement has formed as to the content or construction of world opinion. It remains an entity constantly defined by discourse. Similarly, the global community has no higher level of abstraction to define it or legitimize its existence. It too must derive legitimacy from the discursive practices among nations, and their resulting decisions to allocate resources or power according to its dictates.

However, both concepts do retain some common characteristics in their usage, even as each is viewed through the lens of national interests. Different newspapers may balance or emphasize the components of world opinion in different ways, but the components themselves appear universal to the discourse. The analyses always referred back to the same primary components of world opinion delineated in Chapter 1: the moral component, the pragmatic component, the power of world opinion, the threat of isolation, and references to a nation's image and the world as a unit. In discussions of the Kuwaiti crisis, for instance, the American and Indian newspapers placed different emphases upon the moral and pragmatic components; but the comparison was valid because the terms shared a common meaning in both papers. Similarly, in Chapter 6, I was able to trace the changes in perspectives on world opinion from the Cold War to the post-Cold War era because the components retained their meaning through this transition. Constructions of world opinion may vary with region and time; the elements used to construct world opinion appear constant.

Furthermore, a richer picture of world opinion emerges when one searches for common patterns in the discourses of several newspapers. We began exploring the concept by studying usages in the *International Herald Tribune* and the *Frankfurter Allgemeine Zeitung*; Chapters 5 and 6 added analyses of *The New York Times* and the *Times of India*. The factor analysis in the fifth chapter revealed that all six components of world opinion emerge as relevant factors when all these newspapers' perspectives are combined. Individual newspapers construct the concept according to regional influences, but all six components appear in the shared patterns of their discourse.

The analyses of the Kuwaiti and Bosnian crises underscore the importance of such commonalities. Without shared meanings in discourse, there can be no convergence of perspectives on world opinion across national borders. Absent this convergence, there is little chance that international efforts to address crises will occur. A common understanding of the obligations implied by world opinion makes nations more likely to expend the scarce resources necessary for international collective action. Without this common ground, nations may be likely to take unilateral action, believing the rest of the world shares their perspective, and the concept of world opinion would have little value in the Foucaultian sense of stimulating resource allocations.

Still, if a concept is only revealed fully through the combined discourse of several competing interpretations, who may observe or comprehend it at any given time? Hindsight and comparative analyses seem inadequate for our purposes when our very sense of history demands a coherent accumulation and documentation of our encounters with "the Other." We have suggested, for example, that our national identities are susceptible to the judgments of world opinion and the global public. Beginning with only a partial knowledge of these concepts, individuals will be hard-pressed to understand the changes they are undergoing due to contact with each. We are likely forced to yield our sense of progress toward an ultimate unity or perfection of arrangements in history—a sense which underpins our belief that all previous civilizations lead only to ours, and ours is the most advanced by virtue of being the most recent historically.

Instead, interactions with "the Other" become more random, changing as the individuals within the global public, and those isolated from it, change with the ebb and flow of world opinion. Our positions as "Self" or "Other" vis-à-vis the world community alter with different issues or times. Such mutability transforms the dynamic of recorded history described in the Introduction. For the contact between "Self" and "Other" has traditionally been viewed as one manifestation—and indeed, perhaps the primary manifestation—of motion in the progressive interpretation of history. The idea that notions of identity on the same or different levels may clash and not produce a stable reference group like those accumulated in the past challenges the Hegelian notion of progressive history.

The irony here is that history, as Fukuyama describes it, had not ended heretofore because the designation of "the Other" has occurred in all communities defined by prior opinion publics. Similarly, individuals did not accumulate identities that were set in stone on the path to some universal human identity; as noted in the Introduction, identities, like opinions, are not fixed for individuals, but exist in a constant state of negotiation. The division between the "Self" and "the Other" created conflicts which were, in part, the engine of historical events. This tendency does not end with the emergence of the global public; if anything, it intensifies, since the borders of the international community are defined almost exclusively by who is in conformity with world opinion and who has violated it. Without a higher level of public to legitimize itself, the international community must constantly redefine its borders by designation of "the Other"—the nations or persons isolated from it.

Fukuyama also assumes world opinion will transcend national opinion. The analysis in Chapter 3 suggests this assumption is incorrect. As with all other levels of "public" which influence an individual's actions or identities, the nation continues to hold sway over human activity even as the global public emerges.

It is undeniable, though, that history will now be written in part as a record of the changing boundaries of the "international community." This is not the evolutionary history of Hegel, Marx, and Fukuyama, which progresses toward some ultimate consciousness. Instead, consciousness is defined according to the changing directions of world opinion—and if the direction of public opinion within nations is any guide, one will be challenged to perceive any clear pattern in these changes. The advent of world opinion does not herald an end to history, but rather an end to an *idea* of history as a progress toward a specific goal or final "rationality." For world opinion, just as public opinion, depends upon certain nonrational processes as the fear of isolation, and the resulting negative effects it has upon one's identity. Abandoning the progressive idea of history to world opinion in the postmodern era may prove as important a change in human consciousness as the abandonment of the ancient emphasis upon the Ideal, and the declaration of government by public opinion at the Enlightenment.

If we have not yet defined a "universal discourse" for world opinion, we at least see its "footprints" in the emerging international order. Further, we see enough of the nature of world opinion to raise questions about the direction of past philosophical inquiries in the Western tradition. I have often been asked in the course of my research what criteria determine the issues on the agenda for world opinion. Why, for instance, does genocide in Bosnia attract world attention while genocide in Rwanda does not? Why does the plight of the Palestinians touch the world, while the Chinese suppression of Tibetans is barely noticed? Why are Saddam Hussein's provocative actions routinely condemned, while President Hafez Assad of Syria virtually controls parts of Lebanon? While I cannot answer these questions, I would note that all assume there is one rule, one standard which qualifies an issue for world attention and judgment. But world opinion seems too mercurial a force to define universal standards that are "natural" for all people at all times. The search for the "true" nature of man seems less likely to go to completion. We toil for universals, and discover instead *process*.

Reflecting upon politics and the Western tradition begs the question of how the global forces that have such a significant influence over citizens' lives can be made responsive to their desires, values, and interests. What types of institutional arrangements must exist in order for national governments, and politics, to remain relevant in the emerging international order? It may not be possible to formulate definitive solutions to these problems, but clearly world opinion must figure prominently in any solutions proposed.

WORLD OPINION AND THE EMERGING INTERNATIONAL ORDER: THE CONUNDRUM OF POLITICS IN A NEW HISTORICAL ERA

The study of world opinion leads us to challenges we must meet before the "global public" can become a potent political tool for the world's citizens. The imperfect linkage of national publics with world opinion must be rectified, since world opinion is still filtered through a lens of national interests that limits attempts at integrative efforts across national borders. Furthermore, the model of communication for world opinion, as outlined in Chapter 5, still provides for a "top down" rather than a "bottom up" expression of preferences. If world opinion is to be an empowering force, the flow of information cannot be directed only from elites down to the mass of citizens in individual nations.

One of the most profound questions present generations must confront is whether the national state can meet these challenges. Can the state remain a means by which citizens direct the global forces influencing their lives, identities, and histories? An irony of the trend toward democracy lauded by Fukuyama is that it occurs in a context in which the nation-state's ability to deal with these forces is being questioned. This is not to say that an international trend toward democratization is insignificant. It might prove as important as the world opinion that originally supported the very concept of "nation." However, nation-states are designed to have influence, and be responsive, primarily within national publics. Increasingly, the global public (and its attendant global markets) have significant effects upon citizens' lives which the national state was not designed to address.

Before one dismisses the relevance of the nation-state to the emerging international order, however, a few caveats are needed. Chapter 6 analyzes the endurance of the national idea, even in the context of world opinion and the global public. Nation-states still have significant (and probably primary) sway over individuals' loyalties, and this does not appear likely to change in the near future. Moreover, as noted in Chapter 3, the nation-state retains an important role in the negotiation of an individual's identity. While the construction of national identity involves negotiations between *Selbstbild* and *Fremdbild*, the project itself is prompted by citizens' needs to retain a source of identity and pride in the emerging order. This situation also shows little sign of changing.

The state retains its relevance in the midst of global forces through its function in the process of world opinion. The nation-state remains the entity toward which the threat of international isolation is directed. It is true, as stated earlier, that individuals are isolated, not nations; but these individuals are almost always isolated in their capacity as members or citizens of particular nations. Individuals garner global reputations—fairly or unfairly—as representatives of the Germans, the Americans, the French, the Chinese, or the Iraqis, oftentimes regardless of their own degree of self-identification with their countries. As such, the nation-state operates as a critical vehicle for punishing errant behavior on the international scene.

This function might seem to interpret the state as merely an elaborate and convenient metaphor for individual actions in its name. However, attaching responsibility to a country does allow for some degree of accountability in global public opinion. A fair analogy might be to the role political parties play in certain democratic systems. When a party is punished at the polls, its fate falls upon those in the party who were responsible for its policies as well as those who dissented from them. Similarly, nation-states have the power to make authoritative decisions in their citizens' names. It may seem unfair in many instances for citizens of a particular country to absorb the approbation of fellow actors on the international scene solely due to their identification with the nation-state, but there seems no other identity on the horizon which could fulfill this role of holding those responsible for decisions accountable. If world opinion is a critical means by which global forces affecting citizens' lives may be kept in check, it falls to the nation-state to remain one vehicle through which the power of world opinion is expressed.

Still, the primary question for political and economic theorists is how to make global forces *responsive* to citizens' needs and desires beyond the construction of national identity. Put another way, how can world opinion become a force for citizen control of world events, in the absence of national institutions designed to translate citizen demands on the global level? One institutional means suggested in this regard is international nongovernmental organizations (NGOs) which represent global movements for causes such as human rights and the environment. Associations like Greenpeace and Amnesty International were early examples of these efforts; these groups attempt to influence events by directing world opinion against those who violate perceived international norms on human rights and the environment, respectively. In recent years, the number of NGOs has grown rapidly, aided by communication systems like the Internet and the World Wide Web (see Phan, 1996). Such institutions' influence should only increase in the emerging international order.

International forums and conferences may also provide a means by which world opinion can be expressed and enforced. Thus, the United Nations played a key role in the Kuwaiti crisis, as noted in Chapter 2, and the 1995 UN-sponsored conference on Women's Rights in Beijing had an effect upon the way women's issues are viewed internationally (see Rusciano, Fiske-Rusciano, and Wang, 1997). The effectiveness of this body, though, seems to follow from the unity of world opinion rather than vice versa. Before the United Nations serves as an institution for the translation of world opinion into policy, it must prove its worth as a means for organizing and influencing, rather than just reifying, international consensus.

In 1977, Charles Lindblom ended his analysis of *Politics and Markets* by stating that the multinational corporation, an early manifestation of the global economy, was incompatible with democracy (Lindblom, 1977:356). The challenge for those of us who value the democratic spirit is to find ways to make global forces, including the global economy, responsive to world opinion, and to link world opinion more directly to citizen preferences internationally. The success of this venture may ultimately prove the relevance of democracy—and indeed, the very notion of responsive government—to the emerging international order.

Appendix I
Definition of Terms

The definition of certain terms in the study of world opinion required specific instructions for the coding of references in the news articles. The definitions and coding instructions for several key terms are described below.

Isolation. This term referred to implicit or explicit moves by nations to distance themselves from those who violated the dictates of world opinion. Usually the term "isolation" was stated directly; however, coders were also instructed to watch for synonyms for isolation, such as "quarantined from other nations," "boycotted by other countries," and so on. When specific actions were described as part of this isolation, such as the closing of embassies, the recall of ambassadors, or the denial of airline landing rights, these actions were noted and coded.

Moral component. This term referred to value judgments shared by nations in their expression of world opinion. Examples of moral statements included phrases such as "our shared outrage" or "our consciences are bothered" over certain events.

Nation's Image. This term referred to the manner in which other nations in the world viewed a particular nation, as part of the judgment of world opinion. Sometimes, the word was used directly: "the nation must polish its public image before it may be accepted again." Coders were also instructed to watch for phrases which indicated how other countries perceived the subject nation. Examples include "the world will never regard this nation in the same manner after this affair," "these issues have caused other nations to look at this leader differently," or "the world community will never think of this nation in this way again."

Power of World Opinion. This term referred to any influence or force world opinion was described as exerting in world affairs. Usually, power was referenced directly, or through some synonym—i.e. "force," "influence," or "coercion." However, coders were also instructed to watch for this power stated in terms of an effect world opinion was supposed to create; examples include phrases such as "the nation will react out of deference to world opinion" or "the leader must respect the world's judgment."

Pragmatic component. This term referred to interests shared by nations in their expression of world opinion. Examples of pragmatic statements included phrases such as "all nations would benefit" or "the world economy would be more stable" due to certain actions.

Appendix II
Notes Toward the Measurement
of World Opinion

If the urban, middle-class, and upscale public constitutes the "opinion leaders" in world opinion, then the measurement task becomes dramatically simplified. The homogenized nature of this constituency across nations would allow for the use of a more standardized research methodology than in the study of national public opinion where a greater variety of constituencies have to be surveyed, including those from the lower socioeconomic classes. For example, Sigfredo Hernandez and Carol Kaufman (1990) recommend that survey research methods that work with middle-class European American consumers should not be adopted for consumers who live in Hispanic neighborhoods or barrios in the United States. Cultural differences, lower socioeconomic status, and low levels of acculturation to the dominant culture make barrio Hispanics less likely to respond well to mainstream survey research methods.

Assuming a homogeneity of opinion constituencies across countries facilitates the use of survey research methods in the study of world opinion in three ways: (1) the selection of the method of administration, (2) the development of the questionnaire, and (3) the choice of a sample design.

Regarding administration of the survey, telephone interviews would be easier to conduct across countries since the described public usually possesses and uses telephones. Similarly, while mail surveys can be a problem where illiteracy rates are high and postal services unreliable, it appears that in third world nations like those in Latin America "with proper selection of the areas to be studied (generally large urban areas) and limitation of surveys to middle- and high-income strata, reliable information can be gathered quickly by mail" (Stanton, Chandran, and Hernandez, 1982). Finally, personal interview surveys would be possible, given the concentration of respondents in urban areas, and the further definition of middle-class and upscale areas within these cities.

Individuals in these areas are more likely to be enumerated, and transportation to the interviews is easier, than when one must include isolated rural areas.

While cultural differences must be kept in mind in the design of questionnaires, the design of survey instruments would be facilitated by the homogeneity of this constituency. Questionnaire translation would remain a formidable task, but certain factors reduce the problem of language diversity that one encounters in many national surveys. For instance, the urban upper and middle classes in India, which would form the target for these surveys, tend to speak English. On the other hand, a national survey of India would require questionnaires in 14 different languages, and perhaps many more unofficial languages and local dialects (Cateora, 1993).

The respondents would also be more likely to be familiar with, and receptive to, the typical multipoint scale questions on public opinion surveys. Respondents with lower literacy rates typically tend to have difficulties with fine shades of meaning defined in such questions (Stanton, Chandran, and Hernandez, 1982) or on five-point Likert-type scales (Hernandez and Kaufman, 1990). Also, while questioning styles would certainly be affected by cultural differences in communications styles, individuals in this constituency would have some common communication patterns reinforced by their familiarity with the global media messages they receive.

Perhaps the most difficult problem to surmount in the survey of world opinion is how to draw the sample for study from such a diverse universe. Here, the choice of the described constituency is helpful, but does not address all questions. In the absence of an adequate sampling frame, area samples of middle-class and upscale urban dwellers can be obtained more efficiently than samples of entire country populations. In addition, since telephone ownership is likely to be high in the populations of interest, sampling techniques such as random digit dialing and plus-one sampling can be used in the selection of probability samples.

Any survey of world opinion would require a sampling design that is economically feasible. The urban populations of interest would be geographically dispersed throughout the world. Multiple-stage cluster sampling could be used as a means of reducing costs and time for respondents who are located close to each other. For example, the world could be divided into strata by regions or continents. In a first stage, a number of countries as clusters would be selected randomly from all regions. In a second stage, urban clusters would be chosen at random within the selected countries. The third stage would involve random selection of a number of upper-class and middle-class neighborhoods within the previously selected urban areas. In the fourth stage, blocks would be randomly chosen from the neighborhoods. At this stage, in the absence of city planning maps, a face-to-face survey would require interviewers to canvass the residential addresses within selected blocks for a random selection of residential addresses.

In a telephone survey, selected exchanges in particular neighborhoods could be randomly chosen once middle- and upper-class neighborhoods were selected, and random or plus-one dialing could then be used for the survey. In less developed nations where telephone ownership is often associated with middle- or upper-class status, the third and fourth stages might not be necessary.

References

Allensbach Berichte. "Germans Shun Extremists: No Signs of a New Anti-Semitism." Institut für Demoskopie Allensbach. January 1993.

Anderson, Benedict. "Imagined Communities." In *Nationalism,* eds. John Hutchinson and Anthony D. Smith. New York: Oxford University Press, 1995.

Apple, R.W., Jr. "Bush & Gorbachev, Inc." *The New York Times*. 11 September 1990, 1.

Asch, Solomon. "Group Forces in The Modification and Distortion of Judgments." In *Social Psychology*. London: Routledge and Kegan Paul, 1952.

Avinieri, Shlomo. *Proceedings of the Conference on Europe in the New World Order*. Georgetown University, Washington, DC, 1991.

Baalbaki, Imad B., and Maholtra, Naresh K. "Marketing Management Bases for International Market Segmentation: An Alternative Look at the Standardization/ Customization Debate." *International Marketing Review*. 1 (1993):19-44.

Baldwin, James. *The Price of the Ticket: Collected Nonfiction, 1948-1985*. New York: St. Martin's Press, 1985.

Baldwin, J.M. *The Elements of Psychology*. New York: Henry Holt, 1893.

Barber, Benjamin R. *Jihad vs. McWorld*. New York: Random House, 1995.

Barry, Brian, and Hardin, Russell. *Rational Man and Irrational Society?* Beverly Hills, CA: Sage Publications, 1982.

Becker, Jurek. "My Father, the Germans and Me." *German American Cultural Review*. Winter 1994.

Bell, Daniel. *The End of Ideology: On the Exhaustion of Political Ideas in the Fifties*. New York: Free Press, 1962.

Bell, Daniel. *The Coming of Post-Industrial Society: A Venture in Social Forecasting*. New York: Basic Books, 1973.

Beniger, James R., and Gusek, Jodi A. "The Cognitive Revolution in Public Opinion and Communication Research." In *Public Opinion and the Communication of Consent*, eds. Theodore L. Glass and Charles T. Salmon. New York: Guilford Press, 1995.

Berger, Peter L., and Luckman, Thomas. *The Social Construction of Reality*. Garden City: Doubleday, 1966.

Bergsten, C. Fred. "APEC and World Trade: A Force for Worldwide Liberalization." *Foreign Affairs*. May/June 1994:20-26.

Best, Paul J.; Rai, Kul B.; and Walsh, David F. *Politics in Three Worlds: An Introduction to Political Science*. New York: John Wiley and Sons, 1986.

Bloom, William. *Personal Identity, National Identity and International Relations*. Cambridge: Cambridge University Press, 1990.

Boddewyn, Jean J.; Soehl, Robin; and Picard, Jacques. "Standardization in International Marketing: Is Ted Levitt in Fact Right?" *Business Horizons*. November-December 1986:69-75.

Bogart, Leo. "Is There a World Public Opinion?" *Polls*. 1 1966:1-9.

Brzezinski, Z. "Power and Morality." *World Monitor*. March 1993:23-28.

Canache, Damarys. "Looking Out My Back Door: The Neighborhood Context and Perceptions of Relative Deprivation." Presented at the annual conference of the American Association for Public Opinion Research, Fort Lauderdale, FL, May 18-21, 1995.

Cateora, Philip R. *International Marketing*. Homewood, IL: Richard D. Irwin, 1993.

Childs, Harwood L. *Public Opinion: Nature, Formation and Role*. Princeton: Von Nostrand, 1965.

Connelly, William E. "Identity and Difference in Global Politics." In *International/Intertextual Relations: Postmodern Readings of World Politics*, eds. J. Der Derian and Michael J. Shapiro. Lexington, MA: D.C. Heath, 1989.

Conradt, David P. "Changing German Political Culture." In *The Civic Culture Revisited*, eds. Gabriel Almond and Sidney Verba. Boston: Little, Brown, 1980.

Cooper, Andrew Fenton; Higgot, Richard A.; and Nossal, Kim Richard. "Bound to Follow? Leadership and Followership in the Gulf Crisis." *Political Science Quarterly*. 106 (1991):391-406.

Csepeli, Gyorgy. "Competing Patterns of National Identity in Post-Communist Hungary." *Media, Culture, and Society*. 13 (1991):325-339.

Davis, J.A., and Smith, Tom W. *General Social Surveys, 1972-1982: Cumulative Codebook*. Chicago: National Opinion Research Center, 1982.

Davison, W. Phillips. "International and World Public Opinion." In *Handbook of Communication*, eds. Ithiel de Sola Pool, et al. Chicago: Rand McNally, 1973.

Deutsch, Karl. *Nationalism and Social Communication*. Cambridge: MIT Press, 1966.

Dichter, Ernst. "The World Customer." *Harvard Business Review*. July-August 1962: 113-122.

Doty, R.L. "Foreign Policy as a Social Construction: A Post-Positivist Analysis of U.S. Counter-insurgency Policy in the Philippines." *International Studies Quarterly*. 37 (1993):297-320.

Douglas, Susan P., and Wind, Yoram. "The Myth of Globalization." *Columbia Journal of World Business*. Winter 1987:19-30.

Ebo, Bosah. "Africa and the West in the New World Information Order." Paper presented at the Northwestern University Conference on Communication and Development. Chicago, 1983.

Ebo, Bosah. "The Gulf War and the Third World: Why Does the New World Order Look Like the Old World Order?" *Proceedings of the Association for the Advancement of Policy, Research and Development in the Third World*. Orlando, FL, 1992.

Erdrich, Louise, and Dorris, Michael. Interview in *Bill Moyers: A World of Ideas*, ed. Bill Moyers. New York: Doubleday, 1989.

Foucault, Michel. *The Archaeology of Knowledge* (A.M. Sheridan-Smith, trans.). New York: Pantheon, 1972.

Frankfurter Allgemeine Zeitung. "Ganz neben bei." 6 June 1995, 14.

Friedrich, Carl J. "In Friedrich Hegel." *The Philosophy of Hegel*, ed. Carl J. Friedrich. New York: Random House, 1954.

Fuentes, Carlos. Interview in *Bill Moyers: A World of Ideas*, ed. Bill Moyers. New York: Doubleday, 1989.

Fukuyama, Francis. *The End of History and the Last Man.* New York: The Free Press, 1996.

Gergen, K.J. "Social Construction in Question." *Human Systems: The Journal of Systematic Consultation and Management.* 3 (1992):163-182.

Gilligan, Carol. *In a Different Voice: Psychological Theory and Women's Development.* Cambridge: Harvard University Press, 1992.

Goldmann, Kjell. "International Opinion and World Politics: The Case of the INF Treaty." *Political Studies.* 41 (1993):41-56.

Greenfield, Liah. "Nationalism and Class Struggle: Two Forces or One?" *Survey.* 29 (1985):153-174.

Greenfeld, Liah. *Nationalism: Five Roads to Modernity.* Cambridge: Harvard University Press, 1992.

Gupta, Sunil. "What in the World is a Web User?" Michigan Business School Study. 1995.

Hardin, Russell. *Collective Action.* Baltimore: Johns Hopkins University Press, 1982.

Hassan, Salah S., and Katsanis, Lea Pervel. "Identification of Global Consumer Segments: A Behavioral Framework." *Journal of International Consumer Marketing.* 2 (1991):11-28.

Hedges, Chris. "Serbs Threaten to Boycott Talks." *The New York Times.* 26 July 1995, A8.

Hedges, Chris. "Top Leader of the Bosnian Serbs Now Under Attack from Within." *The New York Times.* 4 January 1996, A1-A8.

Hegel, Friedrich. *The Philosophy of Hegel.* Carl J. Friedrich, ed. New York: Random House, 1954.

Hennessey, Bernard. *Public Opinion*, 5th ed. Monterey, CA: Brooks/Cole, 1985.

Herbig, Paul A., and Miller, Joseph C. "Culture and Technology: Does the Traffic Move in Both Directions?" *Journal of Global Marketing.* 3 (1992):75-104.

Herman, Edward S., and Chomsky, Noam. *Manufacturing Consent: The Political Economy of Mass Media.* New York: Random House, 1988.

Hernandez, Sigfredo A., and Kaufman, Carol J. "Marketing Research in Hispanic Barrios: A Guide to Survey Research." *Marketing Research.* March 1990:11-27.

Hill, Christopher J. "World Opinion and the Empire of Circumstance." *International Affairs.* 72 (January 1996):109-131.

Hill, John S., and Still, Richard R. "Effects of Urbanization on Multinational Product Planning: Markets in Lesser-Developed Countries." *Columbia Journal of World Marketing.* 3 (1984):62.

Hinckley, Ron. "World Public Opinion and the Persian Gulf Crisis." *Proceedings of the American Association for Public Opinion Research.* Phoenix, May 16-19, 1991.

Hirsch, Fred. *The Social Limits to Growth.* Cambridge: Harvard University Press, 1976.

Hite, Robert E., and Frazier, Cynthia. "International Advertising Strategies of Multinational Corporations." *Journal of Advertising Research*. August/September 1988: 9-17.

Hormats, Robert D. "Making Regionalism Safe." *Foreign Affairs*. March/April 1994:97-108.

Hufbauer, Gary C., and Elliot, Kimberley A. "Sanctions Will Bite—And Soon." *The New York Times*. 14 January 1991, A17.

Huntington, Samuel P. "The Clash of Civilizations?" *Foreign Affairs*. Summer (1993a): 22-49.

Huntington, Samuel P. "If Not Civilizations, What?" In *The Clash of Civilizations? The Debate: A Foreign Affairs Reader*. New York: Council on Foreign Relations, 1993b.

Inglehart, Ronald. *The Silent Revolution: Changing Values and Political Styles Among Western Publics*. Princeton: Princeton University Press, 1977.

James, W. *The Principles of Psychology*. New York: Henry Holt, 1890.

Jansen, G.H. "Kuwait May Have Tried to Oust Saddam." *The New York Times*. 5 August 1990, 1.

Jarausch, Konrad H. *The Rush to German Unity*. New York: Oxford University Press, 1994.

Jervis, R. *The Logic of Images in International Relations*. Princeton: Princeton University Press, 1970.

Johnston, William B. "Global Workforce 2000: The New World Labor Market." *Harvard Business Review*. March-April 1991:115-127.

Keegan, Warren J. *Global Marketing Management*. Englewood Cliffs, NJ: Prentice-Hall, 1995.

Kinzer, Stephen. "Germany Ablaze: It's Candlelight, not Firebombs." *The New York Times*. 13 January 1993a, A4.

Kinzer, Stephen. "Stepson of German Politics: Is Fatherland Proud?" *The New York Times*. 22 February 1993b, A4.

Kinzer, Stephen. "As Strife Recedes, Germans Breathe Easier." *The New York Times*. 18 March 1993c, A13.

Kinzer, Stephen. "G.I.'s Abroad: Bosnia on Their Mind." *The New York Times*. 26 October 1995, A8.

Kotler, Phillip. "Global Standardization—Courting Danger." *Journal of Consumer Marketing*. 2 (1986):13-15.

Laczniak, Gene R., and Murphy, Patrick E. *Marketing Ethics: Guidelines for Managers*. Lexington, MA: Lexington Books, 1985.

Levitt, Theodore. "The Globalization of Markets." *Harvard Business Review*. May-June 1983:92-102.

Lewis, Flora. "Steady Against Saddam." *The New York Times*. 21 August 1990, A27.

Lindblom, Charles. *Politics and Markets: The World's Political-Economic Systems*. New York: Basic Books, 1977.

Mackie, J.L. "Fallacies." In *The Encyclopedia of Philosophy*, Vol. 3, pp. 169-179. New York: Macmillan, 1967.

Maier, Charles S. *The Unmasterable Past: History, Holocaust, and German National Identity*. Cambridge: Harvard University Press, 1988.

Malkki, Liisa. "Citizens of Humanity: Internationalism and the Imagined Community of Nations." *Diaspora*. 3 (1994):41-68.

Maslow, Abraham H. *Towards a Psychology of Being.* Englewood Cliffs, NJ: D. van Nostrand, 1962.

Mazrui, A.A. *The Africans: A Triple Heritage.* Boston: Little, Brown, 1986.

Mead, George H. *Mind, Self, and Society.* Chicago: University of Chicago Press, 1934.

Morgenthau, Hans J. "Is World Public Opinion a Myth?" *The New York Times Magazine.* 25 March 1962, 23.

Mowlana, Hamid. *Global Information and World Communication: New Frontiers in International Relations.* New York: Longman, 1986.

Mowlana, Hamid, and Wilson, Laurie J. *The Passing of Modernity: Communication and the Transformation of Society.* New York: Longman, 1990.

The New York Times. "Isolate Iraq." 5 August 1990, E18.

The New York Times. "Mideast: Now a People's Peace." 15 September 1993, A26.

The New York Times. "Clinton's Words: The Promise of Peace." 11 November 1995, A11.

Noelle-Neumann, Elisabeth. *The Spiral of Silence: Public Opinion—Our Social Skin.* Chicago: University of Chicago Press, 1992.

Noelle-Neumann, Elisabeth, and Koecher, Renate. *Allensbacher Jahrbuch der Demoskopie 1984-1992.* Munchen: K.G. Saur, 1993.

Noelle-Neumann, Elisabeth, and Koecher, Renate. *Die Verletzte Nation: Ueber den Versuch der Deutschen, ihren Charakter zu Aendern.* Stuttgart: Deutsche Verlags-Anstalt, 1987.

Obasanjo, O. *Proceedings of the Conference on Europe in the New World Order.* Georgetown University. Washington, DC, 1991.

Ohmae, Kenichi. "Becoming a Triad Power: The New Global Corporation." *The McKinsey Quarterly.* Spring 1985:2-25.

O'Reilly, Anthony J.F. "The Emergence of the Global Consumer." *Directors and Boards.* 2 (Winter 1991):9-13.

Page, Benjamin I., and Shapiro, Robert Y. "Effects of Public Opinion on Policy." *American Political Science Review.* 77 (1983):175-190.

Phan, Chau T. "International Non-governmental Organizations, Global Negotiations, and Global Activist Networks: The Emergence of INGOs as Partners in the Global Governance Process." Paper presented at the annual meeting of the Northeast Political Science Association, Boston, November 14, 1996.

Pollock, John C., and Guidette, Christopher L. "Mass Media, Crisis and Political Change: A Cross National Approach." In *Communication Yearbook IV,* ed. Dan Nimmo. New Brunswick, NJ: Transaction Books, 1980.

Pollock, John; Kreur, Beverly; and Ouano, Eric. "Comparing City Characteristics and Nationwide Coverage of China's Bid to Host the 2000 Olympic Games." *Newspaper Research Journal.* Winter 1997:31-49.

Pollock, John; Shier, Lorena; and Slattery, Patricia. "Newspapers and the 'Open Door' Policy Toward Cuba: A Sample of Major U.S. Cities—A 'Community Structure' Approach." *Journal of International Communication.* December 1995:67-86.

Price, Vincent, and Oshagan, Hayg. "Social-Psychological Perspectives on Public Opinion." In *Public Opinion and the Communication of Consent,* eds. Theodore L. Glasser and Charles T. Salmon. New York: Guilford Press, 1995.

Pross, Harry. "On German Identity." *Media, Culture, and Society.* 13 (1991):341-356.

Quelch, John A., and Hoff, Edward J. "Customizing Global Marketing." *Harvard Business Review.* May-June 1986:59-68.

Reich, Robert B. "What Is a Nation?" *Political Science Quarterly*. 106 (1991):193-209.

Rogers, Everett M. "The Rise and Fall of the Dominant Paradigm." *Journal of Communication*. 28 (1978):64-69.

Rostow, Eugene. *The Stages of Economic Growth: A Non-Communist Manifesto*. London: Cambridge University Press, 1971.

Rousseau, Jean-Jacques. *The First and Second Discourses*, ed. Roger D. Masters; trans. Roger D. Masters and Judith R. Masters. New York: St. Martin's Press, 1964.

Rueb, Matthias. "Die selbstverschuldete Machtlosigkeit der allzu friedlichen Friedensstifter: Ist die UN-Mission auf dem Balken noch zu retten?" *Frankfurter Allgemeine Zeitung*. 13 May 1995a, 6.

Rueb, Matthias. "Der Serben unter Koradzic und Martic bleibt nur die Flucht nach vorn: Die Grenzen die Isolationspolitik." *Frankfurter Allgemeine Zeitung*. 1 June 1995b, 2.

Rusciano, Frank Louis. *Isolation and Paradox: Defining "the Public" in Modern Political Analysis*. Westport, CT: Greenwood Press, 1989.

Rusciano, Frank Louis. "World Opinion on the Kuwait-Iraq Crisis: Does the Third World Have a Voice?" *Proceedings of the Association for the Advancement of Policy, Research, and Development in the Third World*. Orlando, FL, November 18-22, 1992.

Rusciano, Frank Louis; Fiske-Rusciano, Roberta; and Wang, Minmin. "The Impact of 'World Opinion' on National Identity." *Harvard International Journal of Press/Politics*. 2(3) (1997):71-92.

Sandler, Dennis M., and Shani, David. "Think Globally But Advertise Locally?: An Empirical Investigation." *International Marketing Review*. 4 (1992):18-31.

Schelling, Thomas. "The Strategy of Conflict: Prospectus for a Reorientation of Game Theory." *Journal of Conflict Resolution*. 2 (1958):203-64.

Shapiro, M.J. "Textualizing Global Politics." In *International/Intertextual Relations: Postmodern Readings of World Politics*, eds. J. Der Derian and M.J. Shapiro. Lexington, MA: D.C. Heath, 1989.

Simon-Miller, Francoise. "World Marketing; Going Global or Acting Local? Five Expert Viewpoints." *Journal of Consumer Marketing*. 2 (1986):5-7.

Smith, Tom W. "An Experimental Comparison of Clustered and Scattered Scale Items." *Social Psychology Quarterly*. 46 (1983):163-168.

Sneider, Daniel. "As US Troops Pack, Bosnia Doubts Linger." *The Christian Science Monitor*. 22 December 1995, 1.

Snidal, Duncan. "Coordination Versus Prisoners' Dilemma: Implications for International Cooperation and Regimes." *American Political Science Review*. 79 (1985): 923-942.

Stanton, John L.; Chandran, Rajan; and Hernandez, Sigfredo A. "Marketing Research Problems in Latin America." *Journal of the Marketing Research Society*. 2 (1982): 124-139.

Sterngold, James. "The Awakening Chinese Consumer." *The New York Times*. 11 October 1992, 1.

Talmon, J.L. *The Origins of Totalitarian Democracy*. New York: Praeger, 1960.

Tamir, Yael. "The Right to National Self-Determination." *Social Research*. 58 (1991).

Taylor, D. Garth. "Pluralistic Ignorance and the Spiral of Silence: A Formal Model." *Public Opinion Quarterly*. 46 (1982):311-335.

Terpstra, Vern, and Sarathy, Ravi. *International Marketing*. Fort Worth: The Dryden Press, 1994.

Thornton, Thomas P. "India Adrift: The Search for Moorings in a New World Order." *Asian Survey*. 32 (1992):1063-1077.

Times of India. "New Govt. in Kuwait as Pull-Out Begins." 6 August 1990a, 1.

Times of India. "Pressures on Iraq." 11 August 1990b, 10.

Times of India. "New Delhi and Baghdad." 7 January 1991a. 12.

Times of India. "25 Indians for Gulf Peace Team." 12 January 1991b, 15.

Ullman, Richard H. "Flunking World Order 101." *The New York Times*. 12 January 1991, 21.

Unger, David C. "Ferment in the Think Tanks: Learning to Live with No Global Threat." *The New York Times*. January 1991.

United States Information Agency (USIA). "Global media generally support Bush Gulf peace initiative, mixed on U.N. force resolution; See dwindling U.S. support for war." *Foreign Media Analysis*. 11 December 1990.

Verba, Sidney, and Almond, Gabriel. *The Civic Culture*. Boston: Little, Brown, 1965.

Verba, Sidney, and Nie, Norman. *Participation in America: Political Democracy and Social Equality*. New York: Harper and Row, 1972.

Waddel, Eric. "Language, Community and National Identity: Some Reflections on French-English Relations in Canada." In *Canadian Politics: An Introduction to the Discipline*, eds. Alain-G. Gagnon and James P. Bickerton. Lewiston: Broadview Press, 1990.

Wendt, Alexander. "Anarchy Is What States Make of It: The Social Construction of Power Politics." *International Organization*. 2 (1992):393-425.

Whitelock, J.M. "Global Marketing and the Case for International Product Standardization." *European Journal of Marketing*. 9 (1987):32-44.

Whitney, Craig R. "NATO Gives Officials Veto on Air Strikes in Bosnia." *The New York Times*. 26 July 1995, A8.

Wilcox, Clyde; Tanaka, Aiji; and Allsop, Dee. "World Opinion in the Gulf Crisis." *Journal of Conflict Resolution*. 37 (1993):69-93.

Wills, Garry. *Nixon Agonistes: The Crisis of the Self-Made Man*. New York: New American Library, 1979.

Wind, Yoram. "The Myth of Globalization." *Journal of Consumer Marketing*. 2 (1986): 23-26.

Yavas, Ugur; Verhage, Bronislaw; and Green, Robert T. "Global Consumer Segmentation Versus Local Market Orientation: Empirical Findings." *Management International Review*. 3 (1992):265-272.

Yeric, Jerry L., and Todd, John R. *Public Opinion: The Visible Politics*. Itasca: F.E. Peacock, 1983.

Zaller, John. *The Nature and Origin of Mass Opinion*. New York: Cambridge University Press, 1992.

Zukier, Henri. "The Essential 'Other' and the Jew: From Antisemitism to Genocide." *Social Research*. 63(4) (1996):1110-1153.

Index

About the Authors

FRANK LOUIS RUSCIANO is a Professor of Political Science at Rider University. He is a three-time Alexander von Humboldt Fellow, a former Guest Professor at the University of Mainz, and the author of *Isolation and Paradox: Defining "the Public" in Modern Political Analysis* (Greenwood, 1989). His articles have appeared in the *International Journal of Public Opinion Research, Comparative Politics, Political Communication*, Current World Leaders: *International Issues*, and *The Harvard International Journal of Press/Politics*.

BOSAH EBO is a Professor in the Department of Communication at Rider University, where he also teaches in the Baccalaureate Honors, Multicultural Studies, and International Studies programs. He was a Fulbright Fellow in Germany in 1997. He has published several articles and chapters on international communications, and is the author of *Cyberghetto or Cybertopia: Race, Class, and Gender on the Internet* (Greenwood Press, 1998).

ROBERTA FISKE-RUSCIANO is an Adjunct Assistant Professor of Anthropology and Women's Studies at Rider University. She has published articles in the *International Journal of Public Opinion Research* and *The Harvard International Journal of Press/Politics*. She is completing research on women and national identity in the Federal Republic of Germany.

SIGFREDO A. HERNANDEZ is an Associate Professor of Marketing at Rider University. He has been a Fulbright Fellow in Latin America, and received the Lindback Award for Distinguished Teaching from Rider University. He has published several articles and papers in the area of cross-cultural consumer behavior.

JOHN CROTHERS POLLOCK is an Associate Professor of Communications Studies at the College of New Jersey. He is author of *The Politics of Crisis Reporting: Learning to be a Foreign Correspondent* (Praeger, 1981). In addition, he has published articles on the relation between community or city structure and reporting on political and social change in *The Communication Yearbook, Journalism Quarterly, Newspaper Research Journal, The Journal of International Communication*, and *Mass Communication Review*. His forthcoming book is *Newspapers and the Evolution of Public Issues: Media Alignment with Political and Social Change*.

ISBN 0-275-95449-8

EAN

9 780275 954499

90000>

HARDCOVER BAR CODE